7

Christ Our Life

Jesus the Way, the Truth, and the Life

AUTHORS

Sisters of Notre Dame of Chardon, Ohio

Sister Mary Joan Agresta, S.N.D.

Sister Mary Theresa Betz, S.N.D.

Sister Mary Kathleen Glavich, S.N.D.

Sister Mary Verne Kavula, S.N.D.

Sister Mary Patricia Lab, S.N.D.

Sister Mary Andrew Miller, S.N.D.

Sister Mary Renée Pastor, S.N.D.

Sister Mary Patricia Rickard, S.N.D.

Sister Mary Reiling, S.N.D.

THEOLOGICAL ADVISOR

Sister Agnes Cunningham, S.S.C.M.

CONSULTANTS

Reverend Monsignor Joseph T. Moriarty

Timothy E. O'Connell

Reverend Lawrence Tosco, C.S.J.

GENERAL EDITOR

Sister Mary Kathleen Glavich, S.N.D.

LOYOLAPRESS.

CHICAGO

Nihil Obstat: The Reverend Monsignor Joseph T. Moriarty, M.A., Censor Deputatus
Imprimatur: The Most Reverend Anthony M. Pilla, D.D., M.A., Bishop of Cleveland
Given at Cleveland, Ohio, on 3 February 1997

The *Nihil Obstat* and *Imprimatur* are official declarations that a book or pamphlet is free of doctrinal or moral error. No implication is contained therein that those who have granted the *Nihil Obstat* and *Imprimatur* agree with the contents, opinions, or statements expressed.

Christ Our Life
found to be in conformity

The Ad Hoc Committee to Oversee the Use of the Catechism, National Conference of Catholic Bishops, has found this catechetical series, copyright 1997 and 2002, to be in conformity with the *Catechism of the Catholic Church*.

Dedicated to St. Julie Billiart, foundress of the Sisters of Notre Dame, in gratitude for her inspiration and example

Acknowledgments

This present revision of the Christ Our Life series is the work of countless people. In particular, we acknowledge and thank the following for their roles in the project:

- The Sisters of Notre Dame who supported the production of the Christ Our Life series, especially Sister Mary Joell Overman, S.N.D.; Sister Mary Frances Murray, S.N.D.; and Sister Mary Margaret Hess, S.N.D.

- The Sisters of Notre Dame who over the past twenty years have shaped, written, and edited editions of the Christ Our Life series, in particular Sister Mary de Angelis Bothwell, S.N.D., the former editor

- Those who worked on different stages involved in producing this edition, especially Sister Mary Julie Boehnlein, S.N.D.; Sister Linda Marie Gecewicz, S.N.D.; Sister Mary Beth Gray, S.N.D.; Sister Joanmarie Harks, S.N.D.; Sister Mary Andrew Miller, S.N.D.; Sister Mary Agnes O'Malley, S.N.D.; Sister Mary Catherine Rennecker, S.N.D.; and Sister Mary St. Jude Weisensell, S.N.D.

- Those catechists, directors of religious education, priests, parents, students, and others who responded to surveys, returned evaluation forms, wrote letters, or participated in interviews to help improve the series

Scripture selections are taken from the *New American Bible*, copyright © 1991, 1986, 1970 by the Confraternity of Christian Doctrine, Washington, D.C., and are used by license of copyright owner. All rights reserved.

Excerpts from THE JERUSALEM BIBLE, © 1966 by Darton, Longman & Todd, Ltd., and Doubleday, a division of Random House, Inc. Reprinted by Permission.

Excerpts from the English translation of *Rite of Baptism for Children* © 1969, International Committee on English in the Liturgy, Inc. (ICEL); excerpts from the English translation of *The Roman Missal* © 1973, ICEL; excerpts from the English translation of *Liturgy of the Hours* © 1974, ICEL; excerpts from the English translation of *Rite of Penance* © 1974, ICEL; excerpts from the English translation of *Rite of Confirmation (2nd edition)* © 1975, ICEL; excerpts from the English translation of *Pastoral Care of the Sick* © 1982, ICEL; excerpts from the English translation of *A Book of Prayers* © 1982, ICEL; excerpts from the English translation of *Book of Blessings* © 1988, ICEL. All rights reserved.

Excerpt from *The Story of My Life* by Helen Keller, published by Doubleday, a division of Random House, Inc., is in the public domain.

"An I-Opener" on p. 9 is reprinted by permission from *Instant Programs for Youth Groups Volume 1,* copyright © 1988 by Group Publishing, Inc., P.O. Box 481, Loveland, CO 80539.

"The Doughnut Priest" adapted with permission from *Extension Magazine*, published by The Catholic Church Extension Society, Chicago, IL 60616.

All attempts possible have been made to contact the publisher for cited works in this book.

Photographs

© James L. Amos/CORBIS (p. 182); © AP/Wide World Photos (pp. 108 left, 172 left); © Artville LLC. (p. 21); © Davis Barber/PhotoEdit (p. 109); © Billy E. Barnes/PhotoEdit (p. 187); © Leonid Bogdanov/SuperStock, Inc. (p. 146); © The Bridgeman Art Library International, Ltd. (p. 79); © Giulio Broglio/AP/Wide World Photos (pp. 162, 180 top); © Antonio Calanni/AP/Wide World Photos (p. 153); © Myrleen Cate/PhotoEdit (p. 85); © Catholic Worker/AP/Wide World Photos (p. 108 right); © Cleo Freelance Photography (pp. 67, 97, 140); © Corbis Corp. (p. 9 top); © Corel Corporation (p. 188); © dan CHUA Publications (p. 106); © Digital Stock Corp. (pp. 34, 48 middle, 73–74, 95, 116 left, 161); © Donald M. Emmerich/ The Catholic Church Extension Society (p. 66); © EyeWire (pp. 158 bottom, 175); © Sister M. Kathleen Glavich, S.N.D. (p. 130); © Spencer Grant/PhotoEdit (p. 141); © Johnny van Haeften Gallery, London, UK/The Bridgeman Art Library International, Ltd. (p. 81); © Reverend Ignatius Harrington (p. 64); © Ingram Publishing Limited (p. 147); © Erich Lessing/ArtResource, NY (p. 30 middle); © Erich Lessing Culture and Fine Arts Archive/PhotoEdit (pp. 30 left, 158 top); © James Nedresky (p. 38 bottom); © Michael Newman/PhotoEdit (p. 6); © North Wind Picture Archives (pp. 11 left, 48 left); © Nova Stock/PhotoEdit (p. 17); © PhotoDisc, Inc. (pp. 5, 8, 9 bottom, 11 bottom right, 38 top, 63, 88, 98, 111, 119, 120 right, 123, 127, 135, 136 right, 171, 183, 185); © *The Plain Dealer*, Cleveland OH (p. 112); © Eugene D. Plaisted, O.S.C./Crosiers (pp. i, 4, 7, 11 top right, 15, 23, 35, 36, 43–44, 47, 48 right, 52, 59, 69, 72, 80, 87, 89, 96, 103, 107, 116 right, 133, 157, 159, 160, 165–167, 170, 172 bottom, 176, 191); © Private Collection/Jessie Coates/SuperStock, Inc. (p. 41); © Mark Richards/PhotoEdit (p. 84); © Robin L. Sachs/PhotoEdit (p. 100); © James Shaffer/ PhotoEdit (p. 77); Skjold Photographs (pp. 90–91, 115, 136 bottom, 177, 192); © SuperStock, Inc. (p. 134); © Victoria & Albert Museum, London/Art Resource, NY (p. 174); © Rudi Von Briel/PhotoEdit (p. 122 top); © Nancy Wiechec/Catholic News Service (p. 152); © W. P. Wittman Limited (pp. 22 bottom, 25, 27, 29, 30 right, 31, 40, 42, 55, 60–61, 70–71, 92, 105, 121, 144–145, 149, 151, 155, 178, 180 bottom); © David Young-Wolff/PhotoEdit (p. 122 bottom).

Artwork

Cheryl Arnemann (pp. 18, 22, 24, 26, 32, 37, 82 bottom, 104, 137, 138, 139, 217); Sister Mary Megan Dull, S.N.D. (p. 223); Robert Korta (pp. 75, 76); Diana Magnuson (p. 94); Proof Positive/Farrowlyne Assoc., Inc. (pp. 57 right, 58, 124, 137 border); Robert Voigts (pp. 12, 16, 28, 33, 49–51, 56, 57 top left, Beatitudes 104–106, 117, 118, 120, 126, 128, 131, 148, 152, 164, 179, 181, 184, 186, 193, 194, 195, 196, 211, 215, 216, 218).

Cover design by Donald Kye.
Cover art © Eugene D. Plaisted, O.S.C./Crosiers.

05 06 07 DBH 7 6 5

LoyolaPress.

3441 N. Ashland Avenue
Chicago, Illinois 60657
(800) 621-1008

CONTENTS

7

Titles in italics are chapters on the sacraments.

Dear Students,

You are entering the stage of life when you ask the hard questions: Who am I? What is the meaning of life . . . and death? How do I know what is right? Why do people suffer?

Christians believe that Jesus is the whole secret and center of human existence. They gradually find him to be what he called himself—the Way, the Truth, and the Life.

Jesus is the *Way* to the Father, the Way to peace and happiness, and the Way for you to know and fulfill the purpose for which you were created. Jesus is the *Truth*. He reveals the Father, and he teaches the truth everyone seeks. You can rely on his words. Jesus is the *Life*. He promises you a share in divine and eternal life. The source of this life is faith in Jesus and his words. He himself gives you faith and strengthens it through Scripture, prayer, sacraments, and the faith community, the Church.

Jesus the Way, the Truth, and the Life is a tool to help you deepen your friendship with Jesus. It is hoped you will be drawn to adopt his values and base your decisions on them.

As you use this book you will learn more about Jesus as he lived in Palestine. You will learn about the mystery of his death and resurrection that brought us life. You will also learn more about Jesus alive in the world today. You will study the sacraments: those moments when you encounter our risen Lord and are empowered by him to continue his mission of love. You will find out more about the Spirit Jesus sent who is at work in us.

Each day may you respond to the Lord and his great love with an open mind and heart.

Lord Jesus, the Way,
    the Truth,
    and the Life,
we pray,
do not let us stray from you,
    the Way,
nor distrust you,
    the Truth,
nor rest in anything else but you,
    the Life.
Teach us by the Holy Spirit
    what to do,
what to believe,
and where to take our rest.

Prayer of Erasmus, a famous
scholar of the sixteenth century

Jesus Christ the Way

Christians Pray:
Centering Your Family on Christ

Every Friday evening after dinner the Yang family gathers in the living room for fifteen minutes of family prayer. A few years ago the Yangs realized that if they really believed in Jesus, they should pray together. Since beginning this practice, they have found that not only do they feel closer to Christ personally but there is a stronger bond among the family members. Moreover, as a family they have become more active in society and the Church.

Getting started was a little awkward. Mr. and Mrs. Yang probably felt the most uncomfortable. To four-year-old Terry prayer came naturally. Thirteen-year-old Carl resisted praying together at first, but now he sometimes even enjoys it, though he doesn't always let on.

After the family chose a time for their family prayer, they made a commitment to reserve that time each week. They signed a contract: "Knowing how important it is that Jesus be a part of our lives and wanting to grow in our faith, we promise to do our best to be at family prayer on _____." Whenever someone has a good reason for not being there, his or her picture is placed with the family as a reminder that the missing person is with them in spirit.

How does this family pray? Very simply. The members take turns planning the prayer time. They might talk to God about whatever is on their minds. They might pray a favorite prayer, the rosary, or a psalm. They might read from the Bible or a spiritual book. The other day Mrs. Yang played a recording of a hymn about trusting God, and everyone sang along. Terry once led an Easter parade through the house, an idea he got from his preschool class. A moving experience the family had was a reconciliation service. The members prayed a litany for forgiveness for hurting one another by doing such things as slamming the door, forgetting to do chores, and being too busy.

The prayer time the Yang family shares is not perfect. Like the rest of family life, it is sometimes messy. But the family values praying together. The Yangs have come to rely on one another's prayers, and in times of crisis they have more faith, hope, and strength than they had before.

If you wish there were more unity, love, and peace in your family and you do not pray together, try it! You may be surprised.

The Impact of Jesus

For God so loved the world that he gave his only Son,
so that everyone who believes in him
might not perish but might have eternal life.

JOHN 3:16

You are one of God's special gifts to the world. You are unique! You make the world sparkle as no one else ever will. Like a diamond, you have many facets. You have gifts to discover and develop: skills, talents, and qualities. Like a pebble thrown into a pond, your life creates a ripple. What you do affects those around you. You count!

Who you *think* you are has a lot to do with who you are now and who you will become. That's why it is important to have a true picture of yourself. There is no better time than the present for discovering the mystery and the miracle of YOU.

Who Are You?

Check the characteristics found at each level of creation.

	Things	Plants	Animals	People
Exist				
Grow				
Eat/Drink				
Reproduce				
Breathe				
Move				
Have 5 senses				
Think				
Choose				

How do you differ from plants, animals, and the rest of creation? God directly created your soul united to your body within your mother. What makes you human are the powers of your soul: your God-given gifts of **intellect** (ability to think) and **free will** (ability to choose and love). These are divine powers. You are made in God's image. You can share God's truth, goodness, and beauty and can someday share God's glory forever. With your intellect you can make decisions and judgments, and you can laugh. With your free will you can love and sacrifice. Because you have this freedom you are responsible for your acts.

You can see that your soul gives you a dignity that the rest of earthly creations do not have. In fact, God put us over all creation and we can use creation to serve our needs, but we are also responsible to care for it.

It's in Your Hands

God has made you a member of a particular family. From your parents, you received certain traits. This is called **heredity.** You did not choose your inherited traits, like curly hair or a quick temper. It is thought that even the order you were born (first, middle, or last) shapes your personality traits, as the activity "An I-Opener" on the next page might confirm in your case. You also live in a particular area. This is your **environment.** You cannot control many things in your physical environment. But you can control your personal environment: the friends you choose, the movies you see, the books you read, the TV programs you watch. More importantly, you can control your reactions and attitudes. You can decide to develop good or bad habits.

You are growing in many ways: *mentally, physically, spiritually, emotionally, socially,* and *culturally.* You are responsible for what you do with your life. But Jesus is always with you, supporting you, calling you to further growth, and leading you to himself. The key to knowing yourself and becoming the best person you can be is to know Jesus.

> If God had a wallet,
> your picture
> would be in it.

An I-Opener

Do your personality traits match those of others with your same birth order? First circle your birth order. Then go down each column checking the characteristics you feel best describe you. When you are finished, see if you mostly checked the characteristics of people with your birth order. How do you explain the similarities or differences?

I am...

an oldest	a middle	a youngest	an only

an oldest	a middle	a youngest	an only
❏ Am overly serious and mature	❏ Know how to negotiate	❏ Am an "alibi artist"	❏ Often crave solitude
❏ Need a lot of approval	❏ Like to daydream	❏ Enjoy most people	❏ Am self-centered
❏ Get things done	❏ Am a conformist *outside* the family, a maverick within	❏ Seesaw between overconfidence and discouragement	❏ Am tidy and organized
❏ Can manage people	❏ Care too much what people think	❏ Overreact to criticism	❏ Can amuse myself easily
❏ Am a conformist, not very spontaneous	❏ Am easily hurt, but don't show it	❏ Am ambitious, determined to be taken seriously	❏ Really hate competing with others
❏ Have trouble accepting help	❏ Am uneasy about expressing anger or fear	❏ Am spontaneous and creative	❏ Feel uncomfortable in a position of authority
❏ Am assertive and opinionated	❏ Assume people aren't really interested in me	❏ Have a strong sense of justice	❏ Sometimes wonder if I'm too attached to material things
❏ Am a sympathetic listener	❏ Am flexible and open to new ideas	❏ Waste too much time	❏ Sometimes try to manipulate others
❏ Worry too much	❏ Achieve anything I decide to achieve	❏ Cry easily	❏ Am good at following directions
❏ Am super organized	❏ Don't talk a lot	❏ Talk a lot	❏ Don't talk a lot
❏ Talk a lot			

A VIP: ME

Name _____ Birthday _____

Height _____ Hair color _____ Eye color _____

School _____

My favorite:

TV program _____

song or radio station _____

book _____

food _____ color _____

subject _____ sport _____

Scripture verse _____

I am different from everyone else because _____

_____

This year I would like to be able to _____

One important thing I learned from my parents is _____

One important thing I learned from my friends is _____

The quality I like MOST in others is _____

The quality I like LEAST in others is _____

I think I am very good at _____

One thing about my faith that means the most to me is _____

If I could change anything about my life right now, I would change _____

One thing I do not understand about my religion is _____

Ask an important adult in your life 1) to name one of your best qualities and 2) to write what he or she

wishes for you this year: _____

_____

Paste a photo of yourself here

My Friends:	**My Relatives:**

A Carpenter with Influence

Have you ever heard of Rameses the Great? He was king of the Egyptian empire over three thousand years ago. During the sixty-seven years of his reign, Rameses was considered a god. He had many large monuments built as tributes to himself. Carved in these monuments were descriptions of his mighty deeds. When he died at the age of ninety, he had one hundred children. Now Rameses is just a mummy in a museum and a name in a history book.

Jesus Christ lived some two thousand years ago in Palestine. He was a Jewish craftsman who spent about the last three years of his life as a traveling preacher. He taught about the kingdom of God and the laws of love. He healed the sick. But to some religious leaders he was a troublemaker. He attracted crowds and associated with everyone, even outcasts. The Romans executed Jesus as a criminal when he was in his early thirties. After his body vanished from his tomb, some of his followers saw him alive, risen from the dead. They began a movement called the Way, now known as Christianity. Today more than a billion people believe that Jesus is God, and try to live by his teachings.

What are the signs of Jesus' influence in the world today?

_____

_____

_____

Jesus has a powerful and lasting influence because of who he is.

Who Is Jesus?

A fish holds the answer to this question. During persecutions the first Christians used the sign of a fish as a secret means of identification. In Greek, each letter of the word "fish" (ICHTHYS) begins a word in the phrase "Jesus Christ, Son of God, Savior."

The Christ

Jesus is the Christ, which means the **messiah,** the great leader sent by God. He is the one the prophets foretold and the Jewish people awaited. Jesus, however, was much more than the Israelites expected.

Son of God

With the help of the Holy Spirit, the followers of Jesus came to realize that Jesus was the Son of God. Jesus had often referred to God as "my Father." He even called God *Abba,* a Hebrew word for "Daddy."

As Son of God, Jesus was God, too. Like the Jewish and Muslim people, Christians believe in one God. What makes us different is our belief in the **Trinity.** This main Catholic dogma (belief) states *there are three persons in one God: Father, Son, and Holy Spirit.* These divine persons are equal and work together. They have always existed together in a community of love, and they always will be.

At a point in time, God the Father sent his only Son to give us eternal life. This Second Person of the Trinity obeyed the Father and became a man: Jesus. *Jesus then is a person who has both a divine nature and a human nature.* He is completely God and completely human. Jesus is not only Emmanuel, which means "God with us," but he is our brother. The mystery of God becoming human is called the **Incarnation** (*in* + *carn* = in the flesh). God shared in our humanity so that we could share in divinity.

Since Jesus is God, when we look at Jesus we know what God is like. God had revealed himself to us before. *Creation* gives clues about his power and goodness. The Old Testament also tells of God's love through God's words and actions in history. But with the *Incarnation,* God is revealed to us perfectly and fully. Jesus said, "The Father and I are one" (John 10:30). We call Jesus the Word from the Father. Despite God's revelation, God remains a mystery beyond words.

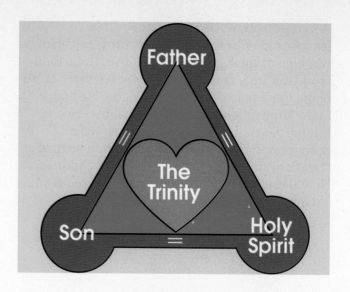

Savior

Jesus is also the **Savior.** Even his name, *Jesus,* means "God saves." By his life, especially through the **Paschal Mystery,** Jesus rescued the human race. The Paschal (Easter) Mystery includes Jesus' suffering, death, resurrection, and ascension. By taking our sins upon himself, and dying and rising, Jesus ended the power of sin and death over us. He made it possible for us to have eternal life. At every Eucharist we, the community of believers, proclaim and celebrate this great mystery of our faith, the Paschal Mystery.

> "He is the image of the invisible God."
> Colossians 1:15

Who Is Jesus for You?

Jesus is your personal Savior. He gives you an *identity*. You are not a "nobody." You are a beloved child of God. Jesus gives you a *destiny*—eternal happiness. He loved you enough to die a painful death for you. And he is always ready to save you again from evil.

Our opinions of people change. For instance, Mark Twain said that when he was fourteen he thought his father didn't know anything. When he was twenty-one, he was surprised how much his father had learned in seven years! You will realize who Jesus is, gradually. Sometimes one aspect of him will be spotlighted, and sometimes another.

Look at page 3. What title of Jesus is your favorite now? Why? How did you first come to know about Jesus? Who helped you to know him? How can you come to know him better?

How Some Seventh Graders See Him

Jesus means love, happiness, and heaven.
—Becky Castell

✜

Jesus is a guide. If I think of doing something wrong, I can ask if Jesus would do it. Then I can make the right decision.
—Teddy Kramer

✜

Jesus means a whole new world opening up.
—Ken Albro

✜

Jesus is someone who believes in you.
—Darren Roger

✜

Jesus means everything to me, for without him I am nothing.
—Kristen Averell

✜

To me Jesus is a friend for life. He is always there for you. Even though he may not always do things your way, he will always do the right thing.
—Cindi Smith

✜

Jesus is a loving man with a heart the size of a mansion. He is a gift of God.
—Amy Olup

Remember

Who is Jesus?
Jesus is the Son of God and the Savior. He is truly God and truly human.

What is the Trinity?
The Trinity is the mystery of one God in three divine persons: Father, Son, and Holy Spirit.

What is the Incarnation?
The Incarnation is the mystery of God becoming human.

What does the Paschal Mystery include?
The Paschal Mystery includes the suffering, death, resurrection, and ascension of Jesus.

Words to Know

Messiah	Paschal Mystery
Incarnation	Trinity

Respond

"Lord Jesus Christ, Son of God, have mercy on me, a sinner." This is the Jesus Prayer, an ancient prayer popular in the Eastern Church. It is recited repeatedly. Try to pray it often.

Reach Out

1. Ask friends or relatives of the Protestant tradition what they think about Jesus and what he means to them.
2. Create a poster or a flyer that calls attention to one of Jesus' titles. Put it where it will cause people to reflect on who he is. A flyer, for instance, can be inserted into your parish's Sunday bulletin.
3. Teach someone the Jesus Prayer.
4. Write a poem-prayer to Jesus in which each letter in his name or one of his titles starts a line. Example:

    Jesus, my God and Savior,
    Each day you call me to love and
    Serve others. Help me to
    Understand what I must do
    So that I might be with you forever.

Review

Know Yourself   Fill in the blanks.

1. Powers that make you in the image of God and above the rest of creation are your

_____ and _____.

2. Some things you can control in your life are _____,

_____, _____, and _____.

3. The key to knowing yourself is to know _____.

A Monogram   Read the statements. If the statement is true, write **T** on the line. If it is false, write **F**. Shade in the areas of the puzzle whose numbers correspond to the true statements. When you are finished, you should see a monogram for Christ.

_____ **1.** Everyone loved Jesus.

_____ **2.** *Abba* means "holy one."

_____ **3.** Christians believe in one God.

_____ **4.** God the Father existed before God the Son.

_____ **5.** In heaven we will fully understand the Trinity.

_____ **6.** The name Jesus means "God saves."

_____ **7.** Christians believe there are four persons in God.

_____ **8.** Jesus is both God and man.

_____ **9.** The Incarnation is the mystery of God becoming human.

_____ **10.** The man Jesus always existed.

_____ **11.** God the Son only pretended to be a man.

_____ **12.** God is revealed best in Scripture.

_____ **13.** There are two persons in Jesus.

_____ **14.** Jesus saved us from sin and death through the Paschal Mystery.

_____ **15.** Jesus saved only Christians by his death.

A Saving Mystery   Number the events of the Paschal Mystery in the order they occurred.

_____ death   _____ ascension   _____ suffering   _____ resurrection

When do we celebrate the Paschal Mystery? _____

Friendship with Jesus

2

And the Word became flesh and
made his dwelling among us.

JOHN 1:14

Suppose you are a brilliant scientist. In your laboratory you are trying to produce a robot like a human being. List the characteristics your robot must have to resemble a real person. (Clue: Think about what makes *you* human.)

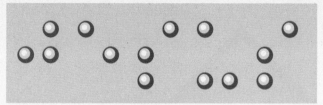

Someone You Can Trust!

When you look at the dots above, you may or may not recognize the word. You might have to look at the Braille key on the bottom of the page. Faith is somewhat like being able to read that word. It is a supernatural power and a *gift.* Not everyone sees Jesus for who he is. Sometimes it requires a little help from others.

That Jesus existed is certain. Some early writings refer to him. But that Jesus is God in the flesh is a matter of faith. **Faith** is believing and trusting when you do not understand. Faith in Jesus is based on Tradition and Scripture. These are two ways that God reveals himself, but they form a single "deposit of faith." **Tradition** is the truths handed down by the Church from generation to generation, from the time of the apostles. It includes teachings, liturgy, writings, and the lives of Christians. **Scripture** is the Word of God, the written testimony of people's belief.

Jesus, Fully Human

Jesus sometimes referred to himself as the Son of Man. In one sense this title means a human being. Jesus had all the traits in your list. *He was like us in all things except sin.* He breathed air, ate food, laughed, and got tired. He knew love, sadness, disappointment, and fear. He faced difficult decisions and had to live with the consequences of his choices. Like us, he had to learn and he had to suffer and die. He was not just pretending to be human. Amazing as it sounds, God the Son really became a man named Jesus.

Since Jesus is God, there is no evil in him. As a perfect person, Jesus reveals to us what we can be. He is our *model* for being human. Anyone who wishes a rich, full life has only to follow in his footsteps. To be like Jesus is not as impossible as it seems because God empowers us through grace. The first step is to have *faith.*

Having faith in Jesus and being committed to him is a lifelong challenge. You can even expect to lose sight of Jesus at times. Staying in touch with Tradition, Scripture, and faith-filled people strengthens faith. So does meeting Jesus in the sacraments. With the grace of the Holy Spirit you will experience a close relationship with Jesus. You and he will be special friends.

A B C D E F G H I J K L M N O P Q R S T U V W X Y Z

Friends, a Human Need

Read these definitions of a friend. Then write your own definition.

Friend (frend), n. **1.** A person whom one knows well and is fond of. (*Webster's New World Dictionary*)

2. A friend is someone who knows everything about you and still accepts you. (St. Augustine)

3. A friend is someone to share with, to share fears and everything—and someone to love. (junior high student)

4. A friend is someone who will always help you and stay with you no matter what happens. (junior high student)

5. A friend _____

_____

_____

One of the most important things in your life right now is your friends. People need friends at every point in their lives. Having friends is a wonderful and necessary part of being human. You may have friendly relationships with many people, but have only a few deep and lasting relationships. A true friend is a gift of God.

The Real Thing

In true friendship, people help each other to become the best they can be. If you usually get into trouble when you are with certain people, they are not true friends. Friends do not lead each other to be selfish, unkind, disobedient, or dishonest. Instead they support each other in choosing good and avoiding evil, even when evil "looks like fun" and "everybody else is doing it." Friends help each other overcome temptation and habits of sin.

Friendship is not always easy. Sometimes you or your friends may be selfish or bossy. You or they may tell a secret or not do a fair share of a job. Sometimes one of you may want to do something wrong. When you fail to be real friends, you are called to repair the damage and keep building your friendship. How?

True Blue Friends

Discuss or role-play situations that challenge friendships like these.

Jean's family has an extra ticket for the Ice Capades. Jean invited Linda, her best friend. Linda has a gymnastics meet that same night. She has a commitment to her team, but Jean will be disappointed if she says no. What are Linda's options? Which choice do you think is better? How can Jean help Linda make her decision?

Miguel and Sam have been friends since third grade. They have always enjoyed playing ball together. This year Miguel made the school track team. Whenever Sam wants to play ball, Miguel is busy. Sam and Miguel still want to be friends. What can they do? Can friends be involved in different activities and still remain close?

Kathy knew something was wrong with Sandra. Then Bob came up and asked to see the treasure Sandra had "picked up" the night before at the mall. Sandra blushed and after a bit of teasing, she admitted shoplifting a poster. Bob left after telling Sandra how clever she was. How will Kathy react if she is a truly good friend? What risks does she take in speaking up? In remaining silent?

Jesus' Friends

Like any other human being, Jesus had friends. He was popular and attracted many people, young and old. Of these, several became his closest friends. From the twelve apostles, he singled out Peter, James, and John to share special events with him. He loved Lazarus and his sisters, Martha and Mary. When Lazarus died, Jesus felt so bad that he cried. Mary Magdalene was another friend. She stayed with Jesus through the crucifixion, and she was the first one he appeared to after the resurrection.

Invitation to Joy

> Look, I am standing at the door, knocking. If one of you hears me calling and opens the door, I will come in to share a meal at that person's side.
>
> Adapted from Book of Revelation 3:20 JB

Jesus invites you to friendship. He knocks at the door of your life, a door that you alone can open. You are free to open it or not. Jesus loves you and wants you to be happy. He wants you to know the joy that comes to those who walk through life with him. With Jesus at your side you can be at peace even when you suffer.

You saw that Jesus' title Son of Man can refer to his being human. It may also refer to his second coming. In the Book of Daniel the Son of Man is someone who comes in glory at the end of the world.

Jesus would like you, his friend, to share his glory, to spend an eternity of happiness with him, his Father, and the Holy Spirit. Will you enter into friendship with him? Will you feast with him at the banquet of heaven?

The Ultimate Test

Like all friendships, friendship with Jesus has its responsibilities. Jesus asks a great deal of you. Read John 15:12–17 in which Jesus speaks to you about being friends. Think about his words and complete these statements:

1. Jesus said that the greatest love a person can

   have for a friend is _____

   _____

2. Jesus said we are his friends if we do what he

   commands, namely, _____

   _____

3. Add two endings to the following statement. Then rank all of them using number one for the most difficult.

   It is not always easy to carry out Jesus' command. I find it difficult to

   _____ help with work around home.

   _____ listen when adults talk.

   _____ be kind when others do not play well in a game.

   _____ be happy when someone gets what I want.

   _____ _____

   _____ _____

4. When I act as Jesus' friend, I know I can count on his Father's help for Jesus said

   _____

   _____

> If you don't feel close to God, guess who moved?

Tips for Journal Writers

1. Plan to spend the time set aside for journal writing doing just that.
2. Be honest with the Lord and with yourself. Write how you really think and feel.
3. Be willing to share anything and everything with the Lord. The Holy Spirit will help you choose what to write.
4. Listen to the Lord. He will speak to you through his Word, through other people, through events of your day, or through your own thoughts.
5. Keep your journal private. Do not plan to show it to others. Write to God alone. You may not feel totally free if you think someone else might read your journal.
6. Make your journal special and neat, but do not worry too much about spelling and punctuation.
7. Reread your journal every now and then to see how God has spoken to you and has been acting in your life.

Growing in Friendship

Being Jesus' friend is more than knowing *about* him. It is knowing him personally. Luke 10:38–42 describes a visit Jesus made to Martha and Mary. While Martha prepared the meal, Mary spent time with Jesus. When Martha complained that Mary was not helping her, Jesus told her that Mary had chosen the better part.

As Jesus' friend you are to serve him, but you are also to spend time with him. This is the only way you will get to know him. Do you see yourself more like Martha or Mary at this time?

Keeping in Touch: A Journal

The time you spend with Jesus is prayer time. A good way to enrich your prayer time is to keep a prayer journal. This is a book you use to write about yourself and your relationship with the Lord. You can write anything you want to say to God. You can tell God what you think and how you feel. You can share your joys and sorrows. You can thank God for gifts and graces. You can praise God and ask forgiveness. You can ask questions. Sometimes you might even write a response God might make to you.

Your journal can be a real treasure. When you reread it, you will come to know yourself better. You will be reminded of God's great love for you and realize how God is working in your life. Best of all, a prayer journal is a way to deepen your love for your friend Jesus.

Remember

What is faith?
Faith is a gift from God to believe and trust when we do not understand.

How does God reveal himself?
God reveals himself in Scripture and Tradition.

What is Scripture?
Scripture is the Word of God in the Bible. It is the written testimony of people's belief.

What is Tradition?
Tradition is the revelation of God through beliefs handed down by the Church from the time of the apostles.

What command of Jesus will you follow if you are his friend?
"Love one another as I love you." (John 15:12)

Words to Know

faith	Tradition
Scripture	journal

Respond

Find a book or a spiral notebook for your prayer journal. Decorate it if you wish. Decide on a time when you will write in your journal.

Reach Out

1. Thank God for the true friends in your life by doing something special for one.
2. Write a composition explaining why Jesus is a good best friend.
3. List reasons why you make a good friend. You might ask your friends to help you.
4. Draw up five rules for making friends and five rules for losing friends.
5. Use one of the following prayer starters each day this week. Write part of your conversation in your journal.
   ✤ Tell Jesus about the beautiful things you saw today.
   ✤ Tell Jesus how you feel and why.
   ✤ Talk to Jesus about something sad that you heard or saw today.
   ✤ If your friend phoned today, what would you talk about? Talk to Jesus about these things.
   ✤ Talk to Jesus about something you fear.
   ✤ Talk to Jesus about gifts God has given you and how you can share them.
   ✤ Think about one wonderful person. Thank God for creating that person.
   ✤ Did you see a lonely or hurting person? Ask Jesus to show you how you could help.

Review

Seeing Double   Complete these statements with the missing pair of words.

1. Jesus was both G_____ and m_____ .

2. Faith is b_____ and t_____ when we don't understand.

3. God reveals himself in T_____ and S_____ .

4. Two of Jesus' friends were the sisters M_____ and M_____ .

5. As Jesus' friends we are to s_____ him and s_____ time with him.

The Right Choice   Circle the item that matches the description.

1. Title of Jesus that may refer to his second coming.   God the Son   Son of Man

2. The written testimony of people's belief.   Scripture   Tradition

3. One thing Jesus did not have in common with us.   pain   sin

4. The sign that we are friends with Jesus.   love   good luck

5. Truths handed down from the apostles by teachings, liturgy, writings, and example.   Scripture   Tradition

True or False   Write **+** if the statement is true and **o** if it is false.

_____ 1. True friends help each other choose good and avoid evil.

_____ 2. Jesus is not a good model for us because he was God.

_____ 3. Faith is a gift.

_____ 4. Jesus never cried.

_____ 5. You can know Jesus better through prayer and journal writing.

Scripture:
A Portrait of Jesus

3

Ignorance of Scriptures is ignorance of Christ.

ST. JEROME

About thirty years after Jesus' death, this conversation might have taken place one day after the celebration of Eucharist:

Mark: Peter was really moved while he was telling about Jesus forgiving that woman. I thought I saw tears in his eyes when he said, "She is forgiven much because she loved much."

Judith: I had never heard that story.

Stephen: I had; but the way I heard it, the woman who poured the perfume on Jesus' feet was Mary, the sister of Lazarus.

Mark: We are really lucky to hear about Jesus from the people who knew him. Our grandchildren won't hear firsthand accounts.

Judith: Right. The apostles won't be with us forever. James has already been killed.

Stephen: I used to think that Jesus was returning to earth soon. Now I realize it might be years before his second coming. Someone should write down for future generations what he said and did.

Mark: I know a Christian who has written a collection of sayings of Jesus.

Stephen: Just think. If we had a record of Jesus' life, the Good News would spread throughout the empire.

Judith: And people interested in joining us could study the scroll.

Mark: I'd love to put together such a document. Excuse me. I'm going to talk to Peter.

By the end of the first century, all the books that formed the **New Testament** (Christian Scriptures) were finished. They testify to the life, death, and resurrection of Jesus. They tell us that Jesus, the Son of God, is the Messiah, the Savior that the people of the Old Testament longed for. Most exciting, they proclaim that Jesus is truly living among us.

The New Testament

Use the table of contents in your Bible to complete this outline of the New Testament. Fill in the name and number of each type of book.

Number	Name
_____	G_____
_____	A_____ of the A_____
_____	L_____ (E_____)
_____	B_____ of R_____

Total _____

Entrance of the Church of the Nativity in Bethlehem

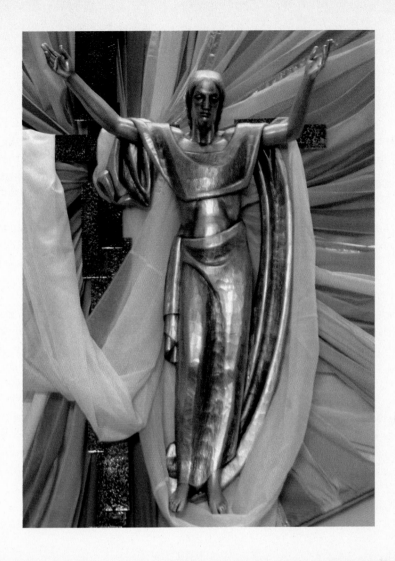

Who Is This Jesus?

He said things like
I am the way. (John 14:6)
I am with you always. (Matthew 28:20)
I am the bread of life. (John 6:48)
Follow me. (Luke 5:27)
[You] hypocrites. . . (Matthew 15:7)
Young man, I tell you, arise! (Luke 7:14)
This is my body. (Luke 22:19)
Whoever has seen me
    has seen the Father. (John 14:9)

He felt
grief (John 11:35)
love (Mark 10:21)
anger (John 2:13–17)
gentleness (Luke 19:5)
sympathy (Matthew 9:18–19)
affection (Mark 6:30–31)
frustration (Luke 13:34)
compassion (Matthew 15:32–38)

He did things like
die on a cross (John 10:14–18)
feed the hungry (Matthew 15:32–38)
curse a fig tree (Matthew 21:18–22)
make breakfast (John 21:1–14)
change water into wine (John 2:1–11)
go to a wedding (John 2:1–2)
pray all night (Luke 6:12)
rise from the dead (Mark 16:1–7)
eat with sinners (Mark 2:13–17)

What kind of person would say, feel, and do things like this?

Gospels: Knowing about Jesus

The word *gospel* means "good news." The Gospels are four accounts of the life and teachings of Jesus. They are *documents of faith.* According to John 20:31, they were written "that you may [come to] believe that Jesus is the Messiah, the Son of God, and that through this belief you may have life in his name." John's Gospel ends:

 There are also many other things that Jesus did, but if these were to be described individually, I do not think the whole world would contain the books that would be written.

John 21:25

The Gospels were not meant to be biographies. They are more like portraits. Each Gospel writer chose incidents and shaped his account to present the features of Jesus that he considered important. In addition, each writer directed his message about the risen Lord to a particular group of people. These are two reasons why the Gospels are different and do not always agree. The Gospels all proclaim the same news: *Jesus is the Messiah, the Son of God who revealed the Father's love for us and saved us.*

Although we are not certain who wrote the Gospels, tradition gives the credit to Matthew, Mark, Luke, and John. These men are called the **evangelists,** which means proclaimers of the Good News. We think that the Gospel of Mark was the first to be written. The writers of the Gospels of Matthew and Luke most likely drew their material from it and from some unknown source that biblical scholars call "Q." Because these three Gospels are so much alike, they are called **synoptic.** *Synoptic* means "same view." John's Gospel, the last to be written, has the style of a deep, religious poem and contains **discourses** (long speeches) and stories not found in the other Gospels.

Did you ever wish that you were alive when Jesus was so you could know him better? Actually, because of the Gospels we probably understand Jesus more than his friends and neighbors did. The Gospels were written after Jesus sent the Holy Spirit. As Jesus had promised, the Spirit instructed the apostles and reminded them of all he had taught. Today, the Holy Spirit is still with the Church Jesus founded, enlightening us so we may know the meaning of Scripture.

	Mark A.D. 63–70	Matthew A.D. 80–100	Luke A.D. 70–90	John A.D. 90–100
Traditional Evangelist	Mark, companion of Peter	Matthew, apostle	Luke, Greek doctor, Gentile, companion of Paul	John, apostle
Symbol from the Opening	Lion (John's voice in the wilderness)	Man (the human ancestry of Christ)	Ox (Zechariah offering sacrifice)	Eagle (the Divine Word, thoughts soaring above Earth)
Main Audience	Persecuted Christians	Jewish converts	Gentile (non-Jewish) Christians	Christians defending their faith
Characteristics	Short, fast-moving	Quotations from Hebrew Scriptures Five sermons	Infancy stories Warm, human portraits	Poetic, symbols Reflective Discourses
Portrait of Jesus	Man of action Man of suffering	Teacher New Moses	Savior and friend of all: sinners, the poor, women, Samaritans	Son of God Giver of life

Gospels: Knowing Jesus

God is the author of the Bible but did not dictate the words to the evangelists and other Scripture writers. God inspired all the books in the Bible. **Inspiration** is the action of God that moves people to communicate what God wants made known, using their own background, culture, language, and style. Inspiration makes the Gospels the Word of God. The Gospels, then, do not only help us know about Jesus. They help us know him personally because they are his all-powerful, living Word. Whenever we read Scripture, we meet God and God speaks to us.

How are the Gospels honored at Mass?

_____

_____

_____

Other Inspired Books

A book called the **Acts of the Apostles** follows the Gospels. It is thought to be a continuation of Luke's Gospel. Acts describes how Peter, Paul, and other disciples founded the first Christian communities. It follows the progress of Christianity from Jerusalem to Rome. Next in the Bible are the **letters,** or **epistles.** Although they appear after Acts of the Apostles, most of the letters were written before the Gospels. These letters apply the message of Jesus to daily life. Most of them are from Paul, a man who never met Jesus, except as the risen Lord.
The last book of the Bible is the **Book of**

Revelation, also called the **Apocalypse.** It is a strange and difficult book to understand because it uses symbols. Written during a time of persecution, Revelation encourages Christians to accept the cross and hope for the triumph of God at the end of the world.

Remember

What is the Gospel?
The Gospel is the Good News that Jesus' life, death, and resurrection have freed us from the power of sin and death.

What is inspiration?
Inspiration is the action of God that directs people to write what he wanted made known through their own language and style.

Words to Know

Gospel	Acts of the Apostles
Synoptic	letters
Q	epistles
evangelist	Book of Revelation
discourse	Apocalypse
inspiration	

Words to Memorize

The evangelists: Matthew, Mark, Luke, and John

Respond

Meet Jesus every day through his word in the Bible. Assemble the Scripture booklet in the back of this book. Use it to know Jesus better.

Reach Out

1. Read Philippians 3:7–9 to find out how St. Paul describes what Jesus means to him. Then answer these questions to yourself:

   - How much does Jesus mean to me?
   - Do I treasure his friendship enough to spend time with him every day?
   - How would I rate my own openness to God?
   - What will I do to know Jesus better?

2. Interview three teenagers or adults who seem to be good friends of Jesus. Ask how Jesus helps them in the problems of daily life.

3. Look into becoming a lector at your parish so you can proclaim the Word of God in your Christian community.

4. Think about something Jesus said or did. Write it in your journal. This statement is Jesus' gift to you. He is telling you something about himself. He wants its meaning to grow in your heart and move you to love him more. Write about his message, including some of these ideas:
   ✢ What it means to you
   ✢ How it makes you feel about yourself
   ✢ How you think Jesus would like you to respond
   ✢ Something you will do to respond
   ✢ Your thanks that he has spoken to you.

Review

Gospel Guess   Write the letter of the Gospel being described.

a. Matthew   **c.** Luke
b. Mark   **d.** John

_____ **1.** The last Gospel

_____ **2.** Probably the first Gospel written

_____ **3.** For Jewish converts

_____ **4.** Is poetic and has discourses

_____ **5.** Shows Jesus as friend to all, including sinners and women

_____ **6.** Is short and fast-moving

_____ **7.** The synoptic Gospels

_____ **8.** Proclaims Jesus as the Messiah, the Son of God who saved us

_____ **9.** Especially for Gentiles

_____ **10.** The symbol of its evangelist is an eagle

1. —

2. — —

3. — — —

4. — — — —

5. — — — — —

6. — — — — — —

7. — — — — — — —

8. — — — — — — — —

9. — — — — — — — — —

10. — — — — — — — — — —

11. — — — — — — — — — — —

12. — — — — — — — — — — — —

Scripture Mount   Write the missing word or number in each sentence on the corresponding blanks above.

1. The New Testament books were probably completed by the end of the _____st century A.D.

2. The Old Testament has 46 books; the New Testament has _____.

3. _____ is the author of the Bible.

4. The _____ of the Apostles is the book that tells the story of the early Church.

5. The Gospels are not history books, but documents of _____.

6. _____ means "Good news."

7. Most _____ were written before the Gospels and apply Jesus' message to life.

8. The first three Gospels are so similar they are called _____ .

9. A long speech in a Gospel is a _____.

10. The last book in the Bible, a symbolic book about the end of the world, is the Apocalypse or the Book of _____.

11. The Gospels' writers are the _____.

12. _____ is the action of God that moves people to communicate what God wants made known.

The World Jesus Lived In

4

The landscape of Jerusalem

Is he not the carpenter's son?
Is not his mother named Mary...?

MATTHEW 13:55

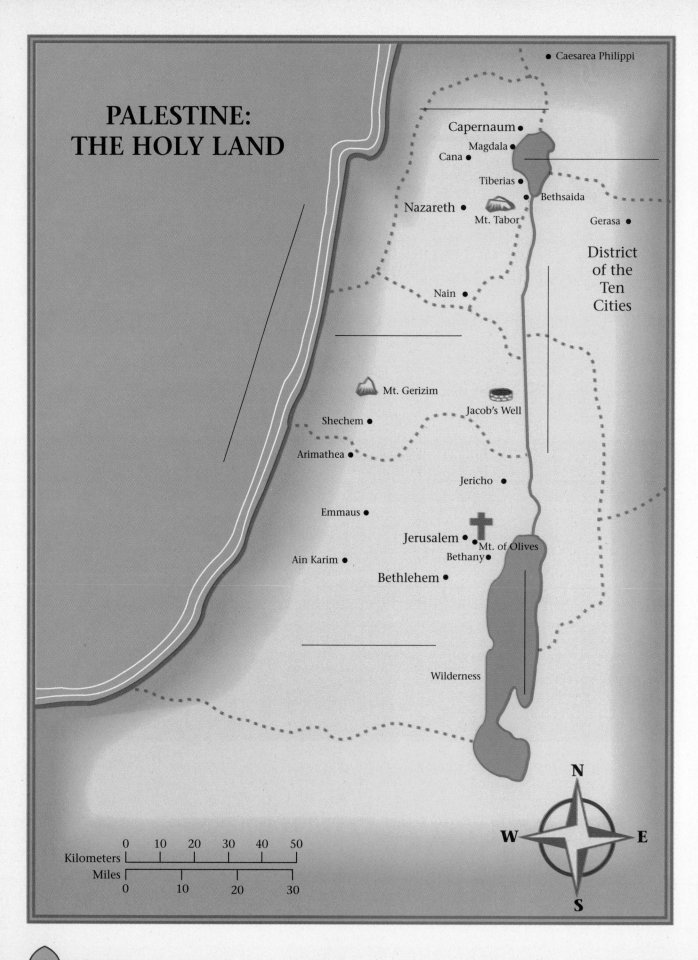

PALESTINE: THE HOLY LAND

• Caesarea Philippi

Capernaum •
Magdala •
Cana •
Tiberias •
Nazareth • Bethsaida
Mt. Tabor
Gerasa •

District of the Ten Cities

Nain •

Mt. Gerizim
Jacob's Well
Shechem •
Arimathea •

Jericho •

Emmaus •
Jerusalem • Mt. of Olives
Bethany •
Ain Karim •
Bethlehem •

Wilderness

N
W   E
S

| | 0 | 10 | 20 | 30 | 40 | 50 |
Kilometers
Miles
| | 0 | 10 | 20 | 30 |

You probably eat with knives, forks, and spoons and not your fingers. Your parents won't be choosing a husband or wife for you. You would be shocked to see nine-year-old children playing outside without clothes. Some customs that you would find strange are perfectly normal for people in other times and countries. The way you live, your habits, attitudes, and values are largely determined by the country and time you live in. What else determines what you are like?

When God became incarnate, he chose to live 2,000 years ago in a country in the Middle East called **Palestine.** The United States is little more than 200 years old, but consider how life has changed since the time of George Washington. Imagine then how different the world that shaped Jesus was from yours! Knowing about life during his time will help you understand Jesus and the Gospels.

The Land Jesus Walked

Palestine is also called Israel or the Holy Land. During Jesus' time it was as large as Vermont and had three main areas: Galilee in the north, Samaria, and Judea in the south. (To remember the order of Galilee, Samaria, and Judea, think "God Sent Jesus.") Nazareth, a town in the hills of Galilee and the home of Mary and Joseph, was where Jesus grew up. During his public ministry his home base was Capernaum, a town near the Sea of Galilee. But Jesus' life began in Bethlehem and ended in Jerusalem, both in Judea.

Find the three main areas of Palestine on the map and label them. Then circle Nazareth, Capernaum, Bethlehem, and Jerusalem.

Galilee is green, mountainous, and beautiful. The freshwater Sea of Galilee (also called Lake Gennesareth) is to the east, and snow-covered Mount Hermon to the north. Although most of Galilee was rural during Jesus' time, major trade routes passed through its large trading cities. Greek and Roman culture was popular in Galilee. And many Galilean Jews were originally non-Jews. For these reasons, Judeans looked down on Galileans with their odd accents.

Samaria was avoided by Jewish people when they traveled. The Samaritans were considered heretics because they had intermarried with foreigners and worshiped in their own temple on Mount Gerizim instead of at the Temple in Jerusalem.

Judea, a hot, dry land, has the Dead Sea to the east and wilderness to the south. **Jerusalem** was the capital city where Israel's kings had lived. It was also the holy city because the Temple was there. Jerusalem is sacred to Jews, Christians, and Muslims.

To the west of Palestine is the Mediterranean Sea. Within Palestine the Jordan River flows south along a very crooked path through the Sea of Galilee and into the Dead Sea. On the map, find these three bodies of water and the Jordan River and label them.

Palestine has two seasons: a cool, wet winter and a summer when the sun shines almost every day. Most of the land is very rocky.

When Jesus lived, towns in Palestine were surrounded by walls. Food and crafts were sold in markets just outside the walls. Every night the city gates were locked and guards kept watch.

The Sea of Galilee

Head of Herod

Augustus Caesar, the first
Roman emperor

The Political Scene

When Jesus lived,
Palestine was occupied by
Rome, which had conquered it in 63 B.C. During
Jesus' lifetime, Augustus Caesar and then his step-
son, Tiberius Caesar, were the Roman emperors.
Herod the Great was king of Palestine until
shortly after Jesus' birth. Although he was a great
builder and rebuilt the Temple, he is remembered
most for his cruelty. He killed many of his family
for fear that they would overthrow his rule. After
his death, Palestine was divided among his three
sons: Archelaus, Herod, and Philip. Archelaus
ruled Judea and Samaria until Augustus replaced
him with Roman procurators like Pontius Pilate,
who sentenced Jesus to death. Herod Antipas,
whom Jesus called "the fox," ruled Galilee. And
Philip ruled the region east of Galilee.

In general, Rome respected Jewish religious practices. Jewish men, for instance, did not have to
serve in the army because their religion did not
permit them to mix with **Gentiles,** or non-Jews.
However, the Jewish people resented the presence
of Roman troops, the Roman laws, and the
Roman taxes. Jewish men who collected taxes for
Rome were the least popular men in town. These
tax collectors, also called **publicans,** were allowed
to keep any money they collected beyond their
quota.

The Wailing Wall in Jerusalem

Some Religious Groups

The **Pharisees** were largely middle-class Jews.
They were known for their love of the **Torah,** or
the Law, the first five books of the Bible. Some
schools of Pharisees interpreted the Law strictly
and added 613 regulations. The Pharisees believed
in angels and in our resurrection. The Gospels
show Jesus scolding them for stressing external
observances instead of a spirit of love and
worship. The Pharisees, however, were sincerely
seeking holiness. It was they who preserved the
Jewish religion after Jerusalem was destroyed by
Rome in A.D. 70. The scholarly teachers among
the Pharisees were called **Scribes.**

The **Sadducees** were wealthy and powerful political leaders. Most were priests. They worked
closely with Rome and, unlike the Pharisees, did
not believe in resurrection and in adding to the
Law. The **Sanhedrin** was a group of seventy-one
Jewish men in Judea who served as a supreme
council. The chief high priest presided. He was
not only a spiritual leader but almost a king.
Caiaphas was the high priest at the end of Jesus'
life, assisted by his father-in-law, Annas. **Zealots**
were freedom fighters who sometimes used
violence to overthrow Rome's control of
Palestine. The **Essenes** were men unhappy with
the way Jewish faith was lived. Seeking a pure life,
many withdrew to the desert. There they lived in
communities doing penance and waiting for the
coming of God.

Jesus' Religion

Jesus was Jewish. Jewish families prayed many prayers together at home. They prayed before and after eating. Morning and evening they prayed the **Shema,** the main commandment:

Hear, O Israel! The LORD is our God, the LORD alone! Therefore, you shall love the LORD, your God, with all your heart, and with all your soul, and with all your strength.

Deuteronomy 6:4–5

On entering and leaving a house, Jewish people touched the **mezuzah.** This was a small case on the right doorpost that held a copy of the Shema. At prayer, devout men put a prayer shawl on their heads and strapped small boxes (**phylacteries**) to their foreheads and arms. These boxes contained the Word of God. People greeted one another with "*Shalom,*" which means "peace."

Everyone who was able traveled to the Temple in Jerusalem to observe the three major feasts: Passover, Pentecost, and Tabernacles. The **Temple,** the symbol of the Jewish faith, was the only place where sacrifices were made. It was a huge and majestic building. Twenty men were needed to open one of its thirteen gates. Twenty thousand people worked there. During the time of Jesus, the Temple was being rebuilt. It was destroyed when Rome attacked Jerusalem. All that was left standing was an outer Western wall that still exists today. At this wall, called the Wailing Wall, Jewish people pray and grieve over the destruction of the Temple. They insert prayer petitions between the giant stones.

Sabbath, the Lord's day, was a day of strict rest. Among forbidden activities were tying a rope, putting out a lamp, and walking over a half mile. Sabbath services were held at local **synagogues.** These were the town centers of prayer, education, and social life. The scrolls of the Torah were read and preached there.

A mezuzah

The Law declared what made a person unclean or unfit for worship. Things like touching a sick or dead person and dealing with Gentiles required special prayers, washings, or passage of time before the person became clean.

List some of your religious customs.

_____

_____

_____

_____

_____

_____

_____

_____

Daily Life in Palestine

Scholars study and describe what life might have been like in cultures long ago. Imagine that you lived in Palestine when Jesus did. Your house is made of clay bricks or stones held together with mud and straw. Its one room has a dirt floor. At night you sleep on a mat on the dirt floor. Your pillow is a piece of wood or a stone. In hot weather you climb the outside steps up to the roof to sleep. The roof is made of sticks bound by long grass and covered with earth. In your house are a table, a spinning wheel, and a wooden bowl for measuring grain. Since there are no windows, an olive oil lamp burns all day on a stand. At the far end of your house a cave shelters your goat and donkey.

You probably belong to a large family. Your father is a farmer, a craftsman, or a fisherman. He has a beard and large brown eyes. He wears a sleeveless gown covered by a long tunic that is fringed at the bottom and tied with a belt. A white cloth on his head is held in place by a cord. A heavy cloak made of camel or goat hair serves him as a coat or a blanket. He leads the family prayers. You and your mother are considered his property.

Your mother cooks outside, grinding grain and baking bread. She wears a decorated tunic and sandals, and she never goes out without a veil over her face. She looks forward to her daily walk to the town well. There she meets and chats with other women before carrying her water jug home

on her head. Your mother cannot know how to read or write, but she memorizes Scripture from the synagogue service.

If you are a boy, you go to synagogue school. There you learn to read and write by studying Scripture under a rabbi. Your father teaches you his trade and how to wrestle. If you are a girl, your mother prepares you to be a good wife. You hope to have many sons. Your parents will arrange a marriage for you. You might not see your husband until your wedding day.

You don't attend public entertainment because the Gentiles are there. Your life revolves around prayer and religious celebrations, especially those that mark stages of life. Weddings can last seven days. For funerals, even poor people hire flute players and mourners for a procession to the stone tombs.

You eat twice a day while sitting cross-legged outside on the ground. Instead of a fork or spoon, you use your hands. Besides bread, your meals include honey, spiced foods, cheese, vegetables, fruit, and fish. You seldom have meat or eggs. Water and wine are the usual drinks.

You probably speak **Aramaic,** but you also know some Hebrew for prayer and perhaps some Greek, which is the language of the land.

3000   2000   1000   1000   2000   3000
Abraham   Moses

The Lord of History

Jesus had to live in a particular time and place, but his life and message are for people in every century and every nation. He lives on in his Church, touching people through the sacraments and through you.

On the timeline of humankind above, put a chi-rho (☧) where you are. Then read each question and check your answer. As you do, you will learn ways to be Jesus for others.

	Yes	Sometimes	No
Do you keep up with world news so that you know about people in other lands?	❏	❏	❏
Do you ever invite someone to church or religion class with you?	❏	❏	❏
Do you talk about Jesus with your friends?	❏	❏	❏
Do you try to do the right thing because that's what Jesus would do?	❏	❏	❏
Do you pray that people might live by Jesus' values?	❏	❏	❏
Do you treat people the way Jesus treated others?	❏	❏	❏

Remember

Who do we believe Jesus of Nazareth is?

And the Word became flesh
and made his dwelling among us,
and we saw his glory,
the glory as of the Father's only Son,
full of grace and truth.

John 1:14

Words to Know

Palestine	Gentiles	Temple
Galilee	Pharisees	Synagogue
Samaria	Scribes	Torah
Judea	Sadducees	Sabbath
Bethlehem	Sanhedrin	Aramaic
Nazareth	Zealots	Shema
Jerusalem	Essenes	

Respond

Create this scene in your mind. You are sitting with Jesus on a grassy hillside overlooking the Sea of Galilee. Hundreds of brilliant wildflowers surround you. Before you the blue lake sparkles in the sun. You hear the water lapping against the shore. The hills across the lake are also blue. You feel very comfortable and relaxed next to Jesus.

What would Jesus say to you? What would you say? Think about it. Then write your conversation in your journal.

> All the way to heaven is heaven because he said, "I am the Way."
>
> St. Catherine of Siena

Reach Out

1. Find out what the Holy Land is like today. Write a report.
2. Ask a Jewish person to tell you about his or her religious customs and feasts. You might be able to visit a Jewish temple or synagogue.
3. Make a relief map of Palestine out of dough and paint it.
4. The Gospel of Mark has Aramaic phrases scattered throughout. Find the meaning of these by looking up the references:
   Talitha koum! (Mark 5:41)
   Ephphatha! (Mark 7:35)
   Golgotha (Mark 15:22)
   Eloi, Eloi, lema sabachthani? (Mark 15:34)
5. Research how Christ's religion has been adapted to other cultures. Visit a Byzantine Catholic church or other Eastern rite church. Attend a liturgy in an African American or Hispanic parish. Ask people about Catholic customs in other countries.
6. What if Jesus had been born in our country and was living now? Where would he live? What would his life be like? How would he teach people? How would he die? Write the story of his life as if it were set in our country.

Review

Who Am I?   Write the letter of the person who fits the description.

a. Publican
b. Sadducee
c. Augustus Caesar
d. Zealot
e. Essene
f. Samaritan
g. Pharisee
h. Scribe
i. Pontius Pilate
j. Herod the Great

_____ 1. I work to overthrow Rome, sometimes by violence.

_____ 2. I am a Roman emperor.

_____ 3. I seek a pure life in a desert community.

_____ 4. I believe in interpreting the Law strictly.

_____ 5. I am a priest who does not believe in the resurrection.

_____ 6. I am a tax collector.

_____ 7. I am a scholarly teacher among the Pharisees.

_____ 8. I am despised by Jewish people for not worshiping at the Temple in Jerusalem.

Jewish Jargon   Circle the correct definition.

1. Sabbath	Saturday	Sunday
2. Shalom	"Rejoice!"	"Peace!"
3. Jerusalem	Holy City	Jesus' birthplace
4. Torah	king	Law
5. Shema	clothing	prayer
6. Galilee	northern region	southern region
7. Synagogue	home	"church"
8. Gentile	non-Jew	priest
9. Sanhedrin	council	army
10. "Kitchen"	outdoors	indoors

The Early Life of Jesus

I proclaim to you good news of great joy
that will be for all the people.
For today in the city of David
a savior has been born for you who is Messiah and Lord.

LUKE 2:10–11

What does Christmas mean to you?

_____

_____

If Jesus had not died and risen, we would have nothing to celebrate at Christmas. But Jesus did rise, showing himself to be the Son of God, our Savior. This is why we celebrate his birthday. The first Christians, however, didn't. The recent, astounding events of his death and resurrection were uppermost in their minds. But as time went on Christians wondered about Jesus' origins and early life. Soon stories were circulating.

Stories of an Infant God

Stories about Jesus' birth and early life are in the Gospels of Matthew and Luke. They are called **infancy narratives.** The evangelists wrote them in a way that shows who Jesus was. They present the mystery of his coming through beautiful and miraculous events:

* The **Annunciation**—Jesus' conception in Mary by the power of the Holy Spirit
* The **Visitation**—the recognition of his presence by Elizabeth and John
* The **Nativity**—Jesus' birth
* The **Presentation**—the offering of Jesus to God in the Temple

Biblical scholars have theories about the infancy narratives. For instance, they discuss who the magi were, where they came from, and whether the story is historical or symbolic. It doesn't matter if there were three kings or not. The all-important truth in the stories is that Jesus did come to save us.

At Jesus' first coming around 4 B.C., there was no video equipment to capture the historic moments. Maybe Mary told Luke the stories of Jesus' birth. Maybe the evangelists added events and symbols to make a point or to fulfill prophecies. Maybe things didn't happen just as the stories say. We don't know. But we do know that the infancy narratives are God's Word and hold a message for us.

Mini-Gospels

The infancy narratives are known as the "Gospels in miniature" because they tell the same Good News as the whole Gospels. They show all the aspects of Jesus' love. They reveal Jesus' identity, his mission, the role of the Holy Spirit in his life, Jesus' concern for all, his suffering, and his rejection. The main message of these stories is the Easter message: _Jesus is Lord, the Son of God who saved us._ This message is proclaimed in many ways. As you review the stories, listen for it and for other messages God may be sending you.

A Photo Album of Jesus

Each picture in this photo album matches a story from the infancy narratives.
Look up the reference and read the verses. Then write a title for the picture.

1. Luke 1:26–28   **2.** Matthew 1:18–25   **3.** Luke 1:36, 39–56   **4.** Luke 2:1–21

5. Matthew 2:1–12   **6.** Matthew 2:13–23   **7.** Luke 2:22–40   **8.** Luke 2:41–52

Gospel Truths

The infancy narratives contain the following Gospel truths. Think of each story above
and write its number before any truth it conveys. Be ready to explain your answers.

_____   **a.** Jesus is God, so extraordinary signs accompany his birth.

_____   **b.** Mary, the mother of God, is someone special.

_____   **c.** Jesus is the Messiah.

_____   **d.** Jesus is sent by the Father.

_____   **e.** The Holy Spirit acts for our salvation.

_____   **f.** Jesus is Savior of all people, not only Jewish people.

_____   **g.** Some people reject Jesus.

_____   **h.** Jesus suffers.

_____   **i.** Jesus comes for the poor and the outcast.

Mary, a Listener

The heroine of the infancy narratives is Mary, a woman who was always open to God's messages. By her yes of faith she became the mother of Jesus. Because Jesus is God, Mary is *Theotokos*, or the Mother of God. When God became the son of Mary, God took the substance of his flesh from her. Jesus bore her features. He lived with her for about thirty years. She made his clothes, cooked his food, and taught him to walk and talk. He took care of her, obeyed her, and loved her. She witnessed his growth, his joys and sorrows, and his prayer. She knew his smile, the touch of his hand, and his thoughts and feelings. Forever he will call her Mother.

We believe that because Mary is God's mother, God gave her special gifts. These privileges of Mary are Catholic doctrines:

> The **Immaculate Conception**—Mary was never in the state of sin, neither original sin, nor personal sin.
>
> The **Virgin Birth**—She conceived Jesus solely through the power of the Holy Spirit. (We believe she was always a virgin.)
>
> The **Assumption**—Mary went to heaven body and soul at the end of her life.

Mary listened to God, which led to action. She was prepared to risk all she had for love of God. She responded to Gabriel, "Let it be," (*fiat*) calling herself God's handmaid. She willingly became the mother of the redeemer, a dangerous and painful mission. Then after the Annunciation Mary did not just sit and think about herself. She went to help Elizabeth. At all times she cooperated with the work of her Son, even when it meant standing at the cross.

Mary's "Let it be" echoed God's "Let it be" that began creation. She made possible the new creation that Christ brought about. As St. Irenaeus put it, "Mary's obedience helped untie what Eve's disobedience had tied."

Do you *listen* to God speak to you in quiet prayer time? Through your parents, teachers, brothers, and sisters? Do you listen to your friends' needs? To calls to share your money or time with the poor? Do you *act*?

It is said that Mary bore Jesus in her heart, before she bore him in her womb. How can you be a Christ-bearer today?

A Modern Mary

After raising four children, Rosemary Koenig felt God calling her to serve others. With little money and at the age of sixty-five she opened the Shelter of God's Love in Chicago. This was a home for eight people with handicaps like Pam, who is blind; Margie, a young girl with cerebral palsy; and Evelyn, a grandmother who has multiple sclerosis. Each evening after dinner the community prayed for the world. A few years later Rosemary started another Shelter where senior citizens could live together. Rosemary trusts God for everything. In surprising ways the Shelters' needs are met: a van, a computer, an assistant director. Like Mary, Rosemary listens to God and then acts. She lets God do great things through her.

Are You Getting the Message?

For each pair of statements put a dot on the line to indicate where you are.
Then connect the dots for a profile of your ability to hear God's word.

I stay close to Jesus.	I keep Jesus far away.
I honor Mary.	I hardly think of Mary.
I do what the Father wants.	I do what I feel like.
I go out to everyone.	I avoid those who don't fit in.
I am humble.	I am proud.
I bear suffering well.	I complain a lot.
I have mercy.	I am unforgiving.
I am a peacemaker.	I cause trouble.
I know that God loves me.	I doubt that God loves me.

Remember

What do the infancy narratives proclaim?
They proclaim the Good News that Jesus is the Son of God and Savior of the world.

What privileges did God give Mary because she was the Mother of God?
Mary's privileges are the Immaculate Conception, the Virgin Birth, and the Assumption.

Why did Jesus come?
Jesus said, "I came so that they might have life and have it more abundantly" (John 10:10).

Words to Know

infancy narratives	Nativity
Annunciation	Presentation
Visitation	Assumption
Immaculate Conception	Virgin Birth

Respond

What might God be saying to you by an infancy narrative person or symbol? Write your thoughts about one in your journal as a prayer. Ideas: Mary, star, Joseph, angel's song, Elizabeth, magi, innkeeper, manger, shepherd, Simeon, holy innocents, Anna.

Reach Out

1. Find out how the celebration of Christmas came to be the way you know it.
2. Research Christmas customs of other countries and cultures.
3. Share the Good News of the story of Christmas:
   - Tell a child the story.
   - Design a Christmas card based on the Gospel story of Christmas. Give it to someone.
   - Make a mural of the events surrounding Jesus' birth or a mobile of Christmas symbols. Put your mural or mobile where it can be seen.
   - Put together a slide presentation or a shadow show telling the story.
   - Plan a Christmas program using carols about the real meaning of Christmas.
4. Survey what Christmas means to people.
5. Pray Mary's Magnificat in Luke 1:46–55. Notice that Mary praises how God treats the poor and lowly.
6. Consult the liturgical calendar or a reference book to find the dates we celebrate the Annunciation, the Visitation, the Nativity, the Presentation, the Epiphany, the Solemnity of Mary, Mother of God, and the feasts of the Holy Innocents and the Holy Family.

Review

The Honest Truth   Write **Y** for yes or **N** for no in answer to each question.

_____ **1.** Was Easter more important than Christmas to the early Christians?

_____ **2.** Does the Gospel of John include infancy narratives?

_____ **3.** Are all of the details in the infancy narratives historically true?

_____ **4.** Do the infancy narratives proclaim that Jesus is Lord, the Son of God who saved us?

_____ **5.** Were the writers of the infancy narratives inspired by God?

_____ **6.** Did Jesus have any brothers or sisters?

_____ **7.** Was Mary always free from sin, even original sin?

_____ **8.** Is the Assumption, Mary's being taken into heaven body and soul, a Catholic doctrine?

A Christmas Crossword

Across

2. A Galilean woman who was sinless and full of grace

5. The holy man who was allowed to see the Messiah before he died and who prophesied sorrow for Mary

7. King who wanted to put the newborn king to death

8. The holy family fled to this place

11. The messenger at the Annunciation

12. Mary was betrothed to this man

14. When Mary became pregnant, Joseph intended to take this action allowed by Jewish law

Down

1. Men who followed a star to Bethlehem

3. A relative of Jesus who was six months older than Jesus

4. Jesus was conceived by this power

5. The first to hear the good news of Jesus' birth

6. Mary helped this relative during the older woman's pregnancy

9. When Jesus was lost in Jerusalem, his parents found him here doing his Father's work

10. When Jesus was born he was laid in this

13. Mary's child was his Son

Jerusalem

The Mission of Jesus

6

My food is to do the will of the one
who sent me and to finish his work.

JOHN 4:34

All of us have a number of roles in life. Your favorite aunt, for instance, might also be a wife, a mother, a lawyer, and the captain of her bowling team. List some of your roles here.

_____

_____

_____

_____

In addition to being God's Son, Jesus is the Christ. *Christ* means "anointed one." The Israelites anointed their prophets, priests, and kings with oil. As God's anointed one, Jesus was a prophet, priest, and king.

The Jordan River

A **prophet** hears God's word and proclaims it. Jesus delivered the Good News that the Father wanted made known. He proclaimed, "Repent, the kingdom is at hand." Like many prophets before him, Jesus was killed for his words.

A **priest** represents people in offering sacrifice to God. Jesus stood for all of us when he offered himself to the Father on the cross.

A **king** has the greatest power and authority. Jesus is Lord of the universe as a result of his incarnation, death, resurrection, and ascension.

Christ is another name for *Messiah*. Jesus was not the Messiah most Israelites expected. In their minds the Messiah would help them overthrow Rome and become the number one superpower. But Jesus' kingdom was not a geographical kingdom. It was the rule of God over our hearts. Jesus was a Messiah who preached humility and love of neighbors and enemies. He was a Messiah who had to suffer and die.

Jesus' mission as Messiah was to proclaim and make present the reign of God. He was to bring about the kingdom of God, in which all people live in peace and love. He began this mission when he was about thirty years old. The Gospels tell how Jesus was strengthened for his mission and how he accepted it.

Launching the Mission

In the Gospel of Luke when Mary, pregnant with Jesus, came to help her relative Elizabeth, the baby within Elizabeth leaped for joy. This baby, John, grew up to be the prophet who prepared the way for Jesus. The following broadcast covers Jesus' baptism by John:

Newscaster: We are on location at the Jordan River to see what it is that attracts the people of Judea to John the Baptizer. Let's find out what they think about this strange man from the desert, who lives on nothing but grasshoppers and honey. Pardon me, madam, may I ask you a few questions?

Woman: Certainly.

Newscaster: When did you first hear about John the Baptizer?

Woman: The day he started to preach here. My son came home all excited and told me I just had to hear him.

Newscaster: What kind of things does John say?

Woman: He says to repent for our sins because the kingdom of God is near.

Newscaster: Do you think John is the Messiah?

Woman: No. He says that the Messiah is greater than he is and that he's not even worthy to untie the Messiah's sandal.

Newscaster: Thank you, madam. (*Turns to a man passing by.*) Sir, may I have a word with you?

Man: Only a minute. I want to get down there before John stops baptizing.

Newscaster: Why do you want to be baptized?

Man: To confess my sins and be ready for the Messiah when he comes.

Newscaster: Do you think that will be soon?

Man: I sure do. John says so.

Newscaster: Thank you, sir. Right down there you can see John in his camel's hair outfit, baptizing at the riverbank. Let's move in a little closer. Yes, here is a better view. There is just one more person waiting for baptism. He is going to the river. Something seems to be wrong. John is shaking his head. (*pause*) I guess it's all right now. They're wading out into the river . . . the man is under the water . . . there, he's up . . . they're back on the riverbank, but look at the faces of these two men! (*Stops a boy.*) Pardon me. Do you know the young man that John just baptized?

Boy: That's Jesus the carpenter. He comes from Nazareth up north.

Newscaster: Thank you. We'll try to find out what happened down there. I don't see Jesus anywhere, but here comes John. Pardon me, sir, was something unusual going on down there? You look as if you've experienced something extraordinary.

John: You're right. I just baptized the Messiah.

Newscaster: How do you know?

John: After my relative Jesus was baptized, the heavens broke open. I saw a dove come down and hover over his head. Then I heard a voice saying, "This is my beloved Son, with whom I am well pleased." Don't you see what that means? Jesus is the Messiah. Praised be the God of Israel!

Newscaster: Praised be the God of Israel! What more can be said? No doubt, we'll be hearing more about this Jesus from Nazareth. This is Pat Smith in Judea signing off.

Anointed for the Mission

Jesus was sinless. Why then did he go to John for baptism? The baptism of Jesus was a sign that he accepted his mission as Messiah. He was ready to proclaim and make present the kingdom of God. Also, Jesus took on the sins of the world. His going down into the water symbolized that he was ready to die for us.

The Gospels proclaim the identity of Jesus by describing an epiphany that occurred after his baptism. An **epiphany** is a revelation or manifestation of God. The Father's voice, the Holy Spirit in the form of a dove, and Jesus the Son are a revelation of the Trinity—the three persons in one God. Through this epiphany the Father strengthened Jesus for his mission and the Spirit anointed him for his work.

The Messiah's Test

After his baptism Jesus was led by the Spirit into the desert. Here, alone, he prayed and fasted for forty days to prepare for his mission. His people, the Israelites, had been formed into God's people by forty years in the desert. Now Jesus would grow into his role in the same way. But where the Israelites often failed their tests, Jesus overcame Satan's attacks and refused to compromise with evil. Faithful to his baptismal commitment, he proved to be the true Messiah whose kingdom was a spiritual one based on faith and love. He walked out of the desert stronger and ready to live his role fully. Here are the temptations according to Matthew:

The Battle

First attack:
Temptation to physical pleasures
Setting: Jesus is hungry after fasting.
SATAN: "If you are the Son of God, command that these stones become loaves of bread."
JESUS: "One does not live on bread alone, but by every word that comes from the mouth of God."
Jesus' kingdom was not based on material goods.

Second attack: Temptation to pride
Setting: Satan takes Jesus to the tower of the Temple.
SATAN: "If you are the Son of God, throw yourself down. Scripture says that the angels will support you with their hands."
JESUS: "Scripture says, 'You shall not put the Lord, your God, to the test.'"
Jesus' kingdom was not based on magic tricks.

Third attack: Temptation to power
Setting: Satan takes Jesus to a high mountain and shows him all the kingdoms of the world.
SATAN: "All these I shall give you if you will prostrate yourself and worship me."
JESUS: "Get away, Satan! Scripture says, 'The Lord, your God, shall you worship and him alone shall you serve.'"
Jesus' kingdom was not based on military power.

Our Test

You will never meet the devil dressed in a red suit and carrying a pitchfork. However, the power of evil is real. Satan, the world around us, and our own weak nature tempt us to sin. **Temptations** are persons, circumstances, and things that entice us to do what is wrong or to omit what is good. Sometimes they do this by making evil appear good. We can recognize temptations because they are contrary to Jesus' teaching. Of themselves they are not sins. Sin is actually choosing to do what is wrong or to omit what is good.

Sins are called **venial** unless they are a serious break in our relationship with God. Then they are called **mortal** (deadly) sins. The degree of our guilt for sin depends on
> the seriousness of the matter,
> our knowledge,
> pressure from outside forces,
> the length of time we reflected,
> circumstances that weaken our willpower,
> our intentions.

For instance, who seems guiltier: someone who steals to provide food for his family or someone who steals in order to buy a Mercedes?

Because **original sin,** the first sin of the human race, left us weak, doing what is right often involves a struggle. Our weapons against temptation are fasting, self-control, the sacraments, prayer, and friendship with Jesus, who knows what it's like to be tempted. Also, the Trinity dwells in us since our baptism. We can rely on God's grace to help us meet the challenge of evil. When we overcome temptation, we fulfill our roles in life—especially our role as a baptized Christian.

Combat Training

Here is a temptation to keep you from fulfilling your role as a son or daughter. Write a response to pass the test. Then choose a role from your list on page 42 and write your own test.

Role: Son or daughter

Tempter: What your mom wants this time is unreasonable. No other kid your age would do that.

You: _____

Role: _____

Tempter: _____

_____

You: _____

_____

Remember

What were Jesus' three roles as the Christ?
Jesus' three roles as the Christ were prophet, priest, and king.

What was Jesus' mission?
Jesus' mission was to proclaim and make present the reign of God.

What do we learn from Jesus' baptism?
From Jesus' baptism, we learn that God is a Trinity and that Jesus is the Son of God, the Messiah.

What is temptation?
Temptation is any person or thing that entices us to do what is evil or omit what is good.

Words to Know

prophet	temptation
priest	venial sin
king	mortal sin
epiphany	original sin

Respond

Author Pearl Buck said, "Youth is the age of temptation." Here are some questions for you to reflect on and respond to in your journal.

- What is my biggest temptation right now?
- What am I doing to resist it?
- What does Christ expect of me?
- With Christ's help, what more can I do to overcome it?

Reach Out

1. At times we need to get away from it all, to find a quiet place to pull ourselves together, to think, and to pray. This "desert place" might be a special place where you can be alone. It might be the early morning, at night when you can't sleep, or a quiet Sunday afternoon. Plan a visit to your desert. Decide where and when you will go, and what you will think about or pray about. Write about your desert experience in your journal.

2. With a group of your friends—or with your family, especially when there is a family problem—conduct a round-robin discussion. A question is written on the bottom of a sheet of paper, and the paper is passed around. Each person writes a response at the top of the paper and folds it over. After the paper has circulated, someone unfolds it and reads the answers, allowing time for comment. Questions might include:
   - How would you reply if someone said, "The devil made me do it!"?
   - At some time or another we all face the temptation to do anything to be popular or admired. How do you handle this temptation?

3. Read Philippians 1:27–28. What do you think St. Paul meant by this advice? How does it apply to your life right now? Think about this during a desert experience or discuss it with your classmates.

4. Show you belong to Jesus' kingdom by doing something to combat an injustice. Write a letter to the editor, write your state senator or representative, or make a phone call to a local official.

Review

Identification   To what do the following phrases refer?

1. Jesus' mission: _____

2. His anointing for it: _____

3. His test: _____

4. His type of kingdom: _____

5. One who speaks for God: _____

6. A manifestation of God: _____

Verdicts   In each case decide if the person is guilty (G), not completely guilty (g), or only tempted (T). Place the proper letter on the line.

_____   **1.** Suellen shoplifts a necklace and doesn't get caught.

_____   **2.** Robert has a bad cold. When his brother picks on him, Robert punches him.

_____   **3.** Jill can't stand Patty. She always has the urge to avoid her and to say things to hurt her.

_____   **4.** Jane considers attending a party where she knows there will be beer.

_____   **5.** Mark joins in when boys on the bus make fun of a student in the special education classes.

_____   **6.** The Sunday after Ann's family returns from camping, Ann says she is too tired to go to Mass. Her mother tells her to stay home, so she does.

_____   **7.** Frequently during the day the sexy scenes from a video Carl saw come into his mind without his willing it.

Tricky Trios   Write a heading that identifies each set of words.

1. _____

prophet • priest • king

2. _____

material goods • magic tricks • military power

3. _____

pleasure • pride • power

4. _____

mortal • venial • original

5. _____

Satan • the world • human nature

6. _____

knowledge • reflection time • intention

7. _____

self-control • sacraments • grace

The Apostles, Mary, and Other Followers

7

Image of the Last Supper from St. Jean Church, Troyes, France

I have called you friends, because I have told you everything
I have heard from my Father. It was not you who chose me,
but I who chose you and appointed you
to go and bear fruit that will remain.

JOHN 15:15–16

Socrates

The Buddha

Jesus and his disciples

You have probably heard of the great teachers Socrates of Greece and the Buddha of India. Every once in a while someone very wise like these men appears on Earth. This person attracts people who hope to learn about the mysteries of life. The teacher is called a **master** and the followers **disciples,** which means learners. Jesus, the world's greatest teacher, had many disciples who were dedicated to him. Excited by what they heard and saw, some disciples left their jobs and families to follow Jesus. They brought other people to him.

The First Disciples

John's Gospel tells how Jesus met his first disciples after his baptism:

 The next day John was there again with two of his disciples, and as he watched Jesus walk by, he said, "Behold, the Lamb of God." The two disciples heard what he said and followed Jesus. Jesus turned and saw them following him and said to them, "What are you looking for?" They said to him, "Rabbi" (which translated means Teacher), "where are you staying?" He said to them, "Come, and you will see." So they went and saw where he was staying, and they stayed with him that day.

John 1:35–39

Something about Jesus drew the disciples to him. They were ready to respond to his invitation, "Come and see." For many months after their first meeting, the disciples walked with Jesus from town to town.

They enjoyed his company. Their understanding of him grew day by day. First they called him teacher. At the Last Supper Jesus called them friends. Eventually they called him Messiah.

What Does It Take?

Many people heard Jesus and saw the signs of his power. Not all believers became followers. What does it mean to be a disciple, a friend of Jesus? Scripture tells us. Read these passages and write the requirements.

A disciple of Jesus Christ must . . .

Matthew 7:21 _____.

Matthew 18:3–4 _____.

Mark 10:43–44 _____.

Luke 9:23–24 _____

_____

_____.

Luke 14:33 _____.

John 13:35 _____.

Do you qualify?

The Twelve

After praying in the hills, Jesus chose twelve from the disciples to be very close to him. They are called the **apostles,** which means "sent." The apostles were to share the ministry of Jesus and preach the Good News of the risen Lord. They were chosen to change the world. They and their successors, the bishops, would be empowered by Christ to carry out his own mission. Because twelve was the number of the tribes of Israel, the twelve apostles symbolized the new people of God.

There is a saying that you can tell a lot about people by the friends they have. The apostles were political nobodies: fishermen, a tax collector—sinners and ordinary people. Sometimes they were jealous and ambitious. Sometimes they were afraid. Sometimes they did not understand Jesus.

Yet Jesus continued to love them. He chose to be alone with them at the Last Supper, and he sent them to act in his name. How do you explain it?

When Jesus looked at Simon, he saw a common fisherman who often spoke without thinking. But he also saw a future leader, a man who could give his all to him. When Jesus looks at us, he sees us as we really are, with our good qualities and our flaws. He also sees us for all we can become.

In Jesus the disciples found compassion and strength. In him they found challenge and purpose. In every age since then, Jesus has continued to touch the hearts of people. Unlike Socrates and the Buddha, Jesus is still with us, inviting us to "come and see." His influence is as strong and real today as when he walked the roads of Palestine.

Portraits of the Apostles

The following sketches of the Twelve are drawn from Scripture and Tradition.

Peter
Feasts: February 22, June 29, November 18

Peter was the apostle Jesus chose to be the first leader of his Church. When Peter met Jesus he was known as Simon. Jesus changed his name to *Cephas,* or Peter, the Greek word for "rock." Jesus said he would build his Church upon that rock.

Peter and his brother Andrew were fishermen from Bethsaida. Later they lived in Capernaum, a city on the northern shore of the Sea of Galilee. Peter often spoke and acted impulsively. Yet he loved Jesus very much and said he would follow him even to death. According to tradition, Peter arrived in Rome during a great persecution of Christians. He was arrested and crucified upside down. Most pictures of Peter show him carrying a pair of keys, the keys of the kingdom of heaven given to him when Jesus made him head of his Church.

Andrew
Feast: November 30

Andrew was one of the first men Jesus called to follow him. After Andrew met Jesus, he brought his brother Peter to meet him. Andrew's name means "manly" and "courageous." His symbol is an X-shaped cross, the type it is believed he died on. Centuries after his death, missionaries taking his relics to Scotland were shipwrecked. They reached shore safely and introduced the Scots to Jesus. So many came to follow Christ that Andrew was named the patron saint of Scotland. He is also the patron saint of Russia.

James the Greater
Feast: July 25

Two apostles were named James. James the Greater was the brother of John. James and John were sons of Zebedee and Salome. With their father, they worked as fishermen and were partners with Peter.

James and his brother once asked Jesus to give them places of honor in his kingdom. Peter, James, and John were the only apostles chosen to witness the Transfiguration of Jesus and the raising of Jairus' daughter from the dead. They were the only three to be near Jesus during his agony in the garden. James was the first of the Twelve to be martyred for Christ. He was beheaded in Jerusalem at the command of King Herod. His symbols are a traveler's staff and a pilgrim's bell. James is the patron saint of Spain.

John
Feast: December 27

John is sometimes called the teenage apostle. Unlike the other apostles, he was not married. Although at one time Jesus called James and John "sons of thunder," John developed into a gentle, sensitive man, an apostle of love. In John's Gospel we think it is John who is referred to as "the disciple Jesus loved." He was the only apostle to stand beneath the cross, and he was the one Jesus asked to care for Mary. The story is told that whenever John was asked to speak in his old age, all he would ever say was, "Little children, love one another. Love one another." He was the only apostle to die a natural death. According to tradition John was the fourth evangelist. His symbol is an eagle.

Philip
Feast: May 3

Philip, like Peter and Andrew, came from Bethsaida. He received a direct invitation from Jesus to follow him. Convinced that Jesus was the one Moses and the prophets had written about, Philip told his friend Nathanael to "come and see." We learn from writers of the early Church that Philip did great missionary work in Asia Minor, where he is buried. His symbol is a column or pillar because of the tradition that he died hanging from one.

Bartholomew
Feast: August 24

Bartholomew is believed to be Nathanael, the man whom Philip introduced to Jesus. *Bartholomew* may mean "son of Tolomai," in Hebrew *bar Tolomai.* Jesus, who knows the thoughts of all hearts, spoke of him as an Israelite without guile. That means he did not try to deceive but was straightforward and honest. Bartholomew traveled east to preach the Gospel. While in Armenia, he was arrested, tortured, and finally put to death. His symbol is a knife, the instrument of his torture.

Matthew
Feast: September 21

Matthew, also called Levi, was a tax collector. He lived in Capernaum where Jesus did much of his public ministry. Matthew is remembered for his prompt response to Jesus' call. He immediately left his money booth and followed Jesus. The first book of the New Testament is the Gospel according to Matthew. Tradition tells us that Matthew died a martyr's death, probably in Ethiopia. His symbol as an evangelist is the head of a man.

Thomas
Feast: July 3

The apostle Thomas is best remembered as "doubting" Thomas. He was not with the other apostles when Jesus came to them after the Resurrection.

Thomas claimed that he would not believe that Jesus had truly risen unless he could touch his wounds. Once he saw Jesus, however, Thomas immediately fell to his knees and exclaimed, "My Lord and my God!"

Thought to be a house builder by trade, Thomas is usually shown carrying carpenters' tools. He is the patron saint of carpenters, architects, and the blind. It is thought that Thomas brought the Good News to India, where he died a martyr and was buried.

James the Less
Feast: May 3

This James is the brother of the apostle Jude. He was given the title "the Less" to distinguish him from the other apostle James. Perhaps he was shorter or younger than the other James. His mother was Mary of Clopas, a follower of Jesus and possibly a cousin of the Blessed Virgin Mary.

According to tradition, James the Less was the first bishop of Jerusalem and wrote the letter in the New Testament that bears his name. This, however, is doubtful. It is said James was beaten to death by Jews who were angry that Paul had escaped death by appealing to Caesar. James's symbol is a cudgel or club.

Jude
Feast: October 28

A brother of James the Less and perhaps a cousin of Jesus, this apostle is also known as Thaddeus. For reasons unknown, St. Jude has become popular as the patron of hopeless cases. He preached the Gospel in Mesopotamia and Persia, and one of the letters in the New Testament bears his name. Some pagan magicians, it is said, killed him for exposing how they were fooling the people. His symbol is an ax, the instrument used in his martyrdom.

Simon
Feast: October 28

Simon from Cana was the only apostle who was a Zealot. When Simon chose to follow Jesus, he had to channel his zeal into the peaceful pursuit of the kingdom of God. He first preached the Gospel in Egypt and then went to Persia with Jude. It was there that he suffered martyrdom when he was beaten with clubs and then sawed into pieces. His symbol is a saw.

Judas

From his name it is believed that Judas Iscariot came from a town in Judea. He was entrusted with the care of the common funds. He helped himself to some of the money that belonged to all. He also betrayed Jesus for thirty pieces of silver. When he realized what he had done, he did not return to Jesus to receive his loving forgiveness as Peter did. Instead, Judas hanged himself. According to Acts, Judas fell and was killed in a field he had bought with his blood money.

Matthias
Feast: May 14

We learn from the Acts of the Apostles that Matthias was selected to take the place of Judas. Matthias had followed Jesus from the beginning and had been a witness of the resurrected Lord. It is believed that he preached in Palestine and was martyred by crucifixion. His symbol is a lance.

The First and Best Disciple

The Acts of the Apostles tells us that on Pentecost when the Spirit came, Mary the Mother of Jesus was with the disciples. This was fitting because she was the first one to believe and follow Christ. Her faith and obedience made her open to God's will in her life. Mary was the first to bring Jesus into the world through the power of the Holy Spirit. She devoted her life to him for thirty years before his public ministry. One of her titles is Queen of Apostles.

The highest praise of Mary is that she fits her Son's description in Luke 8:21. Write Jesus' words here:

_____

_____

_____

True disciples, the real members of Christ's family, believe and act on their belief. Someone whose life gives testimony to his or her beliefs is called a **witness.** Mary was a witness. At a wedding feast, she trusted that her Son would help when the wine ran out. She told the servants, "Do whatever he tells you." During the suffering and death of Jesus many followers fled in fear. But Mary stood faithful at the foot of the cross. There Jesus called her the mother of John, the beloved disciple. From the moment of the Incarnation, when she became the mother of Jesus, Mary was the mother of all members of Christ, the mother of all believers. Mary is the Mother of Jesus and the Mother of the Church, his mystical body.

Mary is the model for all who seek Christ. In our struggles to be faithful disciples, she not only inspires us, but she also prays for us and loves us.

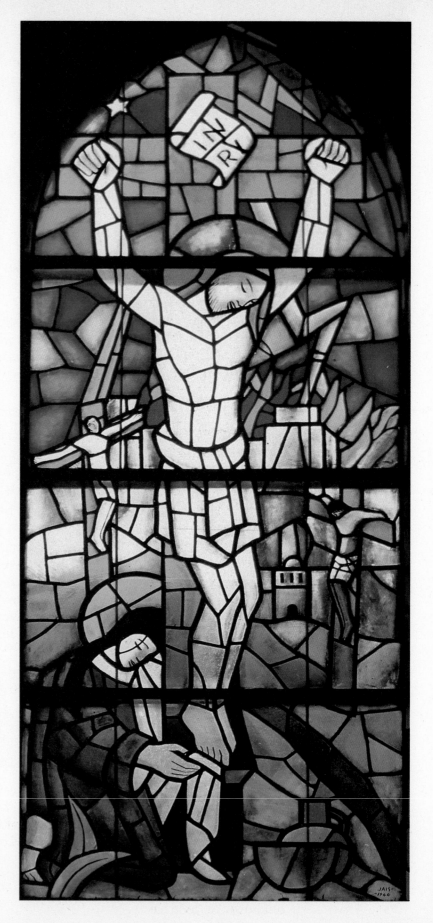

The Way of the Witness

1. Rank the fears junior high students have about seriously following Jesus in order of importance. (1, 2, 3, etc.)

_____ They won't have as much fun.

_____ They may end up without friends.

_____ They will have to treat everyone kindly.

_____ They will be made fun of.

_____ Their families won't understand them.

_____ They will have to work too hard.

_____ They will have to give up too many things.

_____ Other: _____

_____.

How would you answer each fear?

2. If people your age decided to be real friends of Jesus, what things would they most likely have to change in their lives?

   If people your age decided not to grow in their love for Jesus, what things would they be giving up?

3. What do you think is the best way for junior high students to witness to one another? To the world?

Remember

What is a disciple of Jesus?
A disciple of Jesus is a follower of Jesus who is dedicated to him.

What is a witness?
A witness is someone whose life gives testimony to his or her beliefs.

Why is Mary a disciple?
Mary is a disciple because she was open to God's Word and lived it faithfully.

What did Jesus demand of his disciples?
Jesus said, "Whoever wishes to come after me must deny himself, take up his cross, and follow me" (Matthew 16:24).

Respond

Jesus' invitation to you to become his disciple includes an RSVP. It requires a response. Write a letter in your journal responding to Jesus' invitation.

1. Jesus prepared for important events, like choosing his apostles, by praying. Read Luke 6:12–13, Luke 22:31–32, and Luke 22:39–46. When do you pray? If a friend asked you why you prayed, what would you say? Pray to Mary (the Hail Mary, the Angelus, and the rosary) to be a better disciple.

2. Make a poster advertising the job of a disciple. Include the duties, responsibilities, difficulties, and rewards. Hang the poster where people will notice it.

3. As a class, choose a way you will try to witness to one another. You may want to choose a new way to witness each month.

4. Interview three people you know who are Christian witnesses. Find out why they are involved in being of service to others. Write a summary of your findings and share it.

5. At the end of the day think of all the good things you have seen and heard during the day that make you a better person. Decide on one specific thing you will do for the next day to bring the light of Jesus to others.

6. Mary was a woman of action. Get involved in an organization such as Birthright, Bread for the World, Food for the Poor, Habitat for Humanity, or the St. Vincent de Paul Society.

Review

Disciple Rhymes   Fill in the name of the disciple described in each verse.

1. Nathanael might be called _____, too.
He stood by the cross and received Mary as mother.

1. Nathanael might be called _____, too.
Jesus described him as honest and true.

2. Jesus made _____ the head of his flock.
And renamed Simon the fisherman "rock."

3. Peter's brother named _____ was called from his nets,
And died on a cross in the shape of an X.

4. The publican _____ said yes to the Lord,
Left all that he had, followed Christ, wrote God's Word.

5. _____ was one of the favored three,
First martyred apostle, and son of Zebedee.

6. The evangelist _____ was James's brother.
He stood by the cross and received Mary as mother.

7. Apostle to India, St. _____ once doubted.
To Jesus, "My Lord and my God," he then shouted.

8. The brother of Jude, _____, a pacesetter,
Was Jerusalem's bishop and known for his letter.

9. St. _____ preached in Persia. A letter bears his name.
To do the impossible is his great fame.

10. From Cana came _____, a Zealot all-fired.
In Egypt, then Persia he preached and was martyred.

11. _____ invited a friend, "Come and see,"
Right after he answered Christ's "Come, follow me."

12. By _____ Iscariot Christ was betrayed.
To him thirty pieces of silver were paid.

13. _____, our model in answering God's call,
Was the best of disciples and first of them all.

14. _____ was chosen by lot to replace
Judas, the traitor who died in disgrace.

15. "Be my disciple," the Lord calls to _____.
"Take up the cross, love and serve, too."

A Life Commitment to Jesus: Baptism and Confirmation

8

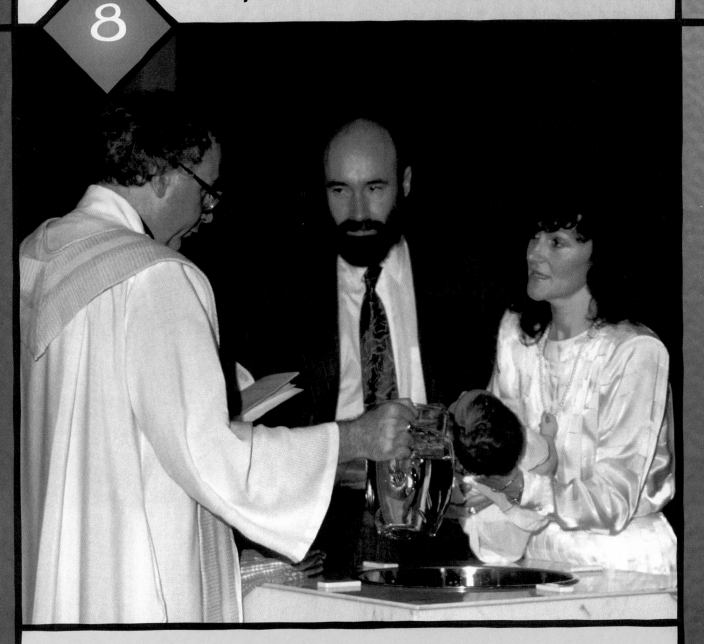

But you are "a chosen race, a royal priesthood,
a holy nation, a people of his own, so that you may
announce the praises" of him who called you out
of darkness into his wonderful light.

1 PETER 2:9

Friendships are built up by signs and words. Think of the last birthday party you went to. Gifts, cards, and a cake with candles expressed your feelings for your friend or relative. So did the words "happy birthday" and the sung words "May the dear Lord bless you." Signs and words celebrate and seal our relationships.

The Seven Sacraments

Our friendship with Jesus grows through the signs and words of the seven sacraments that he entrusted to his Church. **Sacraments** are special encounters with Jesus at key points in our journey of life. Through them he acts in us to save us. He strengthens his grace, his divine life in us, enabling us to carry out our mission as his disciples. In the sacraments we celebrate aspects of God's love for us with the community.

The sacraments are actions of the Holy Spirit. They bring about what they signify whether or not the minister or the one receiving them is worthy, but their fruit depends on the disposition (attitudes) of the recipient. Baptism, Confirmation, and Holy Orders confer a permanent **character** or seal, so they may be celebrated only once.

Finish the outline of the sacraments. Use the clues and the names below.

Sacraments of Initiation

Clue: Through these sacraments we become sons and daughters of God, Christians who share in the ministry of Christ.

_____

_____

_____

Sacraments of Healing

Clue: Through these sacraments we are reconciled to God and the community, healed and strengthened in body and soul.

_____

_____

Sacraments of Vocation

Clue: Through these sacraments we are enabled to accept a lifelong commitment to the ordained ministry or to Christian marriage and family life.

_____

_____

See the sacrament chart on pages 196 and 197.

Holy Orders

Anointing of the Sick

Confirmation

Reconciliation

Matrimony

Eucharist

Baptism

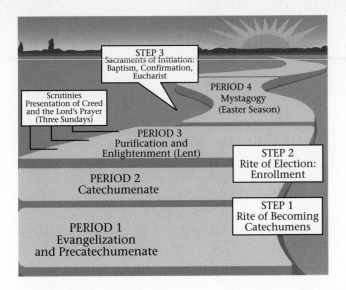

STEP 3
Sacraments of Initiation:
Baptism, Confirmation,
Eucharist

PERIOD 4
Mystagogy
(Easter Season)

Scrutinies
Presentation of Creed
and the Lord's Prayer
(Three Sundays)

PERIOD 3
Purification and
Enlightenment (Lent)

STEP 2
Rite of Election:
Enrollment

PERIOD 2
Catechumenate

STEP 1
Rite of Becoming
Catechumens

PERIOD 1
Evangelization
and Precatechumenate

Christian Initiation

People become disciples of Jesus and join the community of believers through a process called the **Rite of Christian Initiation of Adults (RCIA).** The RCIA takes place in the midst of the parish community. It has three steps: **catechumenate, election,** and **initiation.** The last step is the celebration of the sacraments of Baptism, Confirmation, and Eucharist. Those preparing for initiation are already part of God's household. They are assured of salvation even if they should die before being baptized. They have the baptism of desire. The following story tells about Pat's experiences in the RCIA.

Chris and Pat, high school juniors, rang the doorbell at St. Jude's rectory.

"Relax, Pat. Father Shea's great," Chris encouraged. Before Pat could reply, the door opened and there was Father Shea.

"Hello, Chris, how are you?"

"Fine," Chris replied. "Father, this is my friend Pat. We'd like to talk to you."

"Sure, come in." Father led them to his office.

Chris spoke first. "Pat wants to be a Catholic, Father, and I would like to sponsor him."

Father Shea smiled at Pat, "What made you decide this, Pat?"

Pat began his story. He and Chris had met at basketball. Pat often stayed at Chris's house for supper. He sensed that the spirit he enjoyed so much there was connected with the family's religious belief. One day Pat asked Chris about his religion. Chris explained that faith in Christ helped him understand life and gave him a desire to serve others. He told Pat about the Church. Their conversations led to this meeting with Father Shea.

When Pat finished speaking, Father said that he could begin the Rite of Christian Initiation. Chris would be his **sponsor** and assist him.

Here is part of Pat's journal.

Thursday, September 8
All of us who want to be Catholics met in the church hall tonight with our sponsors. We prayed and were introduced. Mike, the leader, told us how he came to the faith, and then he had us tell our own stories. We're called **inquirers,** ones who are studying the faith. We'll meet every Thursday evening. After the session, members of St. Jude's parish served us cookies and punch and made us feel welcome.

Saturday, October 10
Tonight we became **catechumens.** Before Mass we and our sponsors met at the church entrance. Father Shea called our names. Then he asked, "What do you ask of God's Church?" We said, "Faith." "What does faith offer you?" We answered, "Eternal life." Then Father prayed that we would follow the path of the Gospel under Christ's leadership. He asked everyone if they were ready to help us. They answered, "We are." Then Father Shea made a cross on our foreheads, saying, "By this sign of love Christ will be your strength. Learn now to know and follow him." We entered the church but stayed only until the end of the homily. After we're baptized, we'll stay for the whole Mass.

Friday, February 12
With school, basketball, and catechumen meetings, these months have really been busy. We catechumens know each other well because we have studied the life of Christ and the Church's teachings together, and we have prayed together. Father Shea told us that as followers of Christ we should set a good example. I've been trying to play fair and watch my language. Sometimes I visit Grandpa Reilly in the nursing home and play cards.

Sunday, March 3
Today is the first Sunday of Lent. We had the **Rite of Election** or **Enrollment** at Mass. Chris's mom and dad are my godparents. After the homily, Father Shea called the godparents and us catechumens to the altar. There he asked the godparents if we were worthy of the sacraments of initiation. When they said yes, Father declared that the Church called us to the Easter sacraments of Baptism, Confirmation, and Eucharist. He asked if we wished to celebrate them. We said yes and wrote our names in the book of the elect. I shivered when I wrote because in the early Church, if the book got into the wrong hands, the catechumens could be killed. They called it the "book of life." After that the community prayed for us. We are now the **elect.**

Sunday, March 10
On three Sundays in Lent we have **scrutinies** at the 10:00 Mass. These are petitions and exorcisms. **Exorcisms** are prayers against the evil spirit. They teach repentance, the mystery of sin, and how Christ the Redeemer saved us. The scrutinies strengthen our decision to live for Christ. After them are **presentations.** Today Father Shea presented us with the Creed. On the last Sunday he will give us the Lord's Prayer.

Responding to the Call: Sacraments of Initiation

The night of the Easter Vigil is a momentous one for Pat, Chris, and the community of St. Jude's.

This is a very decisive moment in Pat's life. Following Christ and living his values will be difficult. This is why the faith community is there for support. Pat and the community listen to St. Paul's words about "dying to sin." After the homily, Pat and the other elect go to the baptismal font for a **profession of faith.** There they make their baptismal vows, publicly rejecting Satan and evil and declaring their faith. As the water of Baptism flows over Pat, he remembers that water is a sign of death and life. He is entering into the death of Jesus and experiencing a second birth. He becomes alive in the life of Jesus and shares in the glory of his resurrection. When Pat's godparents put a **white robe** over his head, Pat knows he is being "clothed with Christ." His sins are forgiven and his life is fresh and pure now. His godparents hand him a **lighted candle,** a symbol of his life in Christ. He grins at Chris. Pat is now a full-fledged member of the Church. He may stay for the whole liturgy.

Next Pat celebrates Confirmation. He is anointed with a mixture of olive oil and balsam called **chrism.** He knows that now he is expected to proclaim his faith and that the Holy Spirit will strengthen and guide him.

The Mass continues. During the Liturgy of the Eucharist Pat recalls that Christ died and rose so that he could live. When he receives the Body and Blood of Jesus, he makes an act of faith. He isn't afraid. Surrounding him is the community of believers, who will help him grow spiritually. They will help him live his faith during the next months of the **mystagogy,** a time for sharing in the Eucharist and serving others.

The signs and words of the sacraments of initiation Pat celebrated express our relationship with Jesus as Savior. In Baptism, Confirmation, and Eucharist we receive the new life Jesus won for us. Through each of these sacraments he becomes our personal Savior and we commit ourselves to him.

Baptism: Water and Spirit

Jesus said you must be born of water and the Spirit to enter the kingdom of heaven. When the priest or deacon pours water over you at Baptism, through the Holy Spirit you enter into the dying and rising of Jesus. You are removed from the reign of evil and strengthened against it. You receive divine life, and you are invited to share eternal life with Jesus. You become a new creation. You become a Christian, willing to give witness to Christ, eager to share his teachings with others, prepared to sacrifice all for him. Because Baptism marks you forever as a follower of Jesus you can be baptized only once.

A Flood of Gifts

Do you know all of the tremendous gifts you receive through Baptism?

You become

✣ a temple of the Trinity and share in God's life (grace)
✣ a child of God and heir to heaven
✣ a member of the faith community, the Church.

You

✣ are forgiven original sin and any personal sins
✣ receive the Holy Spirit and gifts
✣ share in the priesthood of Christ
✣ receive virtues like faith, hope, and love.

Signs of Baptism

See how many signs and symbols used at Baptism you understand by matching them with their definitions.

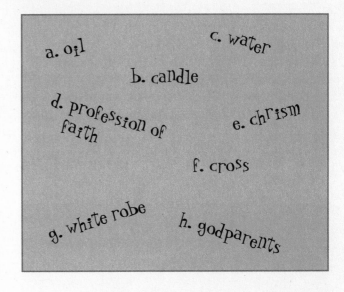

a. oil   c. water   b. candle   d. profession of faith   e. chrism   f. cross   g. white robe   h. godparents

_____ **1.** Symbol of being clothed with Christ and sign of new dignity

_____ **2.** Two people who represent the Christian community and promise to assist the newly baptized to grow in faith

_____ **3.** Symbol that shows that the newly baptized is cleansed of sin, dies with Christ, and is raised up with him to eternal life

_____ **4.** Sign of being strengthened and healed

_____ **5.** Promises the newly baptized makes to reject evil and to believe in the Trinity and the truths of the faith

_____ **6.** Symbol of the light of faith and the call to walk as children of light

_____ **7.** Sign made on the forehead of the newly baptized as a reminder of the saving power of Christ's death and resurrection

_____ **8.** Sign used in anointing that shows that the newly baptized has received the Holy Spirit and shares in the priesthood of Christ

Confirmation: Sealed with the Spirit

Confirmation used to be joined to Baptism. Catholics of the Eastern rites still celebrate it that way. In Confirmation your baptismal gifts are deepened and perfected. The Spirit that came to the Church on Pentecost comes to you more fully. The bishop lays his hand on you, anoints you with chrism, and says, "(Name), be sealed with the gift of the Holy Spirit." You respond, "Amen." The anointing renews your call to witness to Christ through service. Confirmation makes you more like Jesus. You can be confirmed only once because it marks you permanently as God's special possession.

Through Baptism and Confirmation the Holy Spirit empowers you to share your faith with others. You are Christ's follower, constantly growing in your understanding of his message and in your ability to love him and others. You are Christ's witness, showing by your actions his kingdom of justice and mercy.

Eucharist: Made One in the Spirit

The Eucharist completes and fulfills Christian Initiation. As Christians come together to celebrate the Lord's passion, death, resurrection, and ascension and to join with him in offering perfect worship to the Father, they celebrate and express that they belong to the Church. At the Eucharist the Christian community is united, strengthened, and nourished by Jesus present in the forms of bread and wine. The members are prepared to carry on his work.

A Stress Test

How strong a follower and a witness are you? Answer the questions honestly with **A** (always), **S** (sometimes), or **N** (never).

_____ Do you resist making up excuses when your work isn't finished?

_____ Do you try to make your home happy by not losing your temper when you can't get your way?

_____ Do you participate in religion class and share what you believe?

_____ Do you show kindness to people who are unkind to you?

_____ Do you show respect for the teacher no matter how anyone else is acting?

_____ Do you refuse to cheat on homework and tests?

_____ Do you keep from talking back to your parents?

_____ Do you consider family plans before you ask your parents to take you places?

_____ Do you avoid gossiping?

Total Your Score!
3 points for "always"
2 points for "sometimes"
1 point for "never"

How Do You Rate?
21–30 A committed follower
11–20 An acquaintance of Jesus
1–10   Get to know Jesus NOW!

Remember

What are the sacraments of initiation?
The sacraments of initiation are Baptism, Confirmation, and the Eucharist. In Christian Initiation a person is reborn in Baptism, strengthened in Confirmation, and nourished by the Eucharist.

Why are they important?
These sacraments make a person a member of the Church and empower him or her to carry out the mission of Christ in the world.

Words to Know

sacrament	elect
RCIA	scrutiny
sponsor	exorcism
catechumen	mystagogy
rite of enrollment	

Words to Memorize

The sacraments—Baptism, Confirmation, Eucharist, Reconciliation (Penance), Anointing of the Sick, Matrimony, and Holy Orders
(Remember the name B. C. ERAMHO, which contains the first letter of each sacrament in order.)

Respond

The gifts of the Spirit are wisdom, understanding, right judgment (counsel), knowledge, courage (fortitude), reverence (piety), and wonder and awe (fear of the Lord). Choose one of these gifts and write a prayer asking the Holy Spirit to strengthen you in practicing that gift. Write your prayer in your journal.

Reach Out

1. Discuss with your family ways they serve

   * one another
   * the parish community
   * other people.

2. Take a survey of five parish members you know, asking them the following questions:

   * What do you like best about your parish?
   * How does your parish help you?
   * How do you help your parish?

3. Interview someone from another Christian faith tradition about his/her baptism. Discuss with your classmates and teacher the similarities and differences between the Catholic faith ceremony and others.

4. Write a pledge describing your responsibility to serve others because you are a baptized Christian. Design the page. Put it where you will see it.

5. Ask a priest or deacon to explain the Rite of Baptism. Ask him any questions you have concerning the sacrament.

6. Find out how the RCIA is carried out in your parish.

Review

Write the Rite Words   Identify the major terms of the RCIA defined here.

1. The person who assists the candidate in learning about the Catholic faith:

   — — — — — — —

2. The rite involving petitions and exorcisms about repentance, the mystery of sin, and redemption for the "elect" during the third, fourth, and fifth Sundays of Lent:

   — — — — — — — — — — —

3. The process of becoming a Christian (abbreviation):

   — — — —

4. The rite of celebrating the listing of names of catechumens preparing for the sacraments of initiation:

   — — — — — — — — —

5. People interested in studying about the Catholic faith:

   — — — — — — — — —

6. A person who has completed the catechumenate and is ready to enter the Lenten period of intense preparation for the sacraments of initiation:

   — — — — —

7. The Easter season experience when the newly baptized learn more about their faith and how to live it:

   — — — — — — — — —

8. Prayers that the catechumen be delivered from the power of evil and receive the gifts of the Spirit:

   — — — — — — — — — — —

9. The handing on of the ancient documents of the faith, the Creed, and the Lord's Prayer:

   — — — — — — — — — — —

10. Persons selected by the catechumen to help him or her prepare for Baptism and lead a genuine Christian life:

    — — — — — — — — — —

11. A person who studies the teachings of the Gospel and the Church and prepares to receive the sacraments of initiation:

    — — — — — — — — — —

12. Liturgical celebration at which a person celebrates the sacraments of initiation:

    — — — — — — —   — — — — —

Sacrament Match   Write the letter of the sacrament that corresponds to each statement: Baptism (B), Confirmation (C), or Eucharist (E).

_____ **1.** Laying on of hands by the bishop is a sign.

_____ **2.** We receive the Holy Spirit and his gifts for the first time.

_____ **3.** We are anointed with chrism and called to be a witness of Christ.

_____ **4.** The community offers perfect worship to the Father.

_____ **5.** The community is nourished by the Body and Blood of Jesus.

_____ **6.** We become children of God and heirs to heaven.

_____ **7.** The community celebrates the Paschal Mystery of Jesus and makes it present.

_____ **8.** Original sin is forgiven.

Jesus the Way

q

As you received Christ Jesus the Lord, walk in him,
rooted in him and built upon him and established
in the faith as you were taught, abounding in thanksgiving.

COLOSSIANS 2:6–7

Switchword Puzzle on Jesus

How well do you know your friend? Give a clue for each word related to him in the puzzle. Write your answers on a piece of paper under the headings "Across" and "Down."

		[10] W		[1] A	[11] P	O	S	T	L	E	S					[15] P	
		I			H									[14] Z		A	
		T			A		[12] S							E		S	
	[2] I	N	C	A	R	N	A	T	I	O	N			A		C	
		E			I		C					[13] R		L		H	
		S			S		R					C		O		A	
[16] P		S			[3] E	V	A	N	G	E	L	I	S	T		L	
A					E		M					A		S			
L			[4] G	O	S	P	E	L	[18] S							M	
E							N		H							Y	
S		[5] J	O	H	N		T	H	E		B	A	P	T	I	S	T
T							S		M							T	
[6] I	N	F	A	N	[17] C	Y		N	A	R	R	A	T	I	V	E	S
N					H											R	
E			[7] M	A	R	Y				[8] T	R	I	N	I	T	Y	
					I												
			[9] D	I	S	C	I	P	L	E							
					T												

A "Jesus boat" on the Sea of Galilee

Find the Falsehoods

Place an X before any false statements about Jesus.

_____ **1.** Jesus is much too great to be a real friend.

_____ **2.** Jesus is the Son of God, the second person of the Trinity.

_____ **3.** Jesus means "God saves."

_____ **4.** Jesus only pretended to be a man.

_____ **5.** Jesus saved us from sin and death by dying and rising.

_____ **6.** Jesus showed us how to live.

_____ **7.** The Gospels about Jesus always agree on details.

_____ **8.** Jesus sent the Holy Spirit to help us understand him.

_____ **9.** Jesus was Jewish.

_____ **10.** Jesus was accepted as the Messiah by all who knew him.

_____ **11.** Jesus was tempted.

_____ **12.** Jesus associated mostly with common people, the poor, and outcasts.

Sign Readers

What do these sacramental signs mean?

water

_____

_____

"This is my Body . . . This is my Blood."

_____

_____

chrism

_____

_____

_____

First Steps on the Way

Baptism   Confirmation
Eucharist

Can you answer these questions?
1. How is Jesus present today in the sacraments?
2. How are the three sacraments of initiation related?
3. What gifts do we receive in Baptism?

Rite Order

Number the parts of the Rite of Christian Initiation of Adults in order.

_____   Enlightenment

_____   Precatechumenate

_____   Mystagogy

_____   Rite of Election or Enrollment

_____   Catechumenate

_____   Initiation

laying on of hands

_____

"Be sealed with the gift of the Spirit."

_____

bread and wine

_____

_____

"I baptize you."

_____

_____

The Doughnut Priest

Following Jesus the Way can lead to surprising roles. For one man it meant becoming a priest who made doughnuts.

Father Joseph Valine, O.P., ministered to people in Utah in an area larger than Rhode Island. At the age of ninety he was the pastor of three missions. He traveled only 300 miles a week, down from the 600 he used to drive.

Father Valine went to Utah more than forty years ago at the bishop's request. At that time Catholics made up only three percent of the population of Utah, and they lived apart. World War II barracks, a library, a trailer, and parishioners' homes were all "churches" at different missions until a real

church could be built. Father Valine built seven churches with donations and income from his hobbies. For years he farmed more than 200 acres of alfalfa and catered dinners. Then he became a doughnut maker. Every Saturday Father made doughnuts to sell. Farmers and tourists paid whatever they wished for a bag of ten.

In Milford, a town which is ninety percent Mormon, the people once proclaimed "Father Valine Day." This was a tribute to Father's love of God and people. One year Father received an award from the Catholic Church Extension Society. It was the Lumen Christi (Light of Christ) Award. What can you do to help spread the light of Christ to the world? Do you have a doughnut recipe?

Testing Your Strength

How well do you understand what it means to follow Christ? Read each statement. If it is a Christian response, put **C** on the line. If it shows a selfish, unloving attitude, put **S**.

_____ **1.** I can't volunteer for that duty. I want to play basketball during noon recess.

_____ **2.** Here comes the principal! Let's get away from here. She always has a job for everyone she sees.

_____ **3.** I'll sign up for the cleanup committee. I hate that kind of work, but I don't think many will volunteer for it.

_____ **4.** There's a boycott against grapes to support the grape pickers who are treated unjustly. It won't make a difference if I keep eating grapes, my favorite fruit.

_____ **5.** Mother, you look tired! Let me put the baby to bed.

_____ **6.** No, I'm not going to do it. That's stealing!

_____ **7.** I don't have any money for the missions. I need this change for chewing gum.

_____ **8.** I'm good in art. I'll volunteer to make the card from our class.

_____ **9.** The yard's a mess after that storm. Maybe I can get it cleaned up before Mom comes home.

_____ **10.** I can't do what Dad told me. Everyone will laugh at me.

Number right _____ × 10 = _____ points

Looking Back

You have looked at who Jesus is and who he is for you. You have reflected on how the Son of God became human to save us from sin and death. You have heard that he calls you to a close relationship with him. You know ways to deepen your friendship with him and resist evil: prayer, reading Scripture, and celebrating the sacraments. You are coming to understand how Jesus is the Way to the Father, the way to everlasting happiness.

Before you go on, ask yourself three questions. You might write your answers in your journal.

1. How have your thoughts changed about Jesus? About yourself? About others?
2. How do you know Jesus can fill you with peace even when suffering enters your life?
3. What steps are you taking to know Jesus better and follow him?

Personal Inventory

Take an inventory of how well you are following Christ Jesus. Begin to work on points you want to improve.

❏ Do you help your friends become the best people they can be?
❏ Can your friends count on you?
❏ Do you try to make up when you have failed to be a good friend?
❏ Do you open your heart to Jesus and spend time with him each day?
❏ Do you listen to Christ's message read at Sunday Mass?
❏ Do you trust him when you can't understand why he does something?
❏ Do you follow in his footsteps by sacrificing for others?
❏ Do you give loving service to others?
❏ Do you act for peace and justice?

Words to Ponder

Below are some thoughts from people who found that following Jesus is the most important thing in life. Think about them!

"We can only know ourselves through Jesus Christ." (Pascal)

"Prayer is the royal road to God. Let no one mislead you by showing you any other road." (St. Teresa of Avila)

"The most beautiful and stirring adventure that can happen to you is the personal meeting with Jesus, who is the only one who gives meaning to your life." (Pope John Paul II)

"There is only one unhappiness and that is not to be one of the Saints." (Leon Bloy)

"My great luck was to have had him [Jesus] on my mind for so long." (Dorothy Day)

Celebration of Jesus the Way

Song

Leader: Jesus Christ. Everyone who hears about him is faced with a decision. Either Jesus is God or he isn't. Either he is our Savior or he isn't. Whatever we decide about him involves a risk. Our whole life is at stake. Do you, like millions of others, choose to believe that Jesus is the Son of God? Or do you think he was a liar? A fool? A failure? In the Gospels the first Christians share their faith in him.

Reader 1: In the beginning was the Word, and the Word was with God, and the Word was God.
He was in the beginning with God
He was in the world,
and the world came to be through him, but the world did not know him. He came to what was his own, but his own people did not accept him. But to those who did accept him he gave power to become children of God.
(John 1:1, 2, 10–12)

Leader: People who knew Jesus reacted to him in different ways.

Side 1: John the Baptizer said, "Behold, the Lamb of God, who takes away the sin of the world" (John 1:29).

Side 2: The disciples said, "What sort of man is this, whom even the winds and the sea obey?" (Matthew 8:27).

Side 1: The Pharisees said, "He drives out demons by the prince of demons" (Matthew 9:34).

Side 2: His neighbors said, "Where did this man get such wisdom and mighty deeds?" (Matthew 13:54).

Side 1: Some said, "Look, he is a glutton and a drunkard, a friend of tax collectors and sinners" (Matthew 11:19).

Side 2: Peter said, "You are the Messiah, the Son of the living God" (Matthew 16:16).

Side 1: Nathanael said, "Rabbi, you are the Son of God; you are the King of Israel" (John 1:49).

Side 2: The Samaritans said, "We know that this is truly the savior of the world" (John 4:42).

Side 1: The Pharisees said, "Look and see that no prophet arises from Galilee" (John 7:52).

Side 2: Some Jewish people said, "We are not stoning you for a good work but for blasphemy. You, a man, are making yourself God" (John 10:33).

Side 1: Martha said, "I have come to believe that you are the Messiah, the Son of God"
(John 11:27).

Personal Reflection: I say . . .

Reader 2: "Not everyone who says to me, 'Lord, Lord,' will enter the kingdom of heaven, but only the one who does the will of my Father in heaven. Everyone who listens to these words of mine and acts on them will be like a wise man who built his house on rock. The rain fell, the floods came, and the winds blew and buffeted the house. But it did not collapse; it had been set solidly on rock. And everyone who listens to these words of mine but does not act on them will be like a fool who built his house on sand. The rain fell, the floods came, and the winds blew and buffeted the house. And it collapsed and was completely ruined" (Matthew 7:21, 24–27).

Leader: Jesus invites everyone to believe in him. If you believe in Jesus, you will believe in his words and act on them. As a friend and follower of Jesus, you will want to change anything in your life that is against his Father's Law.

Personal Reflection: One way I can do this is . . .

Leader: Jesus is our way to the Father. He proclaimed the coming of the kingdom of God. Let us pray with the words he taught us.

All: Our Father . . .

Song

Jesus Christ the Truth

Christians Pray Always:
Including Christ in Daily Family Life

If the DeLucas are traveling in their car and pass a cemetery, they pray, "Eternal rest grant unto them, O Lord." This is one way they keep before them the union between their everyday life and their spiritual life. They know that God is not someone to think of only at Sunday Mass. Our relationship with Christ can enhance every aspect of our lives.

From the time the children were little, Mrs. DeLuca formed in them the habit of beginning the day mindful of God. They greeted God with a short prayer of praise. When they were older, they prayed the Morning Offering. Night prayers were their chance to thank God for the blessings of the day and to ask pardon for any failings. Meals eaten together always begin by thanking God for all gifts, including the gift of life. Sometimes each family member names something for which he or she is especially thankful.

The DeLucas christen routine actions with prayer. A plaque at their front door reminds them to pray that God blesses their comings and goings. When Mrs. DeLuca gives the children their allowance, she prays a short prayer reminding them to be good stewards.

At times family members pray short prayers spontaneously. For instance, if on the way home from Grandma's they see a spectacular sunset, Mr. DeLuca might pray, "Praise the Lord for the wonders of creation." If the news report is about a tragic situation, Mrs.

DeLuca might pray for the victims. If they hear a siren, the family prays for anyone who might be hurt or sick.

The family marks special occasions with prayer. They pray when they celebrate feasts like Christmas and Easter as well as birthdays and other anniversaries. The day Jay lost his first tooth, they prayed. And the day Joan got her driver's license, the family prayed with her for her protection and the protection of the rest of the world. The DeLucas purchased a few books that have prayers for various times, but usually they just make up their own prayers. These are more creative and from the heart.

Paul exhorts Christians to pray always. To follow his advice your family might choose one of the practices mentioned on this page and bring Christ more actively into your family life.

Parables: Stories Jesus Told

10

Sunrise over the Sea of Galilee

You were once darkness, but now you are light in the Lord.
Live as children of light, for light produces
every kind of goodness and righteousness and truth.

EPHESIANS 5:8–9

What is it like to walk in the dark without being able to see well? What might happen?

_____

_____

_____

Why did Jesus call himself the Light of the World?

_____

_____

Jesus, the Son of God, is the source of all truth. All his life was a teaching. His teachings light our way to the Father. They give us knowledge of human life and of divine things. Jesus revealed the love of God and God's plan for us. He proclaimed the message of salvation. If we follow his teachings, we will know the happiness of his friendship. Walking with him, we will live well on the earth and arrive safely at the kingdom. What God has revealed, especially through Jesus, is the foundation of our faith.

Teachings of Twenty Centuries

Jesus commissioned his apostles to teach the Good News to all nations. The apostles and first Christians handed on Jesus' teachings by their word and by their lives. They expressed these truths in customs, prayers, and **creeds,** or professions of faith. They recorded them in the New Testament.

Bishops, the successors of the apostles, also have the right and duty to teach everything Jesus has revealed. The teaching authority of the Church is called **magisterium.** It is at work primarily in the pope and in the bishops together and in union with the pope. Other members share it as they study and spread the faith. The magisterium is present in liturgy, in the practice of the faith—whenever doctrines contained in Scripture and Tradition are taught. A **doctrine** is a belief the Church holds and teaches. A doctrine that is officially defined by the Church as a truth revealed by God, an article of faith for Catholics, is a **dogma.** Some doctrines are more important than others. It is Church doctrine that Jesus is God. It is also doctrine that Mary was sinless. Which of these two doctrines is more central to our faith?

For two thousand years the Church has preserved the doctrines Jesus taught and has gained new insights. Truth does not change, but the Holy Spirit continually leads the Church to a deeper understanding. On our journey of life, we can look to the Church for truths to guide us—the truths that Jesus taught.

Stories That Teach

Jesus was a master teacher. He used stories about the stuff of everyday life: sowers and seeds, fishermen and nets, shepherds, thieves, and yeast. He spoke of ordinary happenings: looking for a lost object, getting paid for work, and asking a friend for help. These stories Jesus told about God and his kingdom are called **parables.** In a parable a comparison is made between something familiar and a new truth.

B. Deichmann in Trinitatis Kirke, Copenhagen, Denmark

A parable usually also has an unexpected twist that shows the kingdom breaking into everyday life. It teases us to see things differently.

While hearing a parable, we make a judgment about the events in the story and then apply it to ourselves. Often we find that our way of thinking and acting is quite different from God's. This discovery challenges us to change our lives for the better.

How the Short Story Works
Read the parable of the Rich Fool, and then answer the questions on a sheet of paper.

 There was a rich man whose land produced a bountiful harvest. He asked himself, "What shall I do, for I do not have space to store my harvest?" And he said, "This is what I shall do: I shall tear down my barns and build larger ones. There I shall store all my grain and other goods and I shall say to myself, 'Now as for you, you have so many good things stored up for many years, rest, eat, drink, be merry!'" But God said to him, "You fool, this night your life will be demanded of you; and the things you have prepared, to whom will they belong?" Thus will it be for the one who stores up treasure for himself but is not rich in what matters to God.

Luke 12:16–21

1. **A story has a main character and other characters.** Who are the characters in this parable?
2. **A story has a setting.** Where does this story take place?
3. **A story has a plot, the action.** What happens in this story?
4. **The action centers around some struggle.** What problem does our hero face?
5. **A story's main character might have a flaw.** What is the rich man's flaw?
6. **Conversation in a story tells us what a character is like.** How do you know what the rich man is like?
7. **Some stories have surprise endings.** How is the rich man's problem solved?
8. **Stories mirror real life.** Are there people like the rich man? Have you ever been like the rich man? Do you know of anyone who had an experience like the rich man's?

9. **Stories draw us into them and make us think.** How do you think the rich man felt when God spoke? Why was he a fool? What do you think happened after he died?
10. **Stories have a theme, a message.** What meaning do you find in this parable? What questions does the story make you ask yourself?

A parable has layers like an onion. To reveal its meanings, ask questions like those here.

Probing the Parables
Read the parable and match it with a truth.

a. The Pharisee and the Tax Collector (Luke 18:9–14)
b. The Lost Sheep (Luke 15:4–7)
c. The Workers in the Vineyard (Matthew 20:1–16)
d. The Persistent Friend (Luke 11:5–8)

_____ 1. God loves sinners and is glad when they return to a good life.

_____ 2. Even sinners who truly repent at the last minute will have the fullness of joy in heaven.

_____ 3. Beware of being proud of your goodness and judging others.

_____ 4. Keep praying to God and your prayers will be answered.

Kingdom Parables

Jesus proclaimed the kingdom of God, which is already here but not yet fully. In this kingdom God and God's people live together in peace, justice, and love. The following parables give insights into the kingdom. Read them and fill in the blanks in each statement. Notice which Gospel contains all of these kingdom parables.

THE PARABLE	A TRUTH IT TEACHES
Mustard Seed Matthew 13:31 **The Yeast** Matthew 13:33	1. From a small beginning the kingdom _____.
The Net Matthew 13:47 **The Weeds** Matthew 13:24	2. On earth _____ and _____ live together until _____.
The Pearl of Great Price Matthew 13:45 **The Hidden Treasure** Matthew 13:44	3. The person who finds the kingdom feels _____. To possess it, he or she is willing to _____.
The Wedding Feast Matthew 22:2	4. The kingdom is open to _____. We are free to _____.

Write your own comparison:
The kingdom of heaven is like . . .

_____

_____

The Price of Admission

Some parables show what we are to do if we hope to be members of the kingdom.
Read the following two parables and write some advice each one gives.

The Unforgiving Servant (Matthew 18:23–35)

_____

_____

_____

The Three Servants and the Money (Matthew 25:14–30) _____

_____

_____

Some parables encourage us to respond to salvation NOW. Every day is a day to change our ways to be ready for the kingdom. Read the Ten Bridesmaids (Matthew 25:1–13). Then answer the following questions:

1. How were five bridesmaids foolish?

_____

2. How does a wise person prepare for the coming of Jesus?

_____

_____

The Price of Admission

Life or Death?

In Palestine farmers probably scattered seed all over the land and then plowed it under. In the parable of the Sower and the Seed (Matthew 13:3–9, 18–23), Jesus told what happened to one man's seed. Some of it fell on the edge of the path and was eaten by birds. Some fell on rocky ground. It grew, but then withered away for lack of roots. Some fell among thorns and was choked by them. But some seed fell on rich soil and produced a wonderful crop.

The parable shows what happens to the Word of God. Some people do not listen to it at all. Some accept the Word at first but are too weak to live by it. Some accept the Word, and then other people or things of the world kill it in their hearts. But in some people God's Word lives. They spread his kingdom wherever they are. To which group do you belong?

Rich Soil for the Parables

Will the parables take root in your heart? Write how a member of the kingdom would respond to these dilemmas. Then write what might make it difficult to respond that way.

1. Your friends start teasing a classmate who is unpopular.

   Christian response: _____

   _____

   Possible difficulties: _____

   _____

2. Someone hands you pornographic pictures at school.

   Christian response: _____

   _____

   Possible difficulties: _____

   _____

3. You and several others are at a friend's home. Your friend's parents are not there. The friend suggests drinking some liquor. There's a lot of it, and the parents won't miss it.

   Christian response: _____

   _____

   Possible difficulties: _____

   _____

4. A classmate you'd like to be friends with has dared you to do something dangerous. You realize you could seriously injure yourself if you try it and don't succeed.

   Christian response: _____

   _____

   Possible difficulties: _____

   _____

Remember

How do we come to know the teachings of Jesus?
We come to know the teachings of Jesus through Scripture, Tradition, and the teaching of the Church.

What is a parable of Jesus?
A parable of Jesus is a story that teaches about God and the kingdom of God through everyday experiences.

What did Jesus say about listening to God's Word?
Jesus said, "Blessed are those who hear the word of God and observe it" (Luke 11:28).

Words to Know

creed	dogma
magisterium	parable
doctrine	

Respond

Suppose the end of the world were to occur tonight. What would you wish to have changed about yourself to be better prepared to meet Jesus? Write it in your journal. Then list steps you can take to begin to change NOW.

Reach Out

1. The message of Jesus calls us to a way of life that is very different from the way of the world. Bring to class a newspaper story or magazine article about someone whose response to a need was Christlike.

2. All the saints met opposition as they tried to live up to the teachings of Jesus. Sometimes they had to overcome their own personal feelings. Sometimes they met criticism, ridicule, and even persecution. Research the life of a saint or a great Christian who is living today. Suggestions: St. Ignatius of Antioch, St. John Baptist de la Salle, St. Elizabeth Ann Seton, St. Julie Billiart, St. Thomas More, St. John of the Cross, St. Isaac Jogues. Find at least one situation in which that person followed Christ's way even when opposed.

3. The more peace, justice, and love are brought into the world, the more the kingdom is present. What can you do to further the kingdom in your family, your neighborhood, and your world? Brainstorm for ideas and select one or two.

4. Be open to God's Word today. Pay attention to a homily or read a letter from your bishop, part of a Church document, or an article in a Catholic periodical. Share something you learned with someone else.

5. Design a poster that is based on one of the parables. Display it in your parish or school hall.

6. With your classmates present some parables as plays. Be creative in writing the scripts. You might include one or two narrators to tie the plays together. Perform your plays for another class, the school, or a parish audience. Videotape them.

Review

Parables in Art   Choose a parable about God. Write its title and message. Then draw a picture that represents it. Do the same on the kingdom and on the members of the kingdom.

Title: _____

God: _____

_____

Title: _____ Title: _____

The kingdom: _____ Members of the kingdom: _____

_____ _____

True or False   Write **T** if the statement is true and **F** if it is false.

_____ **1.** Scripture was written before Tradition began.

_____ **2.** Magisterium is the teaching authority of the Church.

_____ **3.** The Church can change dogmas.

_____ **4.** The Holy Spirit leads us to new understandings of Christ's teachings.

_____ **5.** Parables are stories meant only for the people in Jesus' time.

_____ **6.** The kingdom of God is already here.

_____ **7.** The parables urge us to listen to God's Word and to get ready for the kingdom.

Miracles: Signs Jesus Worked

11

The Raising of Lazarus by Master of the Prodigal Son

All wonder to see water turned into wine.
Every day the earth's moisture, being drawn into
the root of a vine,
is turned by the grape into wine, and no one wonders.

GREGORY THE GREAT

- The pastor of a poor parish can't pay his electric bill. He prays to the Sacred Heart. The next day's mail brings a check from an anonymous donor for the exact amount of the bill.
- Heavy rains are forecast for the day of the youth picnic. The teenagers pray, and the day arrives full of sunshine and blue skies.
- According to the Gospels, Jesus worked fantastic cures:

> The crowds were amazed when they saw the mute speaking, the deformed made whole, the lame walking, and the blind able to see, and they glorified the God of Israel.
>
> Matthew 15:31

Do you believe in miracles? Why or why not?

_____

What is a miracle?

_____

_____

Miracles Make Sense

The universe is filled with marvelous events and mysteries. Natural wonders, like a spectacular sunset or a newborn baby, make us aware of God's presence. In miracles, God breaks into our world even more dramatically. Since Jesus is the Son of God, it is no surprise that for him, miracles are normal.

While the Synoptic Gospels call miracles acts of power, John's Gospel calls them signs. Jesus' extraordinary acts were signs that the kingdom he proclaimed is among us. Miracles are another way that Jesus teaches us truths about himself, the kingdom, and its members.

Acts that Teach

Jesus' miracles reveal that he is the Holy One. He is Goodness, Mercy, and Life. The miracle stories show him Lord over nature, sin, sickness, Satan, and death.

Some people believed that suffering and death were the result of personal sin. Read John 9:1–3. How did Jesus react to this belief?

_____

_____

_____

Pain, weakness, suffering, and death are the result of **original sin.** All history and each individual bears its weight and suffers its effects. People longed for the Messiah who would free them from their bondage to sin. The disciples of John the Baptizer asked Jesus, "Are you the one who is to come, or should we look for another?" (Matthew 11:3). He replied, "Go and tell John what you hear and see: the blind regain their sight, the lame walk, lepers are cleansed, the deaf hear, the dead are raised, and the poor have the good news proclaimed to them" (Matthew 11:4–5). Jesus' healing of physical evils is a sign of his victory over all evil. Jesus is truly the Savior of the world.

The miracle stories teach some of the same lessons as the parables. When Jesus healed on the Sabbath and touched unclean people, he showed that the law of love surpasses all human laws. When he worked miracles for outcasts, sinners, and Gentiles, he showed that God's kingdom is open to all. When he worked wonders out of pity for people, he showed God's compassion and love. The miracles also teach the importance of _faith_. Jesus performed them when people believed in him. Often he praised their faith. Where there was no faith, he worked no miracles.

The Marriage at Cana by Adriaen Pietersz van de Venne

Miracle Stories

Many people became disciples of Jesus because they experienced his miracles. They watched him heal the sick and bring the dead back to life. They saw him break Satan's hold over people. They realized that in Jesus, God was with them. The following Gospel stories about miracles are rewritten here as eyewitness accounts. As you read them, be open to their teachings. After each one, list the truths that it reveals to you.

Wine Overflowing
as told by Mary (John 2:1–12)

I remember the first miracle Jesus worked. My son, some of his new friends, and I were at a wedding in Cana. Everyone was having a good time, but the wine was getting low. If it ran out, the party would turn into a nightmare for the newlyweds and their families. Thinking my son could help somehow, I merely said to him, "They have no wine." Jesus answered, "Woman, how does your concern affect me? My hour has not yet come." I wasn't sure what he meant, but I knew I could depend on him. I told the servants, "Do whatever he tells you."

Sure enough, Jesus ordered the servants to fill six stone jars with water. These jars, used for ritual washings, each held about twenty to thirty gallons. When they were filled to the brim with water, Jesus told the servants to take some to the headwaiter. I watched the headwaiter sip the wine. He called the bridegroom over and said, "Everyone serves good wine first and keeps the cheaper wine until people have had plenty to drink, but you have kept the best wine until now." When my son does things, he does them well. Not only did he provide a vast amount of wine, but wine of superior quality. He saved the day for the hosts and their guests.

Truths: Jesus has power over _____

_____

_____

_____

_____

_____

Rising from Paralysis and Sin
as told by a friend (Mark 2:1–12)

When we heard that Jesus the healer was home again in Capernaum, four of us decided to take our paralyzed friend to him. With great hope we carried our friend on his mat to the house where Jesus was preaching. To our dismay people packed the house and crowded around the door. We couldn't even get near Jesus. Then we had a brilliant idea. We hoisted our friend up the side steps to the roof. We broke through the clay roof right above Jesus and carefully lowered the mat holding our friend through the opening. You should have seen the look on the people's faces! The crowd made room for our friend then.

Jesus said to him, "Child, your sins are forgiven." We knew that the Scribes sitting there were probably horrified since only God can forgive sins. Jesus seemed to read their minds. He asked, "Which is easier, to say to the paralytic, 'Your sins are forgiven' or 'Rise, pick up your mat and walk'? So that you may know I have authority to forgive sins …" Then he said to our friend, "Rise, pick up your mat and go home." With that, this man, who hadn't even been able to move his little finger, stood and picked up his mat. He passed through the crowd of people and out the door a free man.

Truths: Jesus has power over _____

_____

_____

_____

Stilling a Storm
as told by Peter (Mark 4:35–41)

One evening after a hard day of teaching, Jesus said, "Let's cross the lake." Leaving the crowd on the shore, we got in our boat and sailed off. Jesus was so exhausted that before long he was sound asleep on a cushion. Suddenly a great storm blew up. Huge waves crashed over us, filling our boat with water. We woke Jesus shouting, "Teacher, don't you care that we are perishing?" First he commanded the wind to stop. Then he said to the sea, "Quiet. Be still." At his word the wind ceased and everything became very calm. With disappointment written on his face he asked us why we were terrified. He asked, "Don't you have faith yet?" All we could do was marvel at what we had seen and wonder who he was. Never in all our years of fishing have we met someone whom the wind and sea obeyed.

Truths: Jesus has power over _____

_____

_____

_____

_____

Deviled Ham

as told by an exorcised man (Mark 5:1–20)

I used to be possessed by an evil spirit. I lived in a cemetery where I ran among the tombs, howling and hurting myself. When people tried to chain me down, I broke the chains. One day I saw the Jewish man, Jesus, come to the shore of our Gentile land. I ran to him and prostrated myself before him. A voice came from me saying, "What have you to do with me, Jesus, Son of the Most High God?" Jesus ordered, "Unclean spirit, come out of the man." The spirit begged Jesus not to torment him. When Jesus asked his name, the spirit replied, "Legion. There are many of us." Then the spirits asked not to be sent away but to be sent into the swine nearby. Just like that, the two thousand swine rushed down a slope into the sea and drowned. What a sight! The swineherds ran away.

I was sitting and talking to Jesus when they returned with a crowd. Seeing me perfectly normal, the people were scared and begged Jesus to leave. As Jesus climbed into the boat, I pleaded to go with him, but he told me to go home and tell my family what God did for me. I tell my story over and over.

Truths: Jesus has power over _____

_____

_____

_____

Awakened from Death

as told by Jairus (Mark 5:21–43)

I, an official in a synagogue, put my faith in Jesus. My twelve-year-old daughter was deathly ill. I stepped out of a crowd listening to Jesus and threw myself at his feet. I begged him to lay his hands on my girl and make her well. He came with me, followed by the crowd. To my distress, we were delayed when a sick woman touched Jesus' cloak and was healed. While Jesus spoke to her, people brought the message that my daughter had died. My heart sank, but Jesus said, "Don't be afraid. Just have faith." We continued on.

The mourners were already at the house when we arrived. Jesus asked why they were weeping and carrying on when the child was only sleeping. They mocked him and he made them leave. He let only my wife, Peter, James, John, and me go in with him. Jesus took my daughter's lifeless hand and said, "Little girl, I say to you, arise!" My child opened her eyes, got up, and started walking. Imagine how my wife and I felt. Jesus told us not to tell anyone. Then he said to give our girl something to eat. Thank God I went to Jesus for help.

Truths: Jesus has power over _____

_____

_____

_____

A Man for Others

Compassion is pity or sympathy for people who are suffering and a desire to relieve their pain—even to suffer in their place. It is being one with them in their suffering. Christ showed great compassion for the poor, the sick, the sinners—for anyone who was suffering. His desire to help people often moved him to work miracles. Jesus has the same compassion for us today. He wants us to turn to him with faith when we are suffering. Sometimes he saves us through one another.

As followers and friends of Christ, we will respond to others as he did. We will reach out to the needy with compassion and work the "miracle" of kindness. Our miracles won't be as spectacular as those of Jesus. But with his power in us, we can perform miracles of love like

✤ healing someone with kind words
✤ encouraging sinners by showing them forgiveness
✤ going out of our way to assist someone
✤ doing a hidden act that brightens someone's day
✤ helping a friend overcome temptation and make the right decision
✤ bringing an outsider into the circle of friendship
✤ persuading our family to sponsor a poor child in another country.

What miracles can you work today?

_____

_____

How would they be wonders?

_____

_____

What would they be signs of?

_____

_____

A Burst of Miracles

Learn more about Jesus by reading the miracle accounts below. Summarize the stories using a chart with three columns labeled: Power over . . . , How Christ showed compassion, and Who showed faith.

Luke 5:1–11	Great Catch of Fish
Mark 10:46–52	Blind Bartimaeus
Luke 7:1–10	Centurion's Slave
Mark 9:14–29	Possessed Boy
Luke 7:11–17	Widow's Son

Remember

What do Jesus' miracles show him having power over?
Miracles show Jesus having power over nature, sin, sickness, Satan, and death.

What can we do if we have faith?
Jesus said, "If you have faith the size of a mustard seed, you will say to this mountain, 'Move from here to there,' and it will move. Nothing will be impossible for you" (Matthew 17:20).

Words to Know
miracle   compassion

Respond

Often Jesus worked miracles because of a person's faith. How strong is your faith? Answer these questions in your journal.

Which actions of yours show that you believe in God?

What do you do to strengthen your faith?

When have you turned to Jesus for help in time of need?

How have you given witness to your faith when it was tested by what others said and did?

Do you thank God for the gift of faith and ask that it may be increased?

How have you tried to share your faith with others?

Reach Out

1. Christ and Mary were welcomed guests at the wedding feast of Cana. Would they have been welcome at the last party you attended? Do you think they would have been happy to be there, or might they have been uncomfortable? With a group of friends or with your family, set some ground rules for parties. What are some ways of having a lot of fun without being ashamed to have Christ or Mary walk in on the celebration?

2. Think more deeply about miracles:
   - ✢ What are some natural miracles that amaze you?
   - ✢ How do miracles fit in with the whole pattern and purpose of Jesus' life?
   - ✢ Why do you think the Gospels often say that Jesus told people not to spread the news of his miracles?
   - ✢ What miracles can you pray for today?

3. Plan and present a trilogy of miracle plays. Invite another class, your parents, members of your parish, or a group of people in an institution. You might like to videotape your program.

4. Find out about miracles that have occurred today. Talk to people about them. Look for stories about them in magazines and newspapers. Report to your class.

5. Friends tend to imitate each other. They often like the same music, clothes, books, movies, sports, etc. Sometimes they even think alike. In what ways are you like your friend Christ? How can you be more like him? Think about this during a desert experience and write about it in your journal. Begin by listing qualities or virtues of Christ. Check to see if you have those qualities. Select one or two areas in which you would like to improve. Plan how you will accomplish this.

6. Think of ways to imitate the compassion of Christ and bring healing to others. Perhaps you can involve younger brothers and sisters. Some things you might consider doing are the following:

   Send a card or note to someone who is ill or living alone.

   Make a cartoon or joke scrapbook for a shut-in.

   Offer to read to an elderly person, or write letters for him or her.

   Do something to give someone who cares for you extra rest, especially when he or she seems very tired or isn't feeling well.

   Plan to visit a nursing home. Call to find out times and rules for visiting.

   Invite an adult to be advisor and decide what you will do on your visit.

   Be considerate and quiet around the house when someone is ill or has a headache.

   Send a donation to those who are suffering from a war.

Review

Brainteasers   Use what you learned to answer these questions.

1. Before a person is canonized (declared a saint) usually two miracles worked through the person's prayers must occur. Why are miracles a good test for sainthood?

_____

2. When two persons witness an extraordinary event, one can respond, "It's a miracle," and the other, "It's just a coincidence." What makes the difference in their responses?

_____

3. How are miracles like parables?

_____

_____

Miracle Mix   Unscramble the letters of the words under the blank lines to complete the sentences.

1. A _____ is an act of power, a wonder through which God gives us a sign.
      crliema

2. The miracles of Jesus were a sign of the presence of the _____.
                                                                 gdimkon

3. Pain, suffering, and death are the result of _____.
                                                    ilogarin ins

4. Jesus' miracles show his power over all _____.
                                               live

5. Miracles are closely linked with _____.
                                        tifha

6. Jesus' first miracle was in response to _____.
                                               ayrM

7. When Jesus healed the paralytic, he also _____ him his sins.
                                                voefgar

8. Jesus' calming the storm showed his power over _____.
                                                      etanur

9. Jesus sent evil spirits from a Gentile into _____.
                                                   wiesn

10. Jesus raised Jairus' _____ to life.
        tredhagu

11. Jesus worked miracles because he had _____.
                                             mssoopcnai

12. We are like Jesus when we are _____.
                                      dikn

Jesus' Compassion: Reconciliation and the Anointing of the Sick

Is anyone among you sick? He should summon the presbyters of the church, and they should pray over him and anoint [him] with oil in the name of the Lord, and the prayer of faith will save the sick person, and the Lord will raise him up. If he has committed any sins, he will be forgiven.

JAMES 5:14–15

When was the last time you needed healing?

All people need healing in some way. It may be the healing of a sick and weakened body, or it may be the healing of a spirit wounded by sin and guilt. Jesus came to heal the world of sin and to heal us—body and soul. While on Earth he healed people by word and by touch, showing God's love and mercy. Nearly one-fifth of the Gospels are about healings. Christ's healing ministry continues today especially in the sacraments of Reconciliation and the Anointing of the Sick. This ministry is also carried on in other sacraments, in works of charity, and in the prayer of the community. Being Christian means both being healed and healing.

Healing of Spirit

Every time Steve walked into math class, he saw the boarded-up window. The principal was still trying to find out who had broken it the night of the regional tournaments.

Every day Steve waited to get caught. He was quieter at home. The few remarks he did make to his brothers and sisters were harsh. How they all annoyed him lately! Steve and his friends found themselves tense and quick to argue. The daily reminder of the boarded window and the whispers unnerved them.

Steve was working on his bike when his father appeared. Steve had always found it easy to talk to him, but now he did not even want to look at his father.

"It's a good day for fishing, Steve."

"I'm kind of busy today. Maybe some other time."

Steve's father was patient, but insistent. Soon they were at the lake, waiting for a catch. Now, far away from school, the broken window, and the other guys, Steve found it easier to talk. Before long the whole story poured out. Steve's father listened carefully, looking intently at his son.

Yes, it was an accident, but it was caused by Steve's carelessness. Yes, he had been foolish to run away from it. Yes, in some way he wanted to make up for it.

Already Steve felt the relief of a burden being lifted. Together, he and his father spoke to the principal. Every day after classes, Steve would work in the school until he could pay for a new window.

What kind of healing did Steve need?

_____

_____

Who helped Steve become healed? How?

_____

_____

_____

_____

_____

_____

_____

_____

What were some of the effects of Steve's guilt and who felt them?

_____

_____

_____

_____

_____

_____

If you had been with Steve the night the window was broken, what would you have done?

_____

Healing of Forgiveness

Sin cripples and wounds us. Jesus showed God's mercy and love for sinners. He told his disciples to forgive others in his name. Today, in the Sacrament of Reconciliation (Penance), sins we have committed after Baptism are forgiven through his priests. We are reconciled to God and others. We are healed. Individual confession of serious sins followed by absolution is the only ordinary means of Reconciliation.

Jesus shows in three parables how anxious God is to forgive us after we have sinned: The Lost Sheep (Luke 15:3–7), The Lost Coin (Luke 15:8–10), and The Prodigal Son (Luke 15:11–32), better named The Forgiving Father. Read these, realizing how good it is to be forgiven, to be welcomed home with love and acceptance.

In the Sacrament of Reconciliation, sinners who are sorry for their sins and intend not to sin again can be certain of God's forgiveness. They receive the grace to change their lives and follow Christ more closely. The sacrament is also a sign that the Christian community, which has been harmed by their sin, forgives them, too.

Receiving God's Forgiveness

Four elements must be present whenever Reconciliation is celebrated:

Contrition This is true sorrow for failing to love. You intend not to sin again and are ready to model your life on the life of Jesus. Conversion is at the heart of the sacrament.

Confession When you tell your sins to the priest, it is more helpful to discuss them than just to list them. Talk about things in school, at home, and at recreation spots that keep you from being the kind of person Jesus expects you to be. Ask any questions.

Penance Conversion of heart is shown by an act of penance or satisfaction. This may be a prayer, an act of self-denial, or a work of charity that makes up for damage or pain your sins have caused. It can help you begin again and live more completely for Christ.

Absolution God, through the ministry of the Church and her priest, gives you pardon for your sins with these words:
> "God the Father of mercies,
> through the death and resurrection of his Son
> has reconciled the world to himself
> and sent the Holy Spirit among us
> for the forgiveness of sins;
> through the ministry of the Church
> may God give you pardon and peace,
> and I absolve you from your sins
> in the name of the Father, and of the Son, † and of the Holy Spirit."

Three Rites of Reconciliation

The form of the Sacrament of Reconciliation has changed throughout history. Today there are three possible rites.

For Individual Penitents
In this rite only the penitent (the sinner wanting to change) and the priest are present. The priest represents God and the Christian community in expressing forgiveness and loving support. The penitent either kneels behind a screen or sits face-to-face with the priest.

- The priest welcomes the penitent.
- The penitent or priest may read from the Word of God.
- The penitent confesses his or her sins and expresses sorrow for them.
- The penitent accepts the penance.
- The priest absolves the penitent, who then praises God.

For Several Penitents with Individual Confession and Absolution
This rite stresses the communal aspects of sin and reconciliation. By their presence and prayer, Christians strengthen one another to follow Christ more closely. Communal celebrations are often held in Advent and Lent.

- Introductory rites include a greeting and an opening prayer.
- A reading from Scripture is followed by a homily and an examination of conscience.
- During the Rite of Reconciliation all admit their sinfulness and pray the Lord's Prayer. Then the penitents go individually to the priests for confession, a penance, and absolution.
- The presiding priest leads all in thanking and praising God for showing mercy.
- All are blessed and dismissed.

For Several Penitents with General Confession and Absolution
This rite is used only in exceptional circumstances and with the permission of the bishop. It is similar to the previous one, except that there is no individual confession, penance, or absolution. A common penance and general absolution are given. People who receive forgiveness for mortal sins in this rite must still confess those sins to a priest in an individual confession.

Patching Relationships

The father in the Prodigal Son parable had two bad boys. The older son, who refused to forgive his repentant brother, was refusing to love. He, too, was a sinner.

When were you last called to forgive someone? Did you tell the person he or she was forgiven? Was your relationship restored? Did you try to make the person feel loved and accepted? When were you last forgiven? How did you know you were forgiven? How did you feel?

Christ challenges us to forgive as he forgave—freely, completely, and lovingly. The more we understand God's great love for sinners, the more we will forgive others, ask forgiveness, and rejoice.

Healing of Body

On a warm spring day Lisa was taken to the hospital where she and her family learned she was diabetic. Doctors, nurses, and the hospital staff helped Lisa regain her strength. They formulated diets for her and taught her how to deal with her illness.

Family and friends called and wrote. They visited, bringing cards and flowers and sharing news. Father Johnson, the pastor; Mrs. Snyder, Lisa's favorite teacher; and the cheerleading coach visited her. Everyone listened as Lisa talked about her experiences and what she had learned. Day by day, Lisa became the lively girl they had known before. With loving care and medication she would continue her summer activities and be ready for school in the fall.

Who helped Lisa regain health? How?

_____

_____

_____

A Gift for the Suffering

The book title *Old Age Isn't for Sissies* suggests the difficulty of being weakened by age. Old age and illness often bring frustration, discouragement, and even bitterness. The sick may feel lonely and cut off from everyone else. They may envy others' energy and wonder why God permits them to suffer. Some elderly people fear losing their independence. They may resent younger people who take their places. The aged and sick may be impatient and feel unappreciated. There can be many temptations for them at a time when they feel very weak.

Christ understands suffering. He knows the pain, the stress, and the emptiness that we endure. Through his Church's celebration of the Sacrament of the Anointing of the Sick, he strengthens and comforts the seriously ill, grants them forgiveness, and restores their health if it is God's plan for them.

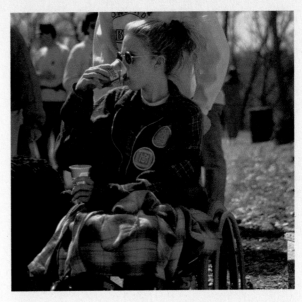

Check the attitudes that apply to you.

What is your attitude toward sickness? Do you

- ❏ refuse to think about it until it happens to you personally?
- ❏ complain when you are ill?
- ❏ think it is a punishment from God?
- ❏ pray when you are sick?
- ❏ thank God for your health?

What is your attitude toward the sick and elderly? Do you

- ❏ pray for them?
- ❏ feel sorry for them, but find it difficult to be around them?
- ❏ find joy in talking to them and listening to them?
- ❏ leave it to other people in hospitals and nursing homes to care for them?

The sick and elderly can unite their sufferings with Christ for the Church. What other gifts can they bring to the community?

_____

_____

_____

_____

_____

_____

The Anointing of the Sick

The Sacrament of the Anointing of the Sick may be celebrated anywhere. At times a parish anointing service is held for all those in need of the sacrament. Normally the *Church* is represented by at least the priest, family, and friends who have *gathered* to pray for the sick person.

The priest *sprinkles* the sick person with *holy water,* recalling Baptism when he or she shared in Christ's passion and resurrection. The sick person may celebrate the Sacrament of Penance at this point. Then *God's Word* is proclaimed, offering comfort and hope to all.

Next, just as Jesus often healed by touching, the priest *lays his hands* on the head of the sick person. This act signifies invoking the Holy Spirit to come upon the sick person. It also signifies the blessing and prayers of the Church and its union with the sick person. Then the priest *anoints the sick with oil* on the forehead and hands saying,

> "Through this holy anointing may the Lord in his love and mercy help you with the grace of the Holy Spirit. May the Lord who frees you from sin save you and raise you up."

The ancient practice of anointing with oil means healing, soothing, and strengthening. It is a sign of the presence of the Holy Spirit. After the anointing everyone prays for the physical and spiritual health of the one anointed.

A person who is dying may receive Holy Communion in a special rite called **Viaticum.** This word means "with you on the way." In Viaticum, Jesus accompanies us through the struggles of the journey's end into the banquet of the heavenly kingdom. The rite includes a renewal of the baptismal profession of faith and may end with everyone giving the dying person a sign of peace.

Do you know someone who is seriously ill or elderly? What can you do to help that person?

_____

_____

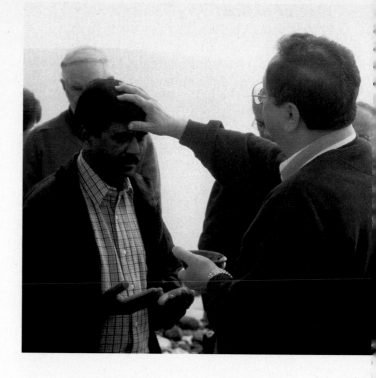

The Gift of Healing

Today Christ's healing ministry is very much alive. Not only does Christ bring healing to us through the Sacraments of Reconciliation and the Anointing of the Sick but through certain persons. At times God gives persons a special gift of healing for the good of others and the Church. Working through them, Jesus responds to the faith and prayers of sick people and their friends. He continues to cure persons with many kinds of illnesses—physical, mental, and spiritual. Often the greatest healing is spiritual.

Each one of us, though, is called to be a healer through our words and actions, our prayers and sacrifices.

When have you been healed?

_____

How have you helped to heal someone else?

_____

Remember

How do the sacraments of healing heal us?
In the Sacrament of Penance, Christ offers forgiveness and reconciliation to those who have turned away from God and the community. In the Anointing of the Sick, Christ offers forgiveness, healing, and strength to those who are weakened by age or sickness.

What are the four elements of the Sacrament of Reconciliation?
The four elements of the Sacrament of Reconciliation are contrition, confession, penance, and absolution.

What is Viaticum?
Viaticum is the rite in which a dying person receives Holy Communion.

How can we bring healing to others?
We can bring healing to others by

✤ being willing to forgive and to ask for forgiveness
✤ visiting, supporting, and caring for the sick and the elderly
✤ practicing the works of mercy
✤ praying for those who suffer physically, mentally, or spiritually.

Words to Know

contrition	reconciliation
confession	conversion
penance	Viaticum
absolution	

Respond

Suffering is a part of life for every descendent of Adam and Eve. Recall one of your own experiences of suffering. Then read 2 Corinthians 4:7–18. In your journal write your reflections on suffering: its mystery, its value, and what it has done for you. Include what can give us hope during times of hardship and pain.

Reach Out

1. Reconciliation begins at home. Try to recognize one good quality of every member of your family. Write a short note to each one thanking him or her for sharing that gift with the family. Plan to celebrate the Sacrament of Penance or a reconciliation ceremony together with your family.
2. Read how Jesus deals with two women who were sinful: the Penitent Woman (Luke 7:36–50) and the Adulteress (John 7:53–8:11). Write a paragraph on Jesus' relationship with sinners.
3. Speak with people in your parish who care for the sick or elderly and ask them to share their experiences with you. Or visit a hospital or home for the elderly. Write your reactions and present them to the class.
4. "Adopt" a parish shut-in. Write to this person, make cards or small gifts, and do things for him or her throughout the year.
5. Make banners, design remembrances, and prepare refreshments for your parish celebration of the Anointing of the Sick.
6. Find examples of times in the news recently when nations, churches, companies, or individuals have asked forgiveness.

Review

Identify the Rite Write the letter of those rites that include the listed features:

a. For Individual Penitents
b. For Several Penitents with Individual Confession and Absolution
c. For Several Penitents with General Confession and Absolution

_____ **1.** Absolution
_____ **2.** Obligation to be followed by individual confession of mortal sin
_____ **3.** Opportunity for getting individual counseling
_____ **4.** Praise of God for showing mercy
_____ **5.** A fuller sign of the forgiveness of community members
_____ **6.** Penance

What Belongs? Underline the answers that match each description.

1. Called a Sacrament of Healing:
Reconciliation   Anointing of the Sick   Holy Orders   Penance

2. The means Christ uses to heal today:
sacraments   works of charity   community prayer   healers

3. Parables of God's forgiveness:
The Net   The Lost Coin   The Prodigal Son   The Lost Sheep

4. Necessary elements of the Sacrament of Reconciliation:
Scripture reading   contrition   confession   absolution   penance

5. Acts of penance:
prayer   work of charity   act of self-denial   sickness

6. Someone who pardons in the Sacrament of Reconciliation:
God   the priest   the penitent   the community

7. Effects of the Sacrament of the Anointing of the Sick:
strength and comfort   forgiveness   health   grace

8. Viaticum:
Holy Communion   exorcism   strength for death   the last sacrament

Sequence of the Rite of Anointing   Each picture depicts a step in the Sacrament of the Anointing of the Sick. On the appropriate line write the name of the step being shown. Then in the circle, number the steps in the order they are performed.

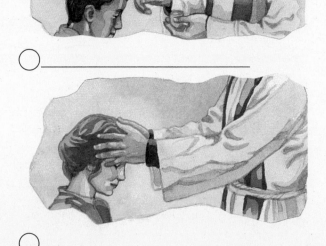

○ _____

○ _____

○ _____

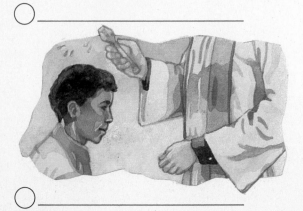

○ _____

○ _____

The Message of Jesus: Choose Life

13

I came so that they might have life
and have it more abundantly.

JOHN 10:10

Complete these statements.

My favorite activity is _bass/violin/sing_

musician

A part of the world I especially like is

home l islands

A person I like to be with is

God I dad

I enjoy eating

French Vanilla bread S
Salad

If you were not alive you would be deprived of all these wonderful things and more. Life is a precious gift. Out of millions of possibilities, the Father called you into being and made you the unique person you are. On top of that, Jesus gave his life that you might live forever. He taught us the secret to fullness of life: love. Read his two great commandments in Matthew 22:36–40.

To love as Jesus means cherishing the gift of life— our own and others'. It means reverencing all human beings and avoiding anything that harms them. We look on every child of God made in God's image as "another self." If we truly love, we will enjoy life, and we will enable others to enjoy it. The following stories show Christlike love in action.

A Modern Love Story

During the Vietnam War a village orphanage was bombed. Several missionaries and children were killed. One eight-year-old girl was badly injured. Without a quick blood transfusion, she would die. The American doctor and nurse who came to help asked in halting language and sign language if anyone would be willing to donate blood. After a long silence, one boy, Heng, volunteered.

As Heng lay on a pallet with a needle in his vein, he began to sob. When the doctor asked if it hurt, Heng replied, "No," and tried to hide his crying. But something was wrong. Finally, a Vietnamese nurse arrived who was able to talk to Heng. She

explained to the Americans, "Heng thought he was dying. He thought you had asked him to give all his blood so that the little girl would live."

"Why would you be willing to do that?" the nurse had asked Heng.

"She's my friend," Heng said.

An Old Love Story

Jesus gave us a model for Christian love in his parable of the Good Samaritan. Read Luke 10:25–37 remembering that the Samaritans and the Jewish people were enemies.

Based on these two love stories, what words would you use to describe Christian love?

family / holy / whole

Go for It!

Christian love is not easy. It is a challenge. Jesus demands an entirely new way of thinking and acting. He admits, "How narrow the gate and constricted the road that leads to life. And those who find it are few" (Matthew 7:14). How are you at accepting challenges?

* When a group invites you to join them in a stunt that would endanger your life, how do you react?
* When a family member, a teacher, or a classmate needs help, how do you react?
* When a friend experiments with smoking, alcohol, or drugs, how do you react?

Daily choices are important. They tell much about your attitudes and beliefs. Because human acts are done in freedom, you are responsible for them. Moreover, you must live with the consequences of these choices. They shape both your present and future life. You can improve your ability to make good decisions through Scripture, personal prayer, and the celebration of the Eucharist and the Sacrament of Reconciliation.

The Sermon on the Mount (Matthew 5–7) contains some teachings of Jesus that guide our decisions. Just as Moses once climbed Mount Sinai and received the Law, Jesus climbed a hillside and gave us a new understanding of the Law. He expects us to do more than follow a set of rules.

Like him, we are to think and act in total love. With his help and the help of the Holy Spirit, we are to do not just the minimum, but the maximum.

Find an example in Matthew 5:21–48 of how Jesus calls us to go beyond the law. Write it here.

_____

_____

Letter or Spirit?

Good laws

* protect the freedom, values, and rights that people hold as important
* protect the common good
* help all people reach goals and live with dignity.

Jesus said he did not come to destroy the law, but to fulfill it. We are to live not so much by the letter of the law as by the spirit. To live by the spirit of the law is to promote the value behind that law. It is to live by what the law calls us to do and be. The motives behind our actions are important. It's the quality of our heart that counts.

Read the Ten Commandments. They express the natural law written in our hearts as a result of our being made in God's image and sharing God's wisdom and goodness. The law is unchangeable and permanent and is the foundation of moral and civil law. What value does each of the Ten Commandments ask us to reverence and promote? If we live according to the truth and the spirit, we grow into the persons we were meant to be. When we fail to love, that is, when we sin, we stunt our growth.

Lovers of Life

"You shall not kill" (Exodus 20:13) is the fifth commandment. Jesus wants us to love and care for all life—physical life and the life of the spirit. We are first of all responsible for our own life. How do you take care of your health?

eat healthy

watch weight

exercise

How do you care for your spiritual life?

pray

go to church/CCD

The following topics are matters of life and death. Some of these issues are debated a great deal. In each case the teaching of Jesus and of his Church upholds the supreme value of life.

Anger and Grudges

Argue. Yell. Hit. Hurt someone's feelings. Get even. These are ways we express anger. Anger is an emotion that can work for good or evil. It can supply the energy you need to change things that are wrong. Jesus was angry at the money dealers in the Temple (Matthew 21:12–13), but his anger was motivated by love.

It is necessary to channel anger properly. Out of control, anger can lead to sin. A few years ago a man who was angry about being fired from his job shot his former boss on a plane. He then killed the pilots. The plane went down, taking the lives of everyone on board.

What advice would you give a friend who has trouble controlling his or her anger?

to calm down/relax

What does Jesus tell us to do instead of holding a grudge?

think about good things/POSITIVE

Scandal

It's easy to see how fights and unkind words hurt people. **Scandal,** or bad example, can harm them just as much. We are influenced, for better or worse, by what others do. Good example encourages and inspires, but bad example damages. Younger children usually try to imitate their older brothers and sisters and friends. Not fully understanding right from wrong, they may simply follow and learn to do wrong. Read Matthew 18:5–7 to find out how serious an offense Jesus considers bad example.

Abortion

Abortion is the killing of a fetus, a developing baby, before birth. A baby has the right to life, the right to know, love, and serve God as a human being in the world. A baby can't defend itself. We must protect his or her right to life.

Are you less important if you have poor eyesight or get poor grades? Are you more important if you are wealthy or popular? The importance of life does not depend on these things. Human life is valuable of itself. Some people believe that babies with handicaps and babies whose parents can't care for them properly are better off not living. We must work and pray that these people will be enlightened to see the value of all human life. Each person deserves a chance to live despite all odds.

In some countries abortion is legal under certain conditions. A law may make it legal, but it cannot make it right. People who abort a baby are excommunicated, that is, cut off from the Church.

Suicide

Life sometimes seems unbearable. Some people see suicide as a way to end their problems. **Suicide** is the deliberate taking of one's own life. It is seriously wrong, but guilt may be lessened because of psychological problems, anguish, or fear. Life is difficult. There are family problems and accidents. There are painful feelings of loneliness, failure, and guilt. There are bad experiences. As you grow, some difficulties seem worse at some times than others. Most problems are temporary; suicide is permanent. Once carried out, it only creates more problems.

What would you say to a boy who wants to die because the girl he likes just ignores him?

to be nice to the girl / move on...! I mean that

How to Get through a Crisis

1. Recall a problem that you solved. Remember how painful it was, but how you handled it eventually. Things do change with time. Give yourself that time.
2. Talk to someone who cares about what you are going through and can help, such as a parent, a teacher, or a counselor.
3. Try to become involved in activities, sports, or hobbies. Be with people who can support you.
4. Reach out to others who may be experiencing pain. This may take the weight from your problem.
5. Bring your concerns to God and ask for help and guidance. Trust that God's love for you is greater than you can ever imagine.

Euthanasia

Euthanasia, or mercy-killing, is direct intervention to end life for the purpose of ending human suffering. It causes a person to die before he or she would die naturally. Although people defend it as a kind way to treat those who suffer, it is wrong. It is contrary to the respect due to a person and his or her Creator.

How can we see illness and aging from a Christian point of view? First of all, God alone creates. God alone has the right over life and death. Second, illness and aging may help the individual and the community in many ways. Pain may call forth love and courage. Third, illness can prepare us for eternal life. It can help us realize that God is the important One in life. Finally, sickness and aging are part of God's plan. There is mystery in much that happens, but we trust that God who has gifted us with life uses all things for our good.

Allowing a person to die without artificial support is not wrong. The Church teaches that extraordinary means that only prolong a person's life need not be used. The decision whether or not to use life-support systems should take into consideration the sick person, the doctor's advice, and the hope of results. Everyone has the right to die with Christian dignity.

War and Violence

A follower of Christ, the Prince of Peace, works against things that destroy peace. War results in death, suffering, and destruction. It is to be avoided unless it is necessary to protect people and their rights. The violence that stalks our streets is evil and creates fear. What are some causes of drive-by shootings, gang fights, murders, and muggings?

Capital Punishment

For the common good a government has the right to punish criminals. The United States Bishops Conference, however, urges an end to the death penalty. As one bishop put it, "Respect for life should be a seamless garment." What do you think he meant?

Life-Threatening "Isms"

Prejudice, unreasonable dislike of a particular group of people, is wrong. It is an attitude that causes harm to people and denies them their rights. Draw a line connecting each "ism" with its description.

racism — Prejudice against older people
ageism — Regarding a race as inferior
sexism — Treating members of a certain sex unfairly

Works of Mercy

Jesus reveals in Matthew 25:31–46 that at the end of the world we will be judged on love. Those of us who have loved him by cherishing the lives of our brothers and sisters will be rewarded. We foster their physical life by the **corporal works of mercy.** We promote their spiritual life by the **spiritual works of mercy.** Read what these works are on page 198. Write one you can practice today.

Remember

What did Jesus teach in the Sermon on the Mount?
In this sermon, Jesus taught us the way to the Father, living a life of love as he did.

Why must life be preserved and respected?
All life is a gift from God to be loved, preserved, and respected for God's honor and glory. Human life is a special gift because we are created in God's likeness, redeemed, and destined to live forever in God's kingdom.

What are Jesus' two great commandments?
Jesus said, "You shall love the Lord, your God, with all your heart, with all your soul, and with all your mind. This is the greatest and the first commandment. The second is like it: You shall love your neighbor as yourself" (Matthew 22:37–39).

Words to Know
scandal   racism
abortion   ageism
euthanasia   sexism
natural law

Words to Memorize
The works of mercy

Respond

God calls us to love as God loves, which is quite a challenge. Read 1 Corinthians 13:4–7. In your journal rewrite the passage, replacing the word "love" with your own name. List one way in which you will try to live what you have written. Ask Jesus to help you grow in love.

Reach Out

1. What is meant by the statement, "It is not enough to be anti-abortion; you must also be pro-life"? Write your response. Then ask a parent, a grandparent, and an older teenager to comment on the same statement.
2. Read Psalm 136 or Psalm 148. Illustrate either one of these or compose your own litany of thanksgiving or song of praise patterned after them.
3. Charity begins at home! Try one of these.
   + Go to bed on time for a week.
   + Pray an original prayer at home before a meal.
   + Use your allowance in some way for your family, instead of for yourself.
   + Offer to do two extra jobs at home to replace the ordinary turn of someone else in your family.
4. Find out what a national or local pro-life group is doing to fulfill Jesus' commandment of love. Write a report. Become involved in their activities.
5. Write a story or play about someone you know who protects and nurtures life.
6. Make a booklet about the works of mercy. Include pictures.

Review

Scripture Search   In Chapters 6 and 7 of Matthew, Christ gives advice for all who would follow him. Read the references and complete the summary sentences.

1. (6:1–4) Do good deeds in _____ .

2. (6:19–21) Work for _____ treasures that alone give real security.

3. (6:24) Serve _____ , not _____ . You cannot serve them both.

4. (6:25–34) Trust in _____ for what you need.

5. (7:1–5) Avoid _____ so that you yourself receive a merciful judgment.

6. (7:6) Treat holy things with _____ .

7. (7:11) Pray to the heavenly _____ .

8. (7:12) Treat others _____ . This is called the _____ rule.

Sentence Sense   Use each of the following terms in a sentence that reveals what you have learned.

1. choices _____

_____

2. challenge of Christ _____

_____

3. good laws _____

_____

4. spirit of the law _____

_____

5. works of mercy _Corporal = physical   {spiritual = spiritual life_

_____

Fifth Commandment Issues   Match the terms in the first column with their definitions.

a. prejudice	_d_	**1.** Direct intervention to end life
b. scandal	_c_	**2.** Regarding a particular race as inferior
c. ageism	_b_	**3.** Bad example
d. euthanasia	_f_	**4.** Unreasonable dislike of a particular group of people
e. suicide	_g_	**5.** The killing of a fetus before birth
f. racism	_e_	**6.** The deliberate taking of one's life
g. abortion	_a_	**7.** Prejudice against older people

Celebrating Life

Leader: The Lord our God has gifted us with life. We are called to care for that precious gift of life in ourselves and others. Let us celebrate life!

Song and Procession with Bible and Candles

Readings

Leader: God has given us life by creating us. Jesus has given us life by redeeming us. The Holy Spirit leads us to the fullness of life in the Father and the Son. Let us listen now as God calls us to choose life.

Reader 1: A reading from the Book of Deuteronomy 30:15–20. *(Passage is read.)*

Leader: Let us pray.

All: Let us choose life today and always. We know that those who follow you, Lord, will have the light of life.

Song or Alleluia

Leader: We know we have love for God if we show love to others. Let us listen to the Word of God calling us to show our love in practical ways.

Reader 2: A reading from the Gospel of Luke 6:27–38. *(Passage is read.)*

Leader: Let us pray.

All: We are your people, Lord, called to love as you love.

Presentation of Symbols

Leader: We bring these symbols, signs of our desire to follow your Word, Lord. Bless them, and bless us as we journey toward you in all we do.
(Symbols of life are placed on a table.)

Litanies of Life

Leader: Let us thank the Lord for his gift of life. Our response is, "Thank you, Jesus, for life."

Reader 1: For the power I have to walk down the street, run through a field, dance, and laugh, I say . . .
For the times I've enjoyed watching a sunset, swimming at the beach, and sitting by a fire, I say . . .
For the experiences of sharing in the Eucharist, being part of a family, and gathering with friends, I say . . .
(Prayers may be added.)

Leader: Let us show gratitude for life by living with love. Our response is, "Jesus, make me fully alive."

Reader 2: Whenever I can lend a hand to help the aged or reach out to help a child . . .
Whenever I can forgive someone who hurt me . . .
Whenever I have a chance to make a friend, say a kind word, or think of others first . . .
(Prayers may be added.)

Leader: For all the "others" in our life, for all who love us and for all who do not, let us pray,

All: Our Father . . .

Song

The Challenge of Jesus:
The Beatitudes

14

Give and gifts will be given to you; a good measure, packed together, shaken down, and overflowing, will be poured into your lap. For the measure with which you measure will in return be measured out to you.

LUKE 6:38

We are programmed for eternity. We long to live forever. Ponce de León crossed the ocean in search of the fountain of youth. Once a rich young man, who obeyed the commandments, asked Jesus for the secret of eternal life. Jesus did not tell him to cross an ocean, or to climb a high mountain, or to find and destroy a monster in order to win eternal life. He set before the young man an even greater challenge. He looked at him, loved him, and said to him, "Go, sell what you have, and give to the poor and you will have treasure in heaven; then come, follow me" (Mark 10:21). The man walked away sad. He had many possessions. He was not prepared to give them up.

How to Be Happy

In Matthew's Gospel, Jesus began the Sermon on the Mount by spelling out how to follow him. He gave us the **Beatitudes,** guidelines for Christlike living that will make us happy and lead to eternal life. Each Beatitude pairs a value with a promise. Those who walk in the light of these values journey safely and surely. Someday they will reach the kingdom of heaven where they will not "need light from lamp or sun, for the Lord God shall give them light, and they shall reign forever and ever" (Revelation 22:5).

Called to Be Happy

Read the Beatitudes in Matthew 5:3–10. On the lines below list the people who will be happy or "blessed."

1. _____

2. _____

3. _____

4. _____

5. _____

6. _____

7. _____

8. _____

_____

The Be-Attitudes

Blessed are the poor in spirit,
        for theirs is the kingdom of heaven.
                                    Matthew 5:3

Jesus was poor in fact and in spirit. Poor people are dependent on others. They are grateful for anything they get, and they share with one another. Although we may not be poor financially, we can still be poor in spirit. This means having the attitudes of the poor. We remember that everything we have comes from our Creator. We depend on and turn to God in our needs. We do not spend our lives collecting as much wealth as we can. Also we are willing to give up the things we have.

Check your responses to these questions.

	Yes	No
Do I let other people help me?	❏	❏
Do I let God help me?	❏	❏
Do I share with others?	❏	❏
Do I thank God for what I have?	❏	❏
Do I regard people as more important than things?	❏	❏

> Blessed are they who mourn,
>   for they will be comforted.
>
> Matthew 5:4

Jesus felt sad when others suffered. He was filled with sorrow for people hurt by sin. He wept when his friend Lazarus died, and he wept for Jerusalem because it would be destroyed for its sin. When we truly love others, their failings and their sorrows make us feel sad.

Why do you confide in other people when something gives you sorrow?

_____

When do you take hurts and sorrows to Jesus?

_____

The Church of the Beatitudes, marking where Jesus gave the Sermon on the Mount

> Blessed are the meek,
>   for they will inherit the land.
>
> Matthew 5:5

Meek means gentle and humble. Jesus was a gentle person. Cardinal Newman wrote that a gentleman is someone who never gives pain to another. A gentle person is not a wimp. On the contrary, being gentle takes great strength and courage. It's easier to be pushy, bossy, inconsiderate, stubborn, and mean. A gentle person is strong enough to suffer out of love as Jesus did.

What else do gentle people do?

_____

_____

> Blessed are they who hunger and thirst
>   for righteousness,
>   for they will be satisfied.
>
> Matthew 5:6

When you're hungry or thirsty, you do something about it. Those who hunger and thirst for what is right act to make the kingdom come in this world. They try to live by the values Jesus taught and to help others live this way. They desire to keep their friendship with God.

> Blessed are the merciful,
>   for they will be shown mercy.
>
> Matthew 5:7

Jesus asked his father to forgive his executioners. He forgives us. He is the friend of sinners, of outcasts, and of the poor. As his imitators, we must have a heart for others. We must give without looking for any return.

> Blessed are the clean of heart,
>   for they will see God.
>
>   Matthew 5:8

> Blessed are the peacemakers,
>   for they will be called children of God.
>
>   Matthew 5:9

Think of a wheel. Every spoke is attached to the hub. Jesus' life is like a wheel. He did many things: curing, preaching, and praying. The center of all his activity was the Father's will. Being pure in heart means having God at the hub of your life. All your days, your thoughts, actions, and decisions are centered on and flow from God. Your gifts are used as God wishes—for the good of all.

What can we foolishly put at the center of our life in place of God?

_____

_____

Jesus made peace between God and us. He brought peace wherever he went. To be a peacemaker we must first be at peace ourselves. Then we can spread peace to the community.

Check the statements that express true peace.

_____ Peace means having everything go the way you want.

_____ Peace means coming to grips with yourself—your strengths and your weaknesses.

_____ Peace means going along with the crowd when there's trouble and praying you don't get caught.

_____ Peace means forgiving those people who hurt you.

_____ Peace can mean conflict—that you will have to stand up for what is right.

_____ Peace means knowing that God made you and that you are valuable to God and others.

_____ Peace means not getting involved.

In June 1988, one hundred seventeen Vietnamese martyrs were canonized. The group includes native Vietnamese and missionaries who died for the faith in the nineteenth century.

> Blessed are they who are persecuted for
>   the sake of righteousness,
>   for theirs is the kingdom of heaven.
>
>   Matthew 5:10

If you live the Gospel seriously, you will be persecuted. People will hurt you by their words and actions. Because Jesus lived and spoke the truth, he was crucified. As his disciples, we are called to take up our cross daily. We do it with joy when we have a personal love for Jesus.

Let Your Light Shine

The teaching of Jesus was revolutionary. It made people see things differently. Today Christian values still sometimes conflict with the world's values. When you live by the Beatitudes, you dare to be different. This will be hard, but as Jesus promised, you will be happy.

Although Jesus is "The true light, which enlightens everyone" (John 1:9), some people prefer to live in darkness. Will you turn away from Jesus like the rich young man, or will you grasp his hand and follow him?

Check those statements that reflect Christlike thinking.

_____ Get even.

_____ Forgive in order to become a stronger person.

_____ Be #1 no matter what.

_____ Welcome people who are different from you.

_____ Take the easy way out.

_____ Make as much money as you can.

_____ Lie or cheat as long as you don't get caught.

_____ Give away some of your possessions to help the poor.

_____ Stand up for the homeless, the imprisoned, and other outcasts.

_____ Mind your own business.

_____ Do whatever makes you feel good.

When we live like Christ, his light shines forth in us. Read Matthew 5:14–16 and fill in the missing words in the following sentence:

Jesus wants us to be . . .

like a city on a _____

and a lamp on a _____ .

Let Your Light Shine

Two Beatitude People

Martin Luther King, Jr.

Dr. Martin Luther King, Jr., a young African American Baptist minister in Alabama, was awarded the Nobel Peace Prize in 1964 for fighting social injustice through nonviolent means. Before the civil rights movement, African Americans had to sit in the back of buses and give up their seats to whites. To change this, King organized a boycott of the buses. At restaurants and businesses that refused to serve African Americans, King staged sit-ins and peaceful demonstrations. To promote fair employment prac-  tices and improved housing for African Americans, he organized strikes and wrote books. He gave speeches, traveled, and met with government leaders. He planned marches to fight for the right of African American people to vote. In the March on Washington 250,000 people joined Dr. King. He was also behind the Poor People's Campaign in which poor whites, Native Americans, and Hispanics went to Washington to demonstrate. King declared, "The ultimate end must be the creation of the beloved community."

King was beaten, stoned, and imprisoned. His house was bombed while his wife and baby were home. Yet King continued to act for what was right.

In a sermon Dr. King once spoke of his own funeral. He said, "I'd like for somebody to say on that day that Martin Luther King tried to love somebody . . . I want you to say that he tried to love and serve humanity . . . Say that I was a drum major for justice. Say that I was a drum major for peace!"

On April 4, 1968, Martin Luther King was gunned down by a racist.

Dorothy Day

Dorothy Day, a remarkable champion for justice, once said of the Church, "There was plenty of charity but too little justice." She showed that loving Christ and living the Gospel call for heroic actions that change society. She believed that the works of mercy were to be lived personally and at  a personal sacrifice. This belief made her a friend to workers, the poor, street people, the sick, and the excluded. It made her one of them, as she dressed in plain clothes and lived simply with them. It led her to begin the Catholic Worker Movement, which opened a House of Hospitality in New York and ran soup kitchens. It led her to protest war and other injustices to the extent that she was sometimes put in jail.

For the first thirty years of her life, Dorothy was searching for a purpose. In 1928 she became a Catholic even though it meant that the man she loved, a nonbeliever, would leave her and their daughter. Five years later she asked God to send her a guide. Peter Maurin was the answer to her prayers. He was a worker from France who lived in homeless shelters. He was intelligent but not interested in making money. What he did care about was the rights of workers. With Peter, Dorothy began *Catholic Worker,* a penny newspaper about Catholic teaching on work and justice. For thirty years, until her death in 1980 at the age of eighty-three, she wrote a column for it.

Dorothy's work lives on. More than sixty Houses of Hospitality now exist, and *Catholic Worker* can still be bought for a penny.

Remember

What are the Beatitudes?
The Beatitudes are a set of guidelines for Christlike living that will make us happy and lead us to eternal life.

What did Jesus say we are to do to have eternal life?
Jesus said, "Go, sell what you have and give to the poor and you will have treasure in heaven; then come, follow me" (Mark 10:21).

Words to Memorize
The Beatitudes

Respond

Do you want world peace? Then promote world forgiveness. Forgive people who hurt you. St. Paul tells us the power of words in Ephesians 4:32. Look up this verse. Think it over. In your journal write about a time you spoke words of forgiveness. Tell how your words helped you and the other person.

Reach Out

1. The Beatitudes tell us to use our gifts to help others. Think about how you can help out more at home. Decide on one new thing you can do. You might talk to your parents about it, or you may wish to make it a "hidden caring." Write it in your journal and check every day to see if you are keeping to it.
2. Read through Matthew 5 and 6. Pick out a favorite quotation. Write it on paper, design it, and hang it in your room. It will be a reminder to share as Jesus did.
3. Kind words heal. They promote peace and show mercy. Write a letter to one of your grandparents or someone who is sick. Share good news with them.
4. The poor in spirit and those who hunger and thirst for justice share with each other. Ask your parents if you can give clothes you do not need to those who need them and can't afford them. Talk to your parents or teacher about where you can take them.
5. Cut out newspaper articles that show people living the Beatitudes. Paste them on paper. Write out a summary of each story. Share them with your class or your family.

Review

The Two Ways   The people following the Beatitudes are on the way to glory. The people not following the Beatitudes are on the way to doom. Indicate which Beatitude group the people on the way to doom could belong to if they would change.

On the Way to Glory

a. The poor in spirit

b. Those who mourn

c. The meek

d. Those who hunger and thirst for justice

e. The merciful

f. The clean of heart

g. The peacemakers

h. Those persecuted for the sake of righteousness.

On the Way to Doom

_____ **1.** John still refuses to speak to his mother after she apologizes.

_____ **2.** José makes choices based on what makes him feel good and not on what God wants.

_____ **3.** Ms. Blake never bothers to write Congress or vote on human rights issues.

_____ **4.** Mr. San's goal in life is to make as much money as he can.

_____ **5.** Phil is afraid to try to stop his friends from making fun of an elderly woman.

_____ **6.** Jane keeps quiet when Sally is blamed for something Sue did.

_____ **7.** Peter is stingy.

_____ **8.** Alice goes the other way when she sees Dorothy struggling up the ramp in her wheelchair.

_____ **9.** Steve always tries to get his own way.

_____ **10.** Linda is secretly happy when she hears that Pam was caught stealing.

_____ **11.** Bill tells a beggar that he hasn't got any change in order to avoid giving him money.

_____ **12.** Maryann tells Sandra the nasty remark Jill made about Sandra.

A Maze with a Message Go through the maze the right way and the letters you pass through will spell an important hidden sentence. Write it below.

Sentence:

_____

_____

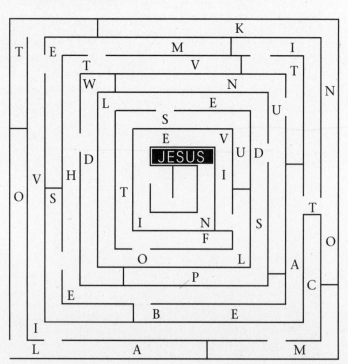

Jesus' Kingdom of Justice and Truth

15

This is what Yahweh asks of you:
only this, to act justly,
to love tenderly
and to walk humbly with your God.

MICAH 6:8 (JB)

One day on the front page of a newspaper was a picture of Mr. John Shultz and a puppy. Mr. Shultz was a dog warden who had received a $2,500 raise. Although he had five children and didn't own his own home, Mr. Shultz decided to split his raise with four assistants because he thought they deserved more pay, too. Why was this front page news?

_____

What if everyone acted like Mr. Shultz?

_____

_____

A sinner named Zacchaeus decided to change his life when Jesus went out to him in love. Zacchaeus' decision cost a lot but gained him the kingdom. Read his story in Luke 19:1–10.

What were signs that Zacchaeus had taken on the values of the kingdom?

_____

_____

_____

_____

Jesus announced, "The kingdom of God is at hand. Repent, and believe in the Gospel." This kingdom is God's dream for us. It is the inbreaking of God's merciful love reaching out to include all, even the poor, rejected, and sinners. God's kingdom is a kingdom of love and peace where everyone lives in justice and truth. People like Mr. Shultz fit in the kingdom. Your values tell if you belong to it.

A Crucial Decision

Are you putting too much value on things that don't matter? The kingdom demands that our values be in line with Jesus' values. We decide whether to live his way or not. Belonging to his kingdom is up to us.

People First

In the eyes of a Christian, persons are more important than things. If you love others, you will respect their right to own property. You will not steal from them or cheat them. Possessions are good. They can help you grow in your friendship with God and others. But possessions must be respected as gifts from God. We must care for our world: its lakes, its wildlife, its atmosphere. We must use all things as God intended.

The seventh and tenth commandments help you to act on these beliefs. The seventh commandment, "You shall not steal," tells you to be honest. You must protect your property and the property of others. You must work honestly to earn things. Work united to Christ's actions can help redeem the world. You must share what you have—not only material goods but also spiritual goods. The tenth commandment is "*You shall not covet anything that belongs to your neighbor.*" It tells you to be honest even in your attitudes toward others and their things. An honest person avoids envy and greed.

Envy Kills

Envy is feeling deprived or sad because of another's belongings or success. When you are envious, you cannot appreciate people. An unhealthy competition grows. Sometimes competition is good because it spurs you on to achieve. But in unhealthy competition you look for the faults of others, compare their talents to yours, and put them down. When you see signs of envy in yourself, remember that God loves you for who you are. Thank God for the gifts given to others. Practice good will, humility, and trust in God's providence.

Greed Destroys

Greed is the desire to possess and control things. It is the root of most wars. Greedy people want more than their neighbor and may be willing to get it unfairly. People who steal and cheat do not respect the rights of others. They break down trust in the community.

To be forgiven for stealing and for damaging property, it is essential to pay restitution. This is paying for or repairing damage to the property. It may be done anonymously. Stolen items must be returned or paid for. Damaged items must be repaired or paid for. If this isn't possible, restitution can be made by contributing to a charity.

A Sinful World

The goods of the earth belong to all. When a group is deprived of food, clothing, shelter, and security, there is injustice. **Social sin** is a term for evil situations that harm people and are opposed to the Will of Christ. As followers of Christ, we are responsible for resisting these situations and promoting justice and respect. We must struggle to change unjust systems and organizations. The first step might be to change our own attitudes.

Priorities

1. Is cheating on a test as wrong as stealing from a store? Explain.

_____

_____

2. What responsibility do you have when you borrow something?

_____

_____

_____

3. What do you own that you could share with others?

_____

_____

_____

4. How does it help other people when we do not waste food or material things?

_____

_____

_____

_____

5. If someone drops a bill and doesn't notice it, why should you return it?

_____

_____

The Power of Words

In the letter of James, the tongue is compared to the rudder that controls a ship. It is small but mighty. The letter also says, "Think how small a flame can set fire to a huge forest; the tongue is a flame like that" (James 3:5, 6 JB). Followers of Christ value truth. They speak the truth to one another and about one another. When they hurt another person by untruths, half-truths, or gossip, they repair the damage that is done.

Truth builds relationships. We depend on one another to tell the truth. **Lying** is saying what is not true with the intention of deceiving. It breaks down trust, causes confusion, and prevents people from knowing what is real. God gave us minds to know the truth and hearts to go out to others in love. That is why the eighth commandment is "*You shall not bear false witness against your neighbor.*" It forbids untrue words and acts and anything that damages another's good name.

Why Do People Lie?

Fear is the number one reason people lie. Some people are afraid others won't like them, so they cover up and exaggerate. Being a phony is much easier than being real. Phonies don't have to say, I'm wrong, I'm sorry, and I don't know.

To be "on top" is another reason people lie. Some people want to impress others and get their attention. They may lie to win, to be popular, to get good grades, or to get out of work or trouble. But a lie only works for the moment. In the end a person loses friends, peace, and, worst of all, even friendship with God.

A Truth Detector

Find out what you know about telling the truth. Check these statements true or false.

	True	False
1. It's all right to lie if you don't get caught.		✓
2. If you love and accept yourself as a friend of God, you will tell the truth.	✓	
3. Adults always tell the truth.		✓
4. You can remain silent about the truth to prevent injustice.	✓	✓
5. To tell the truth means to say anything that comes to mind.		✓
6. A lie hurts only the ones who tell it.		✓
7. Someone who lies can't be trusted.	✓	
8. It is all right to cover up to keep another person out of trouble.		✓
9. Rumors can be lies.	✓	
10. Honesty requires that we tell people all of their faults.		✓

Jill's Campaign

"Look who's running for student council!" remarked Marianne sarcastically as she looked across the room. There stood Jill Woodly handing out campaign buttons.

"Looks decent," said Matt to Marianne as he looked up from doing his homework.

"Shows what you know," answered Marianne. "She really thinks she's something."

"Well, she was class treasurer last year," Carol reminded the group around Marianne. "She was captain of the cheerleaders."

"Kids like her," claimed Bob.

"The teachers like her!" corrected Marianne. "She's so sweet to their faces. The kids don't know about her, or they wouldn't vote for her. That's for sure."

"The kids don't know what?" asked Carol.

Marianne lowered her voice, "Well, I'm only going to tell you. I heard that she took money from the class treasury last year and that she lifts stuff from stores."

"I've never heard that," said Matt.

"I don't believe it," snapped Bob.

"You vote for her if you want, but I'm not," said Marianne firmly.

Carol frowned and muttered, "I didn't know she was *that* kind of person."

1. What did Bob and Carol first think of Jill?

   _____

   _____

2. How has Marianne hurt Jill?

   _____

   _____

   _____

3. Do you think Marianne lied? Explain.

   _____

   _____

   _____

   _____

   _____

4. What do you think will happen because of this rumor?

   _____

   _____

   _____

   _____

   _____

Keeping Secrets and Promises

Sometimes you should not tell the truth! Silence is necessary when you are tempted to spread gossip. It is needed to keep family secrets within the family and to guard other confidences. Priests, doctors, lawyers, secretaries, and other professional people are bound to keep information about their work private. Before telling truths that may hurt others, we should ask, *Is it necessary?* and *Is it kind?*

When someone tells you a secret, it is a way of saying: I trust you, I like you, I respect you. Spreading that secret around would be wrong. It would also be wrong to read another person's private letters, diary, or journal.

Keeping promises is being true to your word. It lets others know they can rely on you.

Silence is not always good, however. When can silence be a lie?

Should people in the news media report everything they find out?

The Truth: What You Get Out of It

Being a truthful person goes hand in hand with strength of character. You have confidence and courage. You take responsibility and cope with consequences. You gain the trust and respect of others. Honesty also builds a better society. By being truthful you show Christ's unselfish love and spread his peace all around you. You further his kingdom.

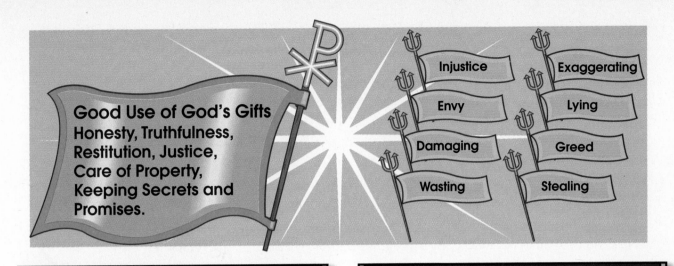

Good Use of God's Gifts
Honesty, Truthfulness, Restitution, Justice, Care of Property, Keeping Secrets and Promises.

Injustice
Envy
Damaging
Wasting
Exaggerating
Lying
Greed
Stealing

Remember

What do the seventh and tenth commandments tell us?
The seventh and tenth commandments tell us to be honest and to respect others' property.

What does the eighth commandment tell us?
The eighth commandment tells us to be truthful in our words.

Where should we have treasures?
Jesus said, "Store up treasures in heaven, where neither moth nor decay destroys, nor thieves break in and steal. For where your treasure is, there also will your heart be" (Matthew 6:20–21).

Words to Know

envy	social sin
greed	lying
restitution	

Respond

Read John 14:23–27. The peace Jesus gives is not free from troubles or difficulties. It is a deep inner peace that comes from being true. In your journal write an experience you had trying to be truthful. Was it hard? Did you ask Jesus or anyone else to help you? How did you handle it? Would you act differently in the future?

Reach Out

1. Jesus often spoke about riches and the kingdom. Read his parable about the rich man and Lazarus (Luke 16:19–31) and decide what the rich man's crime was. Then read these passages: Luke 12:15–21, Matthew 6:19–21, Matthew 6:24, and Matthew 19:23–24. Write a minute talk encouraging people to use the wealth of this world the right way.
2. See how many times during a day you can compliment members of your family, your class, or other people you meet.
3. Make up a short play about someone who stole something and how he or she made restitution.
4. Remember that everything we use is property to be respected. Be careful with the things you have and use. See how well you can take care of them. Try cleaning your room and keeping it neat for one week.
5. Write an article for your school newspaper on the value of honesty as opposed to stealing or cheating. Tell how honesty makes the whole school better.

What does love look like? It has feet to go to the poor and needy. It has eyes to see misery and want. It has ears to hear the sighs and sorrows of others.

St. Augustine

Review

Seven, Eight, or Ten?   Check yes if the person measures up to Christ's standard. Check no if the person doesn't measure up. Record the number of the commandment related to the action: 7, 8, or 10.

	Yes	No	#

1. Mike uses someone else's ID to buy beer.

2. Susan copies from someone's test.

3. Jerry admits he made a mistake.

4. Eddie accepts change for $20.00 when he gave the cashier $10.00.

5. Nita can't eat all of her lunch. She saves it instead of throwing it away.

6. Sam was involved in drinking after the roller skating party. When his parents ask if he was drinking, he says, "Some of the other guys were," implying that he wasn't.

7. Carol says that when her sister uses her things, she takes one of her things to pay her back.

8. Patsy says nice things to a teacher to get what she wants.

9. Rosa knows Jean is hurting herself by taking drugs but doesn't give her good advice for fear of losing her friendship.

10. Ken resents that Carlos has many expensive things.

11. David broke Pete's CD by accident and offers to pay for it.

12. Maria changes the subject when Joe starts criticizing Ann.

13. Megan promised to be home by ten, but she stays out until eleven.

14. Ann copies her history report from the encyclopedia.

15. Nancy reads someone's diary.

16. Julie refuses to tell a secret although many are mad at her.

17. Dan feels happy when other people win. He tries hard not to compare himself to others.

18. George doesn't want to spend his allowance money on school supplies, so he always borrows them.

19. Jeff discovers his brother got into trouble for vandalism. He keeps this a family secret.

20. John scratches words into desks and marks up walls.

21. Mark knows Alex shoplifts but doesn't tell their classmates.

Seventh Commandment
You shall not steal.

Eighth Commandment
You shall not bear false witness against your neighbor.

Tenth Commandment
You shall not covet anything that belongs to your neighbor.

Jesus' Kingdom of Love

16

Let love be sincere . . .
anticipate one another in showing honor.

ROMANS 12:9–10

Do you know a couple who celebrated their fiftieth wedding anniversary? If so, they are probably best friends. Name some qualities of friendship that would help a couple stay happily married:

_____

_____

Friendship is one of the greatest gifts you can give to another person. In sharing your time, your affection, your thoughts and feelings, you are sharing yourself.

Jesus' love is greater than ordinary friendship. He gave his life so that we would be happy. Sometimes you see a heart carved in wood with the initials of two lovers. A heart stands for a person's whole being. When Jesus died on the cross, his heart was pierced by a lance. His sacred heart has symbolized his great love ever since. Add your initials to the heart.

Members of God's kingdom try to imitate Jesus' totally selfless love. In doing so, we find meaning for life and great joy. This deep love exists in a special way between a man and woman who are married.

Marriage: Made in Heaven
"God created man in his image . . . male and female he created them" (Genesis 1:27). Our maleness and our femaleness is our **sexuality.** Every cell in a man's body is marked as male, and every cell in a woman's body is marked female. Our sexuality colors everything we ever do: the way we think, the way we react, the way we move, the way we talk.

God has placed within men and women an attraction for each other. They need and enjoy each other. God wanted them to grow in friendship. But more than friendship, God wanted

a man and a woman
to join in a love
so deep, so selfless,
that their two lives would blend into one
like two streams blending into one river.

This union sealed by a marriage vow would last throughout life.

Read Ephesians 5:25–33 and complete the following comparison:

The love of marriage is like the love of

_____

When God calls a Christian man and woman to make a lifelong commitment in marriage, God blesses their union through the Sacrament of Matrimony. Throughout their lives together, the couple will rely on the strengthening grace of this sacrament. Not all people have an ideal marriage. It is something to strive for.

Married love includes

* sharing all things
* treasuring the other person as he or she is
* meeting the joys and pain of daily life together
* cherishing the children God sends
* being faithful until death.

Married couples use their good qualities to grow in love and to build a good marriage.

Sex: A Gift from God

Carla is talking to her friends by the drinking fountain at school. Ted passes by and says, "Hi." Suddenly Carla's heart begins to beat rapidly. Her face turns red. She feels clumsy, and she can't think of anything to say. Do you think this is love? Explain.

If you ever feel like Carla, congratulations. It is a sign of a change going on within you. Here are other signs of the change. Check the ones you notice in yourself:

❑ I seek more privacy.
❑ I change moods quickly.
❑ I daydream often.
❑ I am easily embarrassed.

These signs point to a special power awakening within you.

God has given each of us special powers that are holy. Among these gifts is **sex,** a power to show and deepen love and to create new persons. In this gift God lets us share in his own power to create life. This power of sharing our deepest selves with another is so sacred that God intended that it be protected by the unbreakable bond of marriage. For those who are called to marriage, sex is a joy that God has given along with the many responsibilities of raising a family. Priests, sisters, brothers, and single people sacrifice this joy in living their vocation. Their love is focused not on another person but on Christ and all his people.

Each new person born needs to belong to a loving family. He or she learns love from seeing the mother and father's love.

Prepare Now!

Five-year-olds can dress up in their parents' clothing and look cute. A recent news report, however, was not so humorous. It told about a nine-year-old boy who made two hundred phone calls to his girlfriend saying he wanted to be her lover. Just as there are natural stages of growth in other areas, mature love requires that we pass through stages. This may be a slow process. Having sex before we are ready is asking for trouble. And we aren't ready until we are free to take on the responsibilities of loving someone for life and being a parent.

You can prepare yourself now for the lifetime commitment of marriage by meeting as many people as possible. At your age it is important to learn about people and how to get along with them. Group dating will make it easier for you to find the right marriage partner, if God is calling you to marriage. It will also give you knowledge and skills needed for forming a lifelong relationship and for dealing with other people.

Another way you can prepare for marriage is by practicing love on other levels. How generous are you in helping your neighbors? How loyal are you to your friends? Do you sacrifice yourself and your time for family members? Can you forgive easily? If you learn how to love now, you have a better chance of experiencing deep, lasting love in your marriage.

If you are a girl, check the moral qualities you most admire in boys your age. If you are a boy, check the moral qualities you most admire in girls your age. Discuss why each good quality appeals to you.

❑ kindness   ❑ honesty
❑ prayerfulness   ❑ truthfulness
❑ gentleness   ❑ self-control
❑ justice   ❑ friendliness
❑ prudence   ❑ forgiveness
❑ courage   ❑ unselfishness
❑ respect   ❑ compassion

A Sign of Total Surrender

Would you wash the family car with motor oil? Of course not. Harm comes from not using items for the purpose for which they were intended.

This same principle applies to the use of our sexual power. The gift of sex comes with instructions, but many people ignore them. They learn the hard way that our happiness in this life and in the life to come depends on using God's gifts correctly.

The gift of sex, the gift of self, is far more precious than any material object. It is a gift that must be treasured and saved for marriage. *The only love that this gift can honestly express is the total surrender of two married people* who are bound to support each other, no matter what. Sex expresses the complete oneness of married couples. It signifies a deep, faithful love. To use it in any other way is a lie.

people who have sex later wish they hadn't. Why, then, do you think young people engage in sex today?

_____

_____

_____

_____

Each person faces the challenge of learning to control his or her sexual drive. Otherwise that power will begin to control the person. What does this mean? It's like riding a bike down a steep hill in the city and discovering that your brakes don't work. Your bike is taking you right into heavy traffic! You'll want to be in control of your thoughts, words, and actions—your human powers. God teaches you what to do and gives you the grace to do it. Jesus was once an adolescent, too. He understands the changes you are going through and sees you learning to deal with the ups and downs of life.

One way to keep your sexual power in control is to participate in good activities such as sports, hobbies, or service. Some other protections for the intimate center of a person are modesty, patience, decency, and good judgment. In what situations could these be practiced?

_____

_____

Who's Boss?

The sexual drive is very powerful. Playing around with it is like playing with dynamite. People who practice sex outside of marriage risk contracting sexually transmitted diseases. In addition they may suffer psychological damage that marks them for life and harms their marriage. Many young

A Double Safeguard

God gave us two commandments to safeguard the sacred gift of sex: the sixth commandment, "*You shall not commit adultery,*" and the ninth commandment, "*You shall not covet your neighbor's wife.*"

In the sixth commandment God forbids any sexual act that is contrary to the sacredness of marriage. **Adultery,** the act of being sexually unfaithful to one's husband or wife, is forbidden by the sixth commandment. So are artificial means of birth control and same sex unions. Any violation of God's plan for the use of sex, either alone or with someone else, is wrong.

God wants us to respect sex, not only in our words and actions but also in our thoughts and desires. God tells us this in the ninth commandment. As all God's laws do, these two commandments protect us from hurting ourselves and others. What problems and heartaches result from not following them?

_____

_____

_____

_____

Perfect Love

These commandments also tell us to practice **chastity.** This virtue is a habit by which we show respect for our God-given power to bring life into the world. A chaste person recognizes that God intended this power to be used only by two partners in the married state and according to the divine plan. All people must practice chastity. For married people, chastity is being faithful to their partner. For unmarried people, it means forgoing the use of the power of sex completely.

Christ challenges us to become perfect as our heavenly Father is perfect. To mirror God's perfect love we must be pure in our thoughts, words, and actions. We must be like Christ, our model of chastity.

Read what Christ teaches in Matthew 5:27–28. Paul, the apostle, explained why we should be chaste. Read 1 Corinthians 6:19–20 and write the reasons Paul gives.

_____

_____

_____

If you really believed that God was within you, would you have sex outside of marriage?

Breaking Through Illusions
Which line is longer?

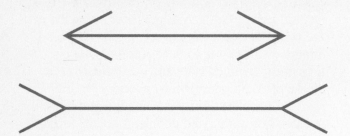

Were you fooled by this optical illusion? The lines are equal. A design can appear to be something it isn't. Illusions are not just found in designs, but also in ideas and opinions. Whenever an idea appears appealing but is contrary to God's plan, it offers only an illusion of goodness. It is a trap.

Don't Be Fooled
Many TV shows, videos, and maybe even the lifestyle of some of your friends and neighbors show that many people do not recognize the true value of the gift of sex. They act on illusions like the following. Can you explain why these ideas are illusions?

✜ Using sexual powers can prove love and popularity.
✜ Sex may be used for entertainment.
✜ Using language that makes fun of sex is adult behavior.
✜ Sex can be used to pay back someone for something.

> Saved sex is safe sex.

Aiming for Real Love
Here is an action plan to help Christians of all ages break through illusions about the gift of sex. Read the plan. Use the word box to complete it.

Word Box
modesty	self-control
praying to Mary	chaste
loved by God	values
receiving Communion	

1. Depend on God to help you practice chastity, make right decisions, and be self-controlled. Make a habit of
   daily personal prayer
   reading the Word of God daily
   celebrating the Sacrament of Reconciliation

   _____

   _____

2. Decide to reverence yourself and all you have been given by God. You are valuable and very precious because you are

   _____.

3. Discipline yourself. Do not always choose the easy way. Strong, unselfish people show

   _____.

4. Do use common sense. Reading books and watching movies and television programs that have a respectful attitude toward sex will help

   you to be _____. If you dress, speak, and act in a way that shows you respect yourself and others, you will be practicing

   _____.

5. Develop healthy friendships with people who

   agree with your _____.

6. Discuss any problems or questions with a mature adult. Name one adult you could possibly consult.

   _____

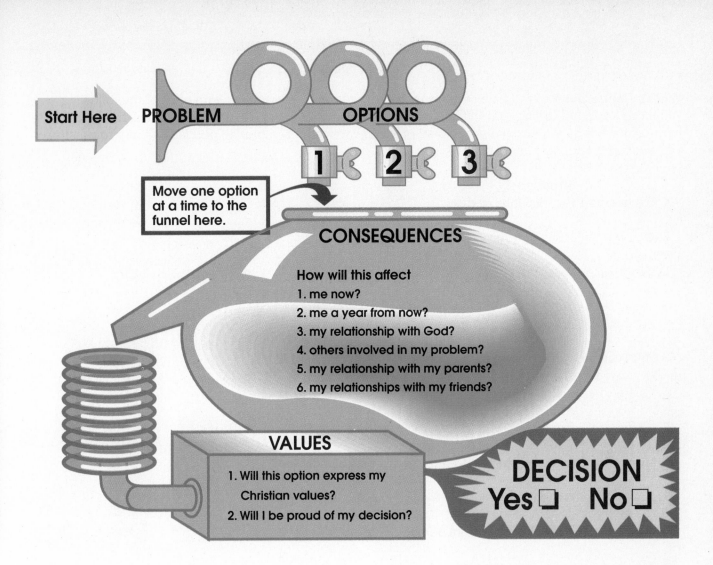

Start Here → PROBLEM OPTIONS

1 2 3

Move one option at a time to the funnel here.

CONSEQUENCES

How will this affect
1. me now?
2. me a year from now?
3. my relationship with God?
4. others involved in my problem?
5. my relationship with my parents?
6. my relationships with my friends?

VALUES

1. Will this option express my Christian values?
2. Will I be proud of my decision?

DECISION
Yes ☐   No ☐

Remember

What is the purpose of the sixth and ninth commandments?
The purpose of the sixth and ninth commandments is to protect marriage, the family, and the sacred gift of sex.

In God's plan, when is the gift of sex to be used?
In God's plan, the gift of sex is reserved for use in marriage.

Words to Know
sexuality   chastity
adultery   modesty

Respond

Choose a point in the action plan. In your journal, list practical ways to carry it out. Then write a note to Jesus asking him to assist you, particularly if there is a situation or a person bothering you.

Reach Out

1. Think of three ways to support your friends in chastity. List them in your journal.
2. Choose a popular song that you think expresses true Christian love. Reflect on why it shows Christ's view of love and how living this song can make you a better person.
3. Research devotion to the Sacred Heart.

Review

What's Dangerous? When are sexually tempting situations dangerous? Rate each of the following situations. Color the traffic light RED if the situation is so dangerous you should stop it. Color it YELLOW if it's somewhat dangerous and you should proceed with caution. Color it GREEN if it's safe to go ahead without being sexually tempted.

Situation	Rating
1. Being under the influence of drugs	
2. Going to an unsupervised party	
3. Going on a group date	
4. Being alone with a person of the opposite sex at your house when nobody else is home	
5. Being alone with a person of the opposite sex in a movie theater	
6. Going to a supervised party	
7. Going to a school dance with friends	
8. Going to a basketball game with a person of the opposite sex	
9. Leaving a school dance with a member of the opposite sex to sit in a car	
10. Walking home after school with a person of the opposite sex	
11. Meeting a person of the opposite sex at the park late at night	
12. Meeting a person of the opposite sex at a restaurant	
13. Drinking alcohol	

Reprinted by permission from JUNIOR HIGH MINISTRY Magazine, copyright 1987, Group Publishing, Box 481, Loveland, CO 80539.

True or False Write **+** if the statement is true and **o** if it is false.

_____ **1.** Sexuality is our maleness or femaleness.

_____ **2.** If a marriage doesn't work out, a Catholic couple may divorce and remarry.

_____ **3.** Sex is sacred.

_____ **4.** Sex outside of marriage is wrong and harmful.

_____ **5.** Some people do not have to practice chastity.

_____ **6.** Through sex, men and women cooperate with God in the act of creation.

_____ **7.** The love between a married man and woman is a symbol of the love of Christ for us.

Jesus the Truth

17

Living the truth in love, we should grow in every way into him who is the head, Christ.

EPHESIANS 4:15

Parable Truths

Which parable do the kind of people listed need to hear? Write the letter of the answer on the line.

_____ **1.** Envious or greedy

_____ **2.** Careless about using gifts

_____ **3.** Selfish, uncaring

_____ **4.** Holding grudges

a. The Rich Man and Lazarus (Luke 16:19–31)

b. The Workers in the Vineyard (Matthew 20:1–16)

c. The Unforgiving Servant (Matthew 18:23–25)

d. The Talents (Matthew 25:14–30)

Change Your Attitude!

Fill in the blanks with a key word from each Beatitude.

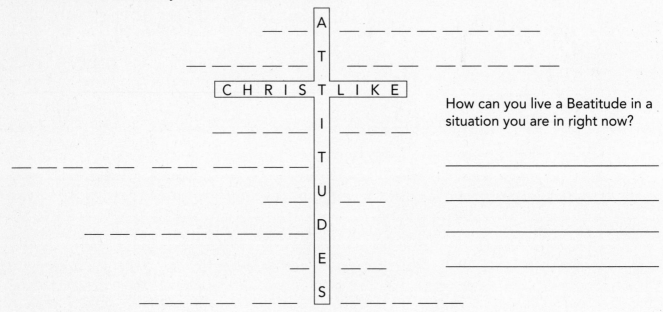

How can you live a Beatitude in a situation you are in right now?

_____

_____

_____

Help Wanted

How would you respond to the following letters? Write your answers on a sheet of paper.

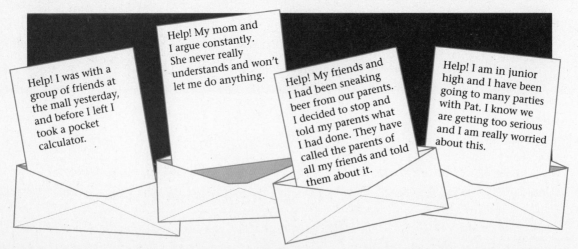

Help! My mom and I argue constantly. She never really understands and won't let me do anything.

Help! I was with a group of friends at the mall yesterday, and before I left I took a pocket calculator.

Help! My friends and I had been sneaking beer from our parents. I decided to stop and told my parents what I had done. They have called the parents of all my friends and told them about it.

Help! I am in junior high and I have been going to many parties with Pat. I know we are getting too serious and I am really worried about this.

Now switch. Imagine yourself in one of the situations. What would you normally do in this kind of situation? How do you wish you could handle such situations?

Puzzling Possibilities

Work the crossword puzzle:

Across

1. What makes it difficult to get into heaven
3. Gift from God to create life
5. Communion for a dying person
7. Sexual unfaithfulness to a marriage partner
11. Who the kingdom is open to
13. The pardon of our sins in the Sacrament of Reconciliation
14. Virtue by which we respect our sexual power
17. Teaching authority of the Church
19. Mercy-killing
21. Kind of sin that is an evil situation that every member of society is responsible for changing
22. Used in the Anointing of the Sick
23. Site of the Beatitudes according to Matthew
24. Subject of a parable that tells of the growth of the kingdom
25. What Jesus is for us as a guide in life

Down

2. Subject of a parable about the kingdom's value
4. Feeling deprived or sad because of something another person has or has achieved
6. True sorrow for sin
8. Repairing damage caused
9. Belief taught by the Church as true
10. Place of the first miracle
12. Bad example
15. The evil one Jesus overcame
16. Stories Jesus told about God and the kingdom
18. What Jesus did for people out of compassion
20. Commandment that protects marriage and the family

A Treasure for the Daring

Jesus promises a treasure to those who live by his truth. To discover what it is, fill in the blanks by unscrambling the letters below them. To check your answer, search John 14.

Whoever _____ me will keep my _____ and my _____ will love him,
　　　　　　seovl　　　　　　　　　　　　　　　　rdwo　　　　　　　　　　　　reahFt

and we will _____ to him and _____ our _____ with him.
　　　　　　　meco　　　　　　　　　　keam　　　　　　　　gliednlw

A Junior High Student Puts Faith into Action

How does someone your age live the message of Jesus today? For Margaret Blazunas, the fourteen-year-old shown here with her pastor, Father John White, S.J., following Jesus' way of love is not only fulfilling but fun.

As the president of Student Council at Gesu School, Maggie leads the student body in carrying out service activities. The students in her school assist with doughnut Sundays at the parish and help promote Red Ribbon week (a "students against drugs" program) in the school.

Maggie has been volunteering at McGregor Home, a retirement community, since she was in the fifth grade. She helps the residents with crafts, takes out their curlers in the beauty parlor, scoops out ice cream at their ice cream bar, and reads letters from their children. Maggie says that she benefits from doing these works of mercy and enjoys listening to the stories the people tell. Her life is also enriched by new friends, such as Mrs. Cooley, one of the residents.

After Maggie volunteered this summer, the director of volunteers at the home wrote a letter to her principal. In it she expressed appreciation for the sixty-seven hours of service that Maggie gave despite having other work and participating in other activities. She commented, "Maggie is always willing to try something new. Our residents enjoyed her enthusiastic manner. She was a joy to have here." Maggie has also worked after school at St. Patrick's Hunger Center, preparing and serving meals for the homeless in Cleveland, Ohio.

Why does this busy teenager make time to help others? Maggie traces her spirit of faith-in-action to her father, who is a Grand Knight in the Knights of Columbus, an organization at the service of the Church. In addition, Maggie's personal convictions motivate her. She thinks serving is really important. She sees it not as something she has to do in order, for instance, to get service points for Confirmation. To Maggie, reaching out to others is something God wants her to do. Maggie believes that being a Catholic requires more than going to Mass. She says we have to take our faith out from the religion class and act on what we hear in the Gospels. She sums it up: "Being a Catholic is doing what Jesus would do."

Maggie encourages other students to try volunteering now so that volunteering will become a habit they will continue to have as adults. Besides, speaking from experience, Maggie says that when you help people in need, you feel great.

Looking Back

In this unit you have taken a look at some of the values and demands of Christian living. You have learned that Jesus calls you to live in his truth. He has called you as a member of the kingdom. Your attitudes, thoughts, and actions should show that you realize you are a member of that kingdom. Jesus asks you to base your decisions on God's law and on his own example. He challenges you to respect life, to respect people and property, to live honestly, and to cherish the gift of sex.

As you complete this unit, ask yourself three questions. Write your answers in your journal.

1. How has this unit helped me understand what Jesus asks of those who follow him?
2. What will I try to remember when I am tempted or when others make it difficult for me to do the right thing?
3. What practical steps can I take to live the life of a disciple?

Personal Inventory

How well do you let the principles Jesus taught guide your judgments and direct your actions? Circle **a** (always), **s** (sometimes), or **n** (never).

Do you think of what Jesus would want you to do or say in situations?

      a   **s**   **n**

Do you go to people you respect for advice?

      a   **s**   **n**

Do you see that little things in life (at home, at school) are opportunities to show respect for others and for property?

      a   **s**   **n**

Do you ever go out of your way to serve others?

      a   **s**   **n**

Words to Ponder

Below are some thoughts from St. Paul, who tried to think and live according to the teachings of Jesus. Read and reflect on them. Then think of situations in which you have shown love, faith, and a desire for purity.

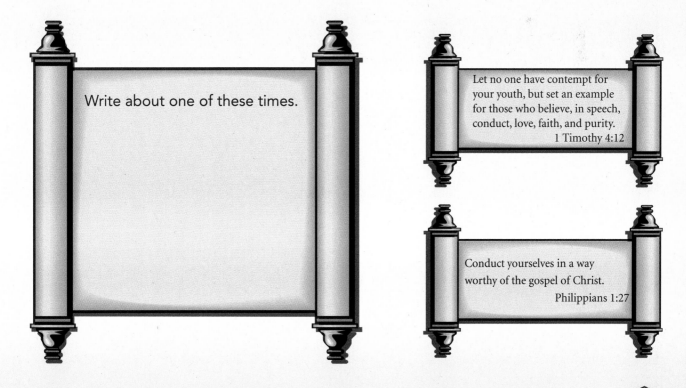

Write about one of these times.

Let no one have contempt for your youth, but set an example for those who believe, in speech, conduct, love, faith, and purity.
1 Timothy 4:12

Conduct yourselves in a way worthy of the gospel of Christ.
Philippians 1:27

Celebration of Jesus the Truth

Song

Leader: Christ Jesus, you are the Truth. You have enlightened our minds and touched our hearts.

Side 1: Thank you for the truth and mysteries you have revealed to us.

2: May we grow in understanding your teachings, the teachings of the Church.

Side 1: Thank you for your parables.

2: May we take their lessons to heart and be good members of your kingdom.

Side 1: Thank you for your miracles.

2: May we always look to you for healing in our lives.

Side 1: Thank you for the Beatitudes.

2: May we be numbered among the happy ones.

Side 1: Thank you for your law of love.

2: May we always walk the way of justice, truth, mercy, and reverence for life.

Leader: Let us each choose one parable, miracle, or teaching of Jesus that has special meaning for us and make a symbol of it out of foil. Let our action be prayer. As we work, let us speak to Jesus about the event or teaching we have chosen, thanking him for it and applying it to our lives.

(*Prayer activity with background music*)

Leader: Let us think of a short prayer based on our symbol.

(*Time for reflection. Then one by one students pray their prayers and place their symbols on the table or bulletin board.*)

Leader: Let us pray.

All: Make known to me your ways, Lord;
  teach me your paths.
Guide me in your truth and teach me,
  for you are God my savior.
For you I wait all the long day,
  because of your goodness, Lord.
Remember no more the sins of my youth;
  remember me only in light of your love. (Psalm 25:4, 5, 7)
You will show me the path to life,
  abounding joy in your presence,
    the delights at your right hand forever. (Psalm 16:11)

Song

Jesus Christ the Life

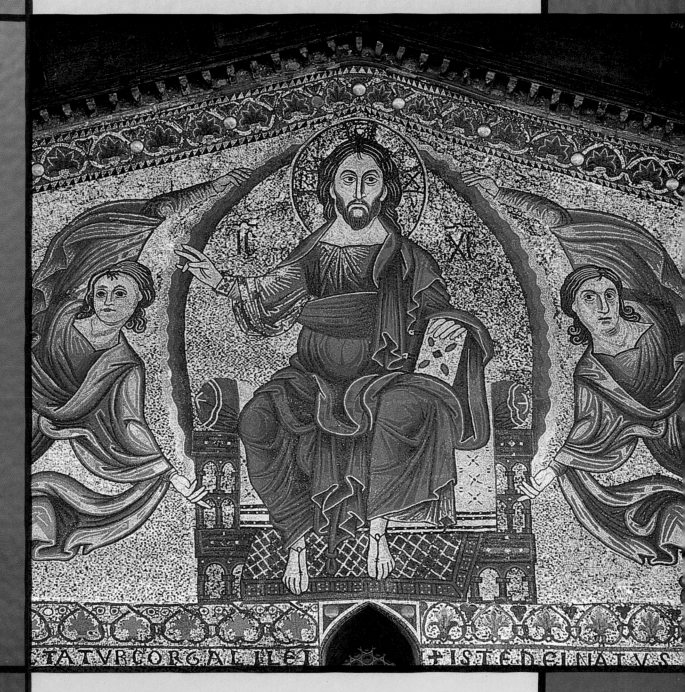

FAMILY FEATURE

Christians Celebrate:
Making Sunday a Special Family Day

Although for many people Sunday is just like another Saturday, the Prebil family has a tradition of celebrating it to the hilt. They know that Sunday is the Lord's Day, time set aside to worship. Every Sunday is a little Easter, a day to remember Christ's death and resurrection that saved us.

A day or two before the Sunday Mass, the family tries to spend some time after a meal preparing the readings of the liturgy. They read them from a missal and discuss what they mean.

The Prebils try to go together to Mass as a family. There they join in offering the sacrifice of Christ and are united by receiving the same Christ in Holy Communion. For the celebration, everyone dresses up so they look and feel different. Often one of the family members has a special role in the Mass. Mr. Prebil is an usher, and Mrs. Prebil and sixteen-year-old Paul are lectors. After Mass the family continues to celebrate by going out to breakfast. They might talk about what they remember from the homily and how to live God's Word heard at the Mass.

The celebration is reflected in the Prebil home. For the family meal they use the good china and silverware placed on a special Sunday tablecloth or table mats. A candle burns on the table in a centerpiece that sometimes features a symbol of the Sunday readings. Everyone helps prepare the meal.

Twelve-year-old Julie is in charge of the background music.

The Prebils also see God's wisdom of ordaining Sunday as a day to relax and rejoice. Enjoying one another's company builds family spirit. Certain games and toys are reserved for Sunday use. Sometimes the family visits relatives and friends or invites them over. They may go to a park, the zoo, a museum, a movie, or just take a drive in the country. Every so often the family spends time on Sunday doing something for people in need. For instance they help at a soup kitchen or search their house for good, reusable items to donate to the poor.

If your family would like to reclaim Sunday as a special day, try some of the ideas on this page. You'll find that your Sunday truly becomes "a pause that refreshes."

Living Faith in Jesus

18

Whoever drinks the water I shall give will never thirst;
the water I shall give will become in him a spring of water
welling up to eternal life.

JOHN 4:14

What if a stranger came to you and told you that tomorrow you would be able to fly, or to read minds, or to be in two places at once? You probably would not believe it. Such superhuman powers are part of science fiction, not real life.

Jesus stepped into our world and told us something just as incredible. He said we could share God's life and live forever. Jesus was a prophet, someone who spoke for God. Those who accept him believe that in Baptism God offers us **grace,** a share in God's own life.

The special grace of God dwelling within us is called **sanctifying grace.** What greater gift can you give than to give yourself?

Sacraments

Spiritual life is friendship with God present within us. Through grace we can speak to God, respond to God, and someday enjoy fullness of life with God eternally.

Your Spiritual Life Inventory

Read the statements below about spiritual life. Check the endings that apply to you.

I think of Jesus
- ☑ often.
- ☐ rarely.
- ☑ when I am in church.
- ☐ when I am happy.
- ☐ when I am in trouble.
- ☑ when I am at home.
- ☑ often throughout the day.
- ☐ when I am with my friends.

I pray
- ☑ in the morning and evening.
- ☑ in church.
- ☐ with my friends.
- ☐ with my family.
- ☑ when I am alone.

I try
- ☐ to help others.
- ☑ to live so that others know I am a Christian.
- ☐ to be understanding and kind.
- ☐ to remember what great love Jesus has shown for me.
- ☑ to make other people happy.

I celebrate Penance and Eucharist
- ☐ occasionally.
- ☐ regularly.

I think of God as
- ☑ very close.
- ☐ far away.

Life Is a Journey

Life is a journey from birth through death to eternal life. For the believer, life is the journey to the Father, through the Son, in the Spirit. Jesus came that we may have eternal life. He invites us to believe in him and to share his friendship and love. Throughout the Gospels people respond to his invitation. The following three stories of encounters with Jesus tell us about faith.

Nicodemus: Night Class

Nicodemus, a Pharisee and probably a member of the Sanhedrin, wanted to know more about Jesus. One night he came to see Jesus.

Why do you think he came at night?

_____

_____

Nicodemus needed faith to see that Jesus was more than a teacher or a miracle worker.

After Jesus died, Nicodemus brought spices for his body and helped to bury it.

Read John 3:1–21.

What did Jesus tell Nicodemus we must do to enter the kingdom of heaven? (John 3:5)

_____

_____

_____

What must happen to Jesus so we may have eternal life? (John 3:14)

_____

_____

_____

Life Is a Journey

The Woman at the Well

The Jews did not associate with Samaritans. (See page 29.) Nor did they speak to women in public. So when Jesus spoke to the Samaritan woman, she was surprised. The Samaritan woman, who had had five husbands, accepted Jesus' invitation to a life of faith. After she came to believe in Jesus, she spread the news to her entire town. At first people believed in Jesus because of what the woman told them. Then when they met him and heard him personally, their faith deepened.

Read John 4:4–30.

What did Jesus tell the Samaritan woman he could offer? (John 4:14)

_____

_____

_____

The Man Born Blind
(Based on John 9:1–38)

(Jesus and Disciples walk past the Blind Man.)

Disciple 1: Rabbi, why is he blind from birth? Has he sinned?

Disciple 2: Or did his parents sin?

Jesus: Neither he nor his parents have sinned. This man's blindness can show how great God's love is for everyone.

(They walk back to the Blind Man. The Blind Man gropes around.)

Jesus: I am the Light of the World. Let me help you.

(Jesus bends down, makes a paste with mud, and gently rubs it on the man's eyes.)

Blind Man: What are you doing to me? Don't hurt me!

Jesus *(smiling):* Go and wash in the Pool of Siloam.

(Jesus and Disciples exit. The Blind Man staggers to the side, kneels, and splashes water on his face.)

Blind Man *(jumping around excitedly):* I can see!

(Neighbors run to him.)

Neighbor 1: Isn't that the man who used to sit and beg?

Neighbor 2: Yes, it is the same man. He can see!

Neighbor 3: No, Simon, you are wrong. He isn't the one. It only looks like him.

Blind Man: I *am* the man.

Neighbor 1: Tell us how you came to see!

Blind Man: The man called Jesus made clay and rubbed it on my eyes and told me, "Go, wash at Siloam." When I went and washed, I could see.

Neighbor 2: Where is Jesus?

Blind Man: I don't know.

(Pharisees enter.)

Neighbor 1: Look, there are the Pharisees.

(Group moves to Pharisees.)

Neighbor 2: Shalom. I hope you are enjoying the Sabbath.

Pharisee 1: Yes, thank you. *(to Blind Man)* Say, you used to be blind. How did you come to see?

Blind Man: Jesus put clay on my eyes.

Pharisee 2: This Jesus cannot be from God. He does not keep the Sabbath.

Pharisee 3: How could a sinner produce signs like this?

Pharisee 1: Blind Man, what do you have to say about this man who opened your eyes?

Blind Man: He is a prophet.

Pharisee 2: He cannot be! You probably were not blind in the first place.

Pharisee 1: Bring this man's parents to us.

(Neighbor 2 exits and returns with Parents.)

Father *(to Mother):* Be careful. Remember the Pharisees said that anyone who says that Jesus is the Messiah will be thrown out of the synagogue.

Pharisee 3 *(to Parents):* Is this your son who was born blind? How does he see now?

Father: Yes, this is our son.

Mother: He was born blind. We don't know how he came to see.

Father: We don't know who opened his eyes.

Mother: Ask him. He's old enough to speak for himself.

(Pharisees huddle to confer, then turn to crowd.)

Pharisee 2: Well, Blind Man, we think the man who cured you is a sinner.

Blind Man: I don't know if he is a sinner. I only know I was born blind and now I can see.

Pharisee 2: What did he do to you?

Pharisee 3: How did he open your eyes?

Blind Man: I told you and you wouldn't listen. Why do you want to hear it again? Do you want to become his disciples too?

Pharisee 3: Fool. *You* can be his disciple. *We* are disciples of Moses.

Pharisee 1: We know God spoke to Moses. But this Jesus? We don't know where he comes from.

Blind Man: Don't know where he comes from? That's amazing! He cured me. God doesn't listen to sinners. God listens to those who do his will. Since the world began no one has given sight to a person born blind. If this man weren't from God, he couldn't do such a thing!

Pharisee 1: How can *you* teach *us?* You have been a sinner from birth.

Pharisee 2: Get away from here.

(Pharisees and Parents exit. Jesus and Disciples enter.)

Neighbor 3 *(to Jesus):* Jesus, the Pharisees threw out the Blind Man.

(Jesus goes to the Blind Man.)

Jesus: Do you believe in the Son of Man?

Blind Man: Sir, who is he that I may believe in him?

Jesus: You have seen him. He is speaking to you.

Blind Man *(kneeling):* I do believe, Lord.

How was the man cured of spiritual blindness?

_____

_____

_____

The Faithful Friend

To these three people—Nicodemus, the Samaritan woman, and the man born blind—and to many others, Jesus reached out to offer life. This is the way it is in your spiritual life: Jesus begins the relationship. Then he is always there, inviting, helping, caring, loving.

Dan's Difficult Day

For Dan, it had been a hard day at school. There had been a surprise quiz in history, he had forgotten his English homework, basketball practice had been canceled, he got in trouble for talking in class, and he had an argument with his friend. By the time he got home, he had had it! But it had been a difficult day for Dan's mother, too. Her work at the office had brought her problems. She had already done the laundry at home and was in the midst of preparing dinner.

When Dan walked into the house, his mother greeted him with a list of jobs to do, reminded him to watch his younger brother, told him to clean his room, and not to play the radio so loud. As Dan heard all this, he felt like arguing. But he also thought about how his mother felt and what would be the right thing to do.

What decision would you have made if you had been in Dan's place?

_____

_____

Grace—It's Free!

Original sin left us with a tendency to do wrong. Dan's urge to do what is right was from the Holy Spirit. It is something that you often experience: God's invitation to deeper friendship—or **grace**. *Grace* has many meanings. You have already seen it as God's life. God's presence in you (sanctifying grace) brings about changes in your life. It prompts you to do what is good. These inspirations are referred to as graces.

Grace is a free gift. God always offers us friendship. But you must be open to it to share in God's life. Grace gives you the desire and the power to lead a Christian life. Grace strengthens you to make decisions and act according to the Father's will. Through grace you can believe Jesus' message, choose to do good, and turn more and more to Christ.

Grace works like human friendship. When you become friends with someone, you often grow alike. You begin to see things the same way. The more you accept Christ's offer of friendship, the more influenced you are by him. You begin to see

things and make decisions as he would. You avoid sin to imitate his obedience to God. You become more like Jesus.

Hints from God

God inspired Dan to do what was good. If he chose to do the right thing, he would grow closer to God. But Dan could reject God's friendship and help. If he did, he would be turning away from God and from all that could make him happy. Even then God would call to him to think over what he had done and start anew.

Can you think of any way you have experienced God's grace today? It may have been a good thought. It may have been something you saw or heard that made you think of God, God's love for you, or all God has done for you. Write it here:

_____

_____

_____

Super Strength for the Journey

You can respond to God and deepen your friendship through virtues, supernatural powers poured into your heart at Baptism. A virtue is a power or a habit for doing good. Virtues grow and develop through graces received through prayer, good works, and the sacraments, especially the Eucharist. You have received theological virtues and cardinal moral virtues. You might think of them as the vitamins of your spiritual life.

Theological Virtues

Theo means "God." The **theological virtues** are powers given by God and centered on God. They lead us to know, love, and trust God in a supernatural way. With their help we reach our journey's end: eternal life with God.

Faith is the power to trust God completely and accept as true all that God has revealed and teaches through the holy Catholic Church. It helps us grow in our understanding of God's goodness. We often use a creed, or profession of faith, to express the truths we believe. We are united not only by what we believe but also in whom we believe.

We believe because we trust a person. When we really trust, we are willing to stake our life on what we believe.

Look at the act of faith on the back inside cover. What words tell why you can believe God?

_____

_____

Hope is the virtue of trusting that God will give you eternal life and all the help necessary along the way. Two sins against hope are **despair** and presumption. To despair is to believe God can't or won't help and so to give up even trying to be saved. **Presumption** is to expect God automatically to give all you hope for even though you do not cooperate with God's grace or make any efforts to live a Christian life. You presume on the goodness of God. It is also presumption to think you can find eternal life without God.

Charity is that virtue that empowers us to love God and to give God first place in our lives. Our model is the love shown in the life and death of Jesus. Paul wrote about the various gifts given by God. Read 1 Corinthians 13:1–13.

What is the most important gift? _____
Why? (See verse 8.)

_____

The Cardinal Moral Virtues

Moral virtues have to do with conduct. The most important ones are called **cardinal virtues.** The word *cardinal* means "hinge." Our spiritual life hinges on the cardinal virtues:

Prudence is the moral virtue that empowers you to decide what is good. Prudent people ask responsible people for advice. They think through their beliefs and reflect before they act.

Justice is the moral virtue that empowers you to respect the rights of others and to give them their due. It gives you the determination to protect those rights and to fulfill your responsibilities to people and to God.

Fortitude is the moral virtue that gives you the courage to do what is right even when it is very difficult. It may mean having patience, being generous, enduring ridicule, and overlooking peer pressure.

Temperance is the moral virtue that empowers you to control your desire for pleasure. Temperance helps keep you from overdoing it in matters such as eating, drinking, sex, money, and the way you dress, act, and speak.

Life Means Growth

It is easy to see how over the years you have grown and changed physically and intellectually. But what about spiritually? How much more do you know about God and your faith now than you did before? How much has your life become a true reflection of your Christian values and ideals? Growing closer to Jesus is vital and takes energy and time—a lifetime.

Remember that life in Christ and prayer are inseparable. Prayer is as necessary to your spiritual life as breathing is to your physical life.

Remember

What is grace?
Grace is a free gift of God's life in us. It is friendship with God that strengthens us and makes us holy.

What are the theological virtues?
The theological virtues are powers given by God at Baptism and centered on God: faith, hope, and charity (love).

What are the moral virtues?
Moral virtues are those gifts received at Baptism that have to do with conduct. The principle ones are the cardinal virtues: prudence, justice, fortitude, and temperance.

Words to Know

virtue	prudence
sanctifying grace	justice
faith	fortitude
hope	temperance
charity	

Words to Memorize
The Acts of Faith, Hope, and Love

Respond

What matters in life is how you respond to Christ. If you respond with love and longing, you will find life. If you respond with indifference or hostility, you will know death. Read Luke 9:18–21. If Jesus were to ask you the same question, what would you say? Write your response in your journal.

Reach Out

1. Look at a creed like the Apostles' Creed or Nicene Creed and on paper design church windows based on it. Or write a creed in your own words. Read these summaries of faith found in Scripture:

   1 Corinthians 15:3–8   Mark 8:29
   Romans 1:3–5 or 8:34   1 John 2:22
   2 Timothy 2:8

2. Jesus offered the Samaritan woman flowing water. Water has many uses. It can destroy life or save it. It can nourish, cleanse, and refresh. Find examples in the Bible and in everyday life where water is used in any of the ways listed. How is it used in Romans 6:4? How did John the Baptizer use it?

3. Make place mats from 14-by-12-inch sheets of paper or plastic. Have each member of the family pick out a favorite faith quote from Scripture and then print it across the top of the place mat. Cut out a nature scene and paste it on. Share the quotes as part of the meal prayers.

4. Compose a prayer service that expresses your faith in God. Include a reading from Scripture, a song, reflection, spontaneous petitions, and teacher or student comments on the reading.

5. Write an autobiography of your faith life. Begin with your baptism and trace the people and events that have helped you grow in faith. Share your story with someone.

6. Tape three cartons end-to-end to make a kiosk, a pillar that serves as a bulletin board. On your kiosk put pictures and captions encouraging people to live their faith, especially by helping the needy. Display your kiosk in your parish.

Review

Framing Words   Eleven key words from this chapter are arranged in irregular shapes in this puzzle. Draw a box around each one. The first one is done for you.

What words are powers from God and centered on God? _____
Color them red.

What words are moral virtues that direct our conduct? _____
Color them blue.

Color green the two sins against hope.

Can you define every word in the puzzle?

```
F   A   P   R   E   S   G   R
I   T   H   U   M   P   A   C
J   U   S   T   I   O   N   E
T   I   C   E   P   R   U   D
C   H   A   R   E   N   C   E
I   T   Y   V   I   T   E   M
F   O   R   R   T   P   E   R
T   I   T   U   E   S   A   N
U   D   E   D   E   H   C   E
S   P   A   I   R   O   P   E
```

Words of Life   Use each word in a sentence that reveals its meaning.

1. grace

_____

2. sanctifying grace

_____

3. virtue

_____

People of Faith   Answer yes or no to each question.

_____ **1.** Did Nicodemus have more faith at the end of Jesus' life?

_____ **2.** Did Jesus tell Nicodemus that we would have eternal life because he would be lifted up?

_____ **3.** Would Jesus be considered a good Jew for talking to the Samaritan woman?

_____ **4.** Did Jesus lead the Samaritan woman to believe in him?

_____ **5.** Did the Samaritan woman bring other people to Jesus?

_____ **6.** Was the man born blind afraid to speak up for Jesus when the Pharisees questioned him?

The Church of the Holy Sepulchre in Jerusalem

Opposition to Jesus

19

The *Via Dolorosa* or "Way of Sorrows" in Jerusalem

If we live, we live for the Lord, and if we die,
we die for the Lord; so then, whether we live or die,
we are the Lord's.

ROMANS 14:8

Name a happy moment in your life.

_____

In moments of joy like this, faith helps you become aware of God's presence—God's power and goodness. It can fill your heart with gratitude to God. But you also have times of sorrow or disappointment. In these moments your faith can help you to believe that God is with you and will bring good out of these sorrows. It can help you accept them with trust. Through sorrows you may become the person God has called you to be.

Making It with Faith

Suffering was part of Jesus' life. Words from the prophet Isaiah apply to him:

> Because of his affliction
>> he shall see the light in fullness of
>>> days;
> Through his suffering, my servant shall
>> justify many,
>> and their guilt he shall bear.
>>>> Isaiah 53:11

Because Jesus suffered he received glory. This was difficult for the apostles to understand until the Spirit came at Pentecost. When Jesus first predicted what he must undergo as the suffering servant, Peter would not hear of it. The apostles needed stronger faith for the trials to come. So, Jesus took Peter, James, and John to a mountain (possibly Mount Tabor) where they saw him transfigured. Read Matthew 17:1–8. Then answer these questions:

1. What happened to Jesus? (Matthew 17:2)
2. Read Luke 9:31. What were Moses and Elijah discussing with Jesus?
3. What did Peter want to do to prolong the moment? (Matthew 17:4)
4. What did the voice from the cloud say? (Matthew 17:5)
5. How did the event confirm the disciples' faith?

The choice Jesus made to suffer and die for us is part of his glory. It shows his love for the Father and us. The Transfiguration teaches us that glory comes from the cross. Just as the Israelites passed from death to life in the Exodus, Jesus passed from death to resurrection. Suffering accepted

with faith can make you strong, open, and loving. It can lead you to share in the glory of Christ.

The Transfiguration

Faith Builders

The Father tells us how to meet joys and sorrows. He says, "Listen to my Son." Jesus speaks to us and strengthens our faith especially in Scripture, in prayer, and in the sacraments. We believe, though, that Jesus is with us in all the events of life.

Check those events in which you have experienced the presence or guidance of Jesus.

- ❏ being misunderstood by parents
- ❏ taking a test
- ❏ participating in the Sunday Eucharist
- ❏ losing a game
- ❏ doing homework
- ❏ receiving a compliment
- ❏ having a good time with a friend
- ❏ celebrating the Sacrament of Reconciliation
- ❏ reading Scripture
- ❏ praying with the family
- ❏ losing a friend
- ❏ making a decision
- ❏ being left out of a team or a group
- ❏ hearing about suffering people

Tell how faith could help you to come closer to Jesus in one of these situations.

A Wall of Opposition

Jesus suffered throughout his public life. Sometimes people didn't understand him or accept him. From the beginning, the religious leaders watched his every move with suspicion. They didn't like his popularity and his criticism of their rigid view of the law. Instead of being open and changing their narrow-minded attitudes, they gradually built a wall of opposition.

For each stone, look up the reference and write the form of opposition that Jesus faced. Choose from the box below.

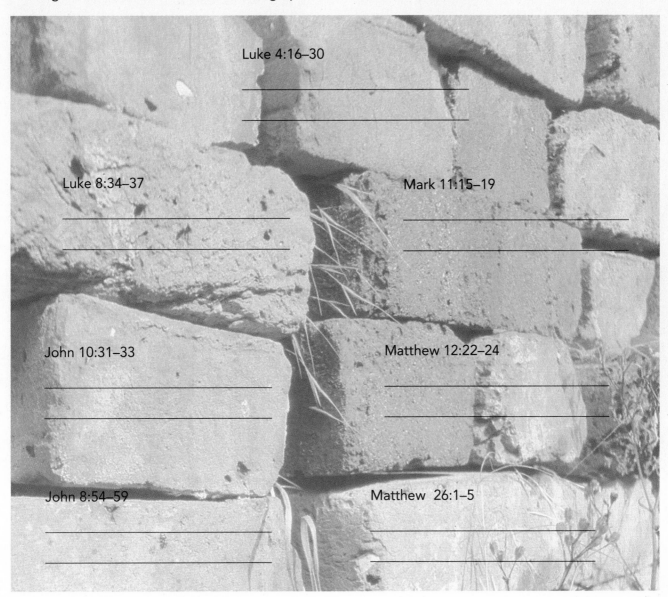

Luke 4:16–30

_____

_____

Luke 8:34–37

_____

_____

Mark 11:15–19

_____

_____

John 10:31–33

_____

_____

Matthew 12:22–24

_____

_____

John 8:54–59

_____

_____

Matthew 26:1–5

_____

_____

Opposition Box

✣ picked up rocks to throw at him
✣ asked him to leave town
✣ said he had power from the devil
✣ made plans to arrest and kill him
✣ accused him of blasphemy
✣ attempted to throw him off a cliff
✣ planned to destroy him

In the face of this opposition, Jesus remained true to his goal—to do the will of the Father and to work for the kingdom. The raising of his friend Lazarus from the dead united the forces of the opposition and was the immediate cause of Jesus' death. In the account of the event, suffering and glory, life and death are intertwined.

MAN DEAD FOUR DAYS LIVES!

BETHANY—A man dead for four days here was restored to life yesterday by the Galilean preacher and wonder-worker, Jesus of Nazareth.

Yesterday Jesus, a close friend of the family, arrived and requested that the tomb be opened. It is said that the deceased man's sister Martha objected, for she knew what the body would be like after four days.

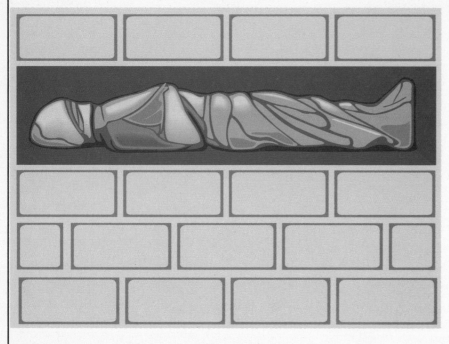

Nevertheless, at Jesus' insistence, the stone was removed. Observers said that Jesus commanded Lazarus to come forth. Seconds later the corpse appeared in its burial clothes at the entrance of the tomb. At the order of the Galilean, the sisters of Lazarus unwound the burial linens and found themselves face-to-face with their brother, alive and whole!

Excitement runs high today as people discuss proclaiming Jesus as the Messiah. The Sanhedrin is expected to convene to address the issue and determine the action it will take. A reliable source has disclosed that the members fear Jesus' power to draw crowds will attract Rome's attention.

Lazarus, a distinguished citizen of Bethany, died Monday after a brief illness. Prescribed Jewish burial rituals were performed, and the body was laid in the family tomb outside the city.

From Death to Life

Behind a front page news article, there is an inside story. To find out the inside story about the raising of Lazarus, read John 11:1–53. Then answer the following questions:

1. Why didn't the apostles want Jesus to go to Lazarus?
2. What encouraging message did Jesus give Martha?
3. What were Jesus' emotions at the tomb?
4. How did Jesus show that he was following his Father's will?
5. What attitude toward death did Jesus have? Mary and Martha?

You can imagine how people flocked to Jesus after he raised Lazarus from the dead. According to the Gospels, when Jesus rode into Jerusalem on a colt near the feast of Passover, a great crowd greeted him. They waved palm branches, a sign of welcome for a conqueror. They shouted, "Hosanna! Blessed is he who comes in the name of the Lord, the king of Israel." The Pharisees were helpless to stop the demonstration. They cried, "Look, the whole world has gone after him."

A Dead End?

If you took a poll asking "How do you view death?" you might find answers like these:

Death is beautiful. It's coming home to God.

Death is cruel and meaningless. It's a total end of life.

Death is frightening. The body and soul separate. I don't want to think about it.

Death is a mystery that I can't understand.

Death means good-bye. I don't want to lose what I have.

Death is confusing. There must be life after death, but I'm not sure what kind.

Raising Lazarus was a sign of Jesus' power to give eternal life to those who would believe in him. Not long after this miracle, Jesus freely and obediently offered his life to the Father in order to free us from our sins and give us eternal life. By doing this he changed death into a doorway leading to happiness with God. It became a friend not an enemy.

The Christian Views Death

Through Baptism you share in the life won by Christ's death and resurrection. God has called you to live in friendship with him beyond death and forever. Death can be your final "yes" to God. You can accept it and offer your life to the Father as Jesus did. Here are four advantages of death for faithful Christians.

† You are united with God in the kingdom of love forever.
† You are freed from evil's power forever.
† You deepen your relationship with all those who have already died and are united with Christ.
† You have a new relationship in love with those who have not yet died.

If death means all these good things, why are we afraid? Death, the result of sin, brings pain and suffering. It leads us into the unknown, away from all that is familiar and loved.

Even Jesus dreaded death. The night before he died he went to the garden of Gethsemane. There he faced the fact of his coming death and was overwhelmed with fear. As he prayed, he was strengthened to accept death, and he willingly gave his life to the Father. Like Jesus we must accept our fear and give ourselves with trust into the hands of our Father. Our faith and our hope in eternal life strengthen us to do this.

When Someone You Love Dies

How empty and lonely life can be when your best friend moves away. A similar experience on a deeper level is the loss through death of someone you love. The emptiness and loneliness are great. At these times it helps to remember that through your union with Christ, you remain united to the one you love. And someday suffering will give way to a life of glory together.

Remember

What is the Christian view of death?
For a Christian, death is a final chance to accept God's Will and offer oneself freely to God, following the example of Jesus.

What is Jesus' promise of eternal life?
Jesus said, "I am the resurrection and the life; whoever believes in me, even if he dies, will live" (John 11:25).

Word to Know
Transfiguration

Respond

Thomas, the apostle, had a special meeting with Jesus. Read John 20:19–29. What did Thomas say to Jesus when he met him? What did Jesus say to Thomas? Did you ever have to believe without seeing? What did you feel like? What helped you to have faith in Jesus? Answer these questions in your journal.

Reach Out

1. Read Luke 7:11–17, Luke 8:49–56, and John 11:1–41. Create a front page news feature for one of the stories from Luke. Or, with a small group, make up a skit for one of the three stories.
2. Make a photo album of the main events in Jesus' life. Draw the photos and add captions. Include the times of opposition.
3. When did you face opposition for acting as a Christian? How did you respond? Reflect on the incident in your journal. Write a prayer asking to meet opposition courageously.
4. Imagine that your friend has lost a loved one through death. Write a sympathy note, sharing the Christian view of death.
5. Participate in the funeral for someone in your parish. Pray for him or her as a representative of the faith community. Report on what you observed that strengthened your faith.

Review

Sorting Events   If the statement refers to the Transfiguration, write **T** on the line. If it refers to the raising of Lazarus, write **L**.

_____ **1.** Moses and Elijah spoke with Jesus.

_____ **2.** Jesus proclaimed that he was the resurrection and the life.

_____ **3.** Peter wanted to stay on the mountain with Jesus.

_____ **4.** The apostles learned that glory comes from the cross.

_____ **5.** The Pharisees were determined to kill Jesus.

_____ **6.** The apostles' faith was confirmed.

_____ **7.** The Father told us to listen to his Son Jesus.

_____ **8.** Jesus appeared in glory.

_____ **9.** People in Jerusalem greeted Jesus as the king of Israel.

_____ **10.** Jesus showed his humanness.

Not Wanted   Give proof that Jesus was rejected.

_____

_____

_____

_____

Riddles   Answer these questions.

1. Why is death a comma, not a period?

_____

2. Why can we say Jesus "loved us to death"?

_____

3. Why is life after life better than life?

_____

_____

4. How do you turn death into a "yes"?

_____

Jesus' Gift to Us: The Eucharist

20

Whoever eats this bread will live forever;
and the bread that I will give is my flesh
for the life of the world.

JOHN 6:51

* During Pope John Paul II's visit to the United States in 1995, a Eucharistic celebration was held outdoors. Thousands of people in Baltimore, Maryland, participated.
* In Uganda, Father Dan, a missionary, parks his truck where Catholics have gathered for Mass. He sets up an altar alongside the road, and the people celebrate the Eucharist.
* The Fields celebrated their sixtieth wedding anniversary with a home Mass. Friends and relatives gathered around the table to break bread together.

What celebration of Mass has impressed you?

_____

What made it special for you?

_____

More Than a Remembrance

Really, all Masses are special. Before Jesus died, he gave us a precious gift—a way he could remain with us. He gave us the Eucharist. In this sacrament he is present with us under the appearances of bread and wine. Jesus acts in every eucharistic celebration. He continues to teach us by his word and example. He, our one and only Mediator, makes the offering of his life present to us. He nourishes us with his body and blood, and he unites us with himself and with one another in the Christian community. The Eucharist is a sign of Jesus' permanent love for us. It is the perfect act of worship and the heart of Christian life.

Meals that Made History

God prepared humankind for the gift of the Eucharist. Long ago God rescued the Israelites from slavery in Egypt and brought them to freedom. To commemorate this great saving event, Jewish people celebrate a special Passover meal. Another hint of the Eucharist occurs in the story of the Israelites' journey to the Promised Land. God fed them in the desert with manna, a bread-like substance.

A more immediate preparation for the Eucharist was Jesus' miracle of feeding great crowds with bread and fish.

Read Mark 6:30–44. How is this miracle like the Eucharist?

_____

_____

_____

In John's Gospel, after this miracle Jesus promised the Bread of Life. When he said, "Whoever eats my flesh and drinks my blood has eternal life," many left him. Choose one passage and design the banner to reflect its message.

| John 6:35 | John 6:54 | John 6:58 |
| John 6:40 | John 6:56 | |

people. At the Last Supper Jesus gave us a new commandment. He said, "Love one another. As I have loved you so you also should love one another." Humankind entered a new covenant with God sealed by the blood of Jesus. All who have died and risen with Christ at Baptism share in the celebration of this covenant. They offer Christ's sacrifice and grow in love.

The Last Supper

Jesus' last meal with his friends, the apostles, was probably a Passover meal. At that meal Jesus put a towel around his waist and washed the feet of the apostles like a servant. He said, "If I, therefore, the master and teacher, have washed your feet, you ought to wash one another's feet." Then Jesus showed a greater proof of his love. He took bread, blessed it, broke it, and gave it to the apostles saying, "This is my body which will be given for you; do this in memory of me." Then he took a cup, passed it to the apostles and said, "This is my blood of the covenant which will be shed for many." The next day Jesus would die on the cross for us. The sacrifice offered at the Last Supper was the sacrifice of Calvary.

Jesus now offers this same sacrifice to the Father for us and with us in the Eucharist. Each time we celebrate the Eucharistic liturgy we come in contact with the dying and rising of Jesus. Only validly ordained priests can preside at Mass and can consecrate bread and wine.

A New Covenant

Sacrifices and covenants were familiar to the Jewish people. They considered their birthday as God's people the **covenant,** or agreement, God made with them at Sinai. There God revealed the divine name to the Israelites and gave them the Law. They agreed to live by this Law. The covenant was sealed by a ritual in which the blood of sacrifices was sprinkled on the altar and on the

A Thanksgiving Meal

Eucharist means "thanksgiving." This sacrament is the greatest act of praise and thanksgiving we can offer God. We are bound to participate in the Eucharist for the Lord's Day and for every holy day of obligation. Some people celebrate Mass on other days and benefit from the grace it offers. Any time something wonderful happens and your heart is full of joy and gratitude to God, you might consider celebrating Mass to give God thanks.

What days might you make special by the Eucharist?

_____

_____

The celebration of the Eucharist has two main parts, the **Liturgy of the Word** and the **Liturgy of the Eucharist.**

The Liturgy of the Word

During the Liturgy of the Word God speaks to us in the readings. In the Gospel, we are assured of God's love for us. We hear Jesus teach us what the Father wants us to know and what he wants us to do to lead a new life. The homily gives us insight into what God's words mean for us. Then we ask God's help in the General Intercessions. Nourished and strengthened by God's Word, we are fed with the Bread of Life.

The Liturgy of the Eucharist

Jesus' words and actions of the Last Supper are repeated at every Eucharist. By them we not only call to mind the Paschal Mystery, but Jesus makes it actually present. We offer Jesus to the Father and ourselves with him. Then we receive Christ's Body and Blood under the appearances of bread and wine. By sharing this meal we form the Church. Just as many grains make one bread and many grapes make one wine, so we are made one in Christ. Together we become more like him. Together we are sent to bring his love to the world.

Read John 15:4–7. What symbol did Jesus use to describe our relationship with him?

_____

Use these answers for activities in the next sections on the Liturgy of the Eucharist:

The Great Amen.

Lord, I am not worthy to receive you, but only say the word and I shall be healed.

Blessed be God forever.

Holy, holy, holy Lord.

Christ has died, Christ is risen, Christ will come again.

He Takes Bread

The Liturgy of the Eucharist begins with the **Preparation of the Gifts.** We take bread and wine to the priest. Then he says a prayer over each gift. These prayers remind us that the bread and wine symbolize the gifts of God and the work of our hands. They symbolize each one of us and our offering with Jesus. What do we respond to each of these prayers?

_____

He Gives Thanks

Then the priest says a prayer of thanks called the **Preface.** With him, we offer thanks and praise through Jesus to the Father. We thank the Father for his Son Jesus who became man and redeemed us through his cross and resurrection. Then we join the angels and saints in a song of praise.

What is its first line?

_____

He Offers Himself

The Preface leads into the **Eucharistic Prayer,** the high point of our act of worship. The priest stretches his hands over the gifts and calls on the Holy Spirit to make them holy. Then he prays the words of the institution at the Last Supper, and Jesus' Body and Blood become present on the altar under the forms of bread and wine. This change in substance is called **transubstantiation.** Jesus is present living and glorious, soul and divinity.

The Eucharistic Prayers are found in the **Sacramentary,** the official book of prayers and directions for Mass. Here are the words of the Consecration:

Over the bread he says,
> Take this, all of you, and eat it:
> This is my body which will be given up for you.

Over the wine he says,
> Take this, all of you, and drink from it:
> this is the cup of my blood,
> the blood of the new and everlasting covenant.
> It will be shed for you and for all
> so that sins may be forgiven.
> Do this in memory of me.

The Sacramentary

At this, the priest usually invites us to proclaim the mystery of faith that we celebrate. Write one of the four memorial acclamations.

_____

As the priest continues the Eucharistic Prayer, united with Jesus we give praise to the Father. We pray for the Church on Earth, for those who have died, and we remember Mary and the saints. The priest concludes this prayer with the hymn of praise (a doxology):

> Through him,
> with him,
> in him,
> in the unity of the Holy Spirit,
> all glory and honor is yours,
> almighty Father,
> for ever and ever.

What do we sing to voice our agreement with all that is taking place? _____

Jesus Gives Himself to Us

In the Communion Rite of the Mass, Jesus gives us himself as food and drink. We prepare for this by praying together the prayer Jesus taught us, the Lord's Prayer. As a community united in faith and love, we exchange a sign of Christ's peace. We are called to reconciliation and unity as we pray for peace for one another. While the priest breaks the bread, we pray that Jesus, the Lamb of God, will have mercy on us and grant us his peace. Before receiving Jesus in Holy Communion, we pray together a prayer that expresses both our weakness and our trust in God. What is it?

_____

_____

The Church encourages us to receive Communion at every Mass. When we receive Jesus, we praise and thank and love him. We tell him of our needs, confident that he will help us. All who share the Body and Blood of Jesus are drawn into union with the Father and the Holy Spirit and with one another. Here is a mystery. As we accept Christ in Communion, we also agree to accept and support one another in the Christian community and others in the world. If we permit him, Jesus will gradually change us into the people he calls us to be.

He Sends Us to Love and Serve

Having been opened to Jesus' love and transforming power, we are more aware of others' needs and more able to serve them. With Jesus, we go forth to bring the Good News to all.

A Feast without End

In the Eucharist, we share in the communion of saints. We are united with all the members of the Church in heaven and on Earth. We can pray for those in purgatory. At Mass we carry out the same liturgy or praise of God's glory that echoes through heaven. Our thanks and praise are a foretaste of the time when we will give God glory forever. The Eucharist is a sign and pledge of the banquet of God's kingdom. There those who have been faithful to the covenant will share in a love feast forever.

Remember

What is the Eucharist?

The Eucharist is the sacrament in which the Paschal Mystery of Jesus is both called to mind and made present under the appearances of bread and wine. We offer Jesus with ourselves to the Father, and we are united through eucharistic communion with Jesus, the Father, and the Holy Spirit, and with one another.

What is the new commandment of Jesus?

 I give you a new commandment: love one another. As I have loved you, so you also should love one another. This is how all will know that you are my disciples, if you have love for one another.

John 13:34–35

Words to Know

Passover   covenant
transubstantiation   Sacramentary
Liturgy of the Word
Liturgy of the Eucharist

Respond

Think of a symbol that represents you. Maybe it is a football, a pizza, a computer, or a rainbow for your interest in many things. Draw your symbol in your journal and write a prayer offering yourself to the Father.

Reach Out

1. Invite someone to celebrate the Eucharist with you. Perhaps afterwards you could eat together at home or at a restaurant.
2. Think of someone you can love and serve this week. Write three things you will do for that person and then do them!
3. Participate in a Eucharist in a rite other than your own or at another parish.
4. Pay close attention to the readings and homilies of the next Eucharistic celebration. Write a paragraph explaining what God was saying to you personally that day.
5. Compile quotations on the Eucharist from John 6 and 1 Corinthians 10, 11. Use one to design a card for someone celebrating a First Communion.

Review

Matching   Match the definition with the correct term. One term is used twice.

a. transubstantiation   **d.** mediator
b. Sacramentary   **e.** Passover
c. covenant   **f.** Eucharist

_____   **1.** A meal that makes the sacrifice of Calvary present again
_____   **2.** The official book of prayers and directions for Eucharistic worship
_____   **3.** A go-between for two opposing parties
_____   **4.** An agreement between God and human beings
_____   **5.** An act of worship that means thanksgiving
_____   **6.** The change in substance from bread and wine to the Body and Blood of Jesus
_____   **7.** The Hebrew meal that commemorates God's saving actions

Ordering Meals   Number these special meals in the order they occurred.

_____   the Last Supper

_____   the manna in the desert

_____   the heavenly banquet

_____   the Passover

_____   the last Mass you celebrated

_____   the multiplication of loaves

_____   the Eucharist of the early Christian community

Liturgy in Outline   Complete the outline.

Liturgy of the (1) _____
    Old or New Testament reading(s)

    The (2) _____

    Homily

    General (3) _____

Liturgy of the Eucharist

    Preparation of the (4) _____

    Eucharistic Prayer

        The (5) _____

        Holy, Holy, Holy

        (6) _____

        Memorial Acclamation

        Great (7) _____

Communion Rite

    The (8) _____ Prayer

    Sign of (9) _____

    (10) _____ of God

    Communion

Jesus the Lamb of God

The Final Hours of Jesus

21

The way we came to know love
was that he laid down his life for us;
so we ought to lay down our lives
for our brothers.

1 JOHN 3:16

Sally covered her face with her hands and sobbed. "I can't move again. I just can't! Not another town and school! Just when I find friends! Just when I make the team! We always move just when I finally *belong!*"

Moving can be painful. Being separated from familiar places and people can seem like dying. Every person meets "little deaths" as a part of life. Through these "deaths" a person gains new opportunities for life.

Write one good thing that may come from moving.

_____

What "little death" have you suffered that resulted in something good?

_____

What good result came from it?

_____

The Garden of Olives outside Jerusalem

His Passion

 Unless a grain of wheat falls to the ground and dies, it remains just a grain of wheat; but if it dies, it produces much fruit.

John 12:24

Like the grain of wheat, Jesus had to suffer and die in order to enter into his glory. He died as a result of sin. By his obedience and love he brought all humankind back to God. He won for us forgiveness, salvation, and eternal life. The Jewish people sacrificed animals and the first fruits of their crops to God. Jesus offered himself to the Father for us. As other sacrifices, his was to make up for sins and to gain benefits. Jesus was the Lamb of God—the perfect sacrifice. The events from the Last Supper to Jesus' death on the cross are called his **passion**. *Passion* means "suffering."

Love for his Father and us led Jesus to accept his passion. Love demands courage, truthfulness, and constancy in suffering. The **passion narratives** are the four Gospel accounts of Jesus' final sufferings and death. Read the passages that follow and write how Jesus responded to the situations.

The mob came to arrest him. (John 18:1–9)

_____

Judas betrayed him. (Luke 22:47–48)

_____

Peter denied him. (Luke 22:59–61)

_____

Pilate questioned him. (John 18:33–37)

_____

Soldiers tortured him. (Mark 15:16–20)

_____

He saw others suffering. (Luke 23:27–28)

_____

Many people caused his pain and death.
(Luke 23:34)

_____

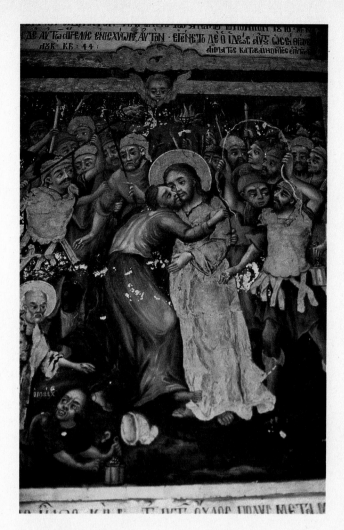

His Source of Strength

Under the pressure of exhaustion, rejection, loneliness, and evil, where did Jesus find the strength
to go on? How could he keep loving and forgiving?

The answer lies in his union with his Father. Jesus
knew the depth of his Father's love. Through
prayer, he received strength to suffer and die for
us. He prayed,

"My Father, if it is possible, let this cup pass
from me; yet, not as I will, but as you will."
Matthew 26:39

Our Response

Suffering will always be a mystery, something we
cannot fully understand. Only when we, like
Jesus, trust in the Father's love and accept the
suffering he permits does suffering have any
meaning. As his followers, we can

✢ work to eliminate the evil around us
✢ try to relieve the pain of others
✢ unite our suffering with his in love
✢ accept suffering without self-pity or anger
✢ offer our sufferings for other people
✢ gain strength as Jesus did, through prayer and
   union with our Father.

OBITUARY

Jesus of Nazareth died about 3:00 P.M. Friday as a result of crucifixion at the hands of Roman soldiers. Jesus, a former carpenter, was a controversial Jewish figure. He was popular in Galilee and Judea for his teachings and his healings. On Thursday, Judas Iscariot, one of Jesus' followers, led soldiers to him. They arrested him in a garden and brought him to the Jewish leaders. The Sanhedrin accused him of blasphemy because he claimed to be the Son of God. The high priest Caiaphas sent him to Pilate for execution. Finding him innocent, Pilate offered to release him, but most of the people demanded that Barabbas, a revolutionary, be freed instead. After having Jesus scourged, Pilate ordered him crucified on the charge that he had declared himself a king. At Jesus' death, his mother Mary, a disciple named John, and some women were present. Burial was immediate since the next day was the Sabbath. Soldiers guard the tomb because the man predicted he would be raised in three days.

Free to Love

> Nothing . . . can ever come between us and the love of God made visible in Christ . . .
>
> Romans 8:38–39 (JB)

Jesus wants you to share his glory, his joy. The best response you can give is to love him—not because you are afraid, or because you have to, or because others do, but because he is so good and you really *want* to love him.

How can you tell if you really love God?

Read 1 John 4:20–21. Compare your answer.

> I asked Jesus, "How much do you love me?" He stretched out his arms on the cross and said, "This much."

A Lifetime Project

> Out of his infinite glory, may he give you the power through his Spirit for your hidden self to grow strong.
>
> Ephesians 3:16 (JB)

On your journey to the Father, you have many chances to love him and others. Your choices make you what you are. How does this happen? Each time you choose to be honest, it is easier to be honest in the future. You are becoming a more honest person. On the other hand, each time you choose to be unkind, you make it easier to be unkind again. Gradually you could become a cruel person.

The change is so gradual that you and others may not be aware of it. But with every decision you grow stronger or weaker in the Lord. As you respond to God's grace or reject it, you set a pattern for your life.

After Death, Then What?

At the moment of death you will see your hidden self and realize how much you have become like Jesus. Then, based on that likeness, you will realize before God how you fit or do not fit into the kingdom of love. This moment is called the **particular judgment.**

After death there are three possibilities:

+ People who have become like Jesus by loving perfectly can enter God's presence, see God face to face, and know a boundless joy. This is called **heaven.**
+ People may need to be purified of remaining selfishness, because only those totally transformed by love can enter the kingdom. This purification is called **purgatory.**
+ People who have freely refused in serious ways to follow God's command to love are in the state of mortal sin. Anyone in this state cannot enter heaven but will be outside of it forever. This eternal separation from God for whom we long is called **hell.**

The End of the World

At the end of time, Jesus will return in glory to judge the living and the dead. At this Second Coming, or **parousia,** the resurrection from the dead will take place. God will reveal the plan of salvation in all its glory. The eternal destiny of the human race and of every person will be revealed in the **Last Judgment.** The souls of the just will be reunited with their glorified bodies. The universe will be transformed, and God will be "all in all." Christians long for the parousia when God "will wipe every tear from their eyes" (Revelation 21:4). We pray, "Come, Lord Jesus" (Revelation 22:20). If you knew Christ would return next week, how would you live differently?

> Make ready for Christ, whose smile, like lightning, sets free the song of everlasting glory that sleeps in your paper flesh like dynamite.
>
> Thomas Merton

The Last Things

Can you answer these questions?

1. What will you learn about yourself from God at the moment of your death?
2. What is the moment called when a person finds out about his or her eternal destiny?
3. Describe the three alternatives for a person at the moment of death.
4. What is the parousia and its purpose?
5. What is the Last Judgment?

The Thief Who Stole Heaven

Read Luke 23:39–43.
How did the good thief show that he was on Jesus' side?

_____

_____

Write Jesus' response to the good thief.

_____

_____

No matter what the good thief had done in the past, Jesus welcomed him into the kingdom because the thief reached out in love. The same Jesus is always ready to forgive you and offer you his love, even to the moment of death. Will you turn to him?

Remember

What is the supreme act of God's love for all people?

The supreme act of God's love for all people is Jesus' death on the cross. In obedience to the Father, Jesus offered his life for our sins, so that all could have eternal life.

How does the Gospel explain this act of love?

God so loved the world that he gave his only Son, so that everyone who believes in him might not perish but might have eternal life.

John 3:16

Words to Know

passion   purgatory
passion narratives   parousia
particular judgment
Last Judgment

Respond

Imagine that you are standing on Calvary while Jesus is dying. Experience the sights and sounds around you. Now focus your attention on Jesus in his suffering. Realize that your sins are part of the burden he is carrying. Be with him now, supporting him with your love, knowing that your love can ease his burden. Record your thoughts and feelings in your journal.

Reach Out

1. Find the traditional "Seven Last Words of Christ" in Scripture. See Mark 15:34; Luke 23:34, 43, 46; John 19:26, 28, 30. Compose a prayer or make a mobile based on the meaning of Jesus' words for today.
2. The mystery of Jesus passing through death to glory is the core of Christian belief. Using a missalette, list references to the death and resurrection of Christ in the prayers of the Eucharistic liturgy.

3. Take a survey of five people of various ages. Ask each one to complete these statements:
   - ✤ When I was younger, I thought heaven was like . . .
   - ✤ Now I think heaven is . . .
   - ✤ I look forward to heaven because . . .
4. Read about the Last Judgment in Matthew 25:31–46. Imagine you are one of the sheep or goats. How would you feel?
5. Pray the prayer below. What title would you give it? Learn it by heart and pray it.

> O God, I love you for yourself,
> And not that I may heaven gain,
> Nor because those who love you not
> Must suffer hell's eternal pain.
>
> You, O my Jesus, you did me
> Upon the cross embrace;
> For me did bear the nails and spear
> And manifold disgrace,
>
> And griefs and torments numberless,
> And sweat of agony,
> Even death itself—and all for one
> Who was your enemy.
>
> Then why, O blessed Jesus Christ,
> Should I not love you well?
> Not for the sake of winning heaven,
> Nor of escaping hell;
>
> Not with the hope of gaining things,
> Not seeking a reward;
> But, as you yourself have loved me,
> O ever-loving Lord.
>
> And so I love you, and will love,
> And in your praise will sing,
> Solely because you are my God
> And my eternal king.

Review

Jeopardy   Write a question each term answers.

1. Judas
2. particular judgment
3. Simon
4. Last Judgment
5. Pontius Pilate
6. parousia
7. purgatory
8. Mary
9. John
10. Barabbas

Symbols of the Passion   Write how each symbol is related to the Passion.

INRI   1. _____

2. _____

3. _____

4. _____

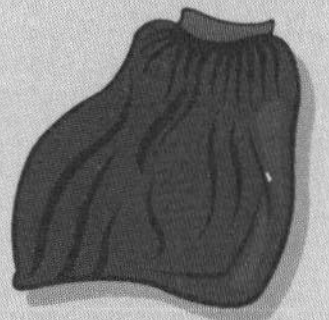

5. _____

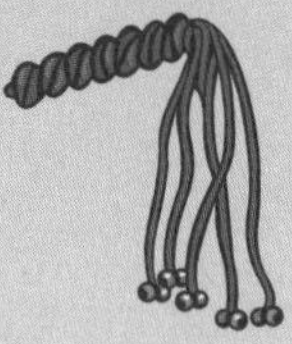

6. _____

7. _____

8. _____

9. _____

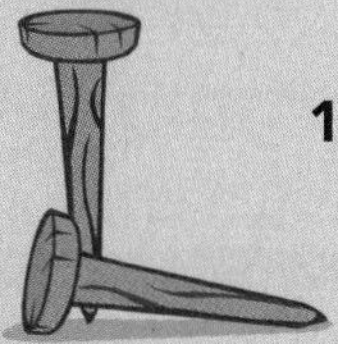

10. _____

11. _____

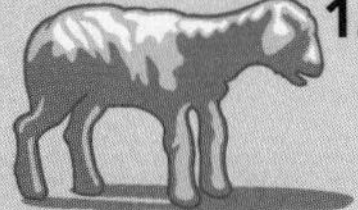

12. _____

Victim or Victor?   Suppose the doctor tells you that you have an incurable disease. What Christian attitudes would help you cope with this cross? What can you expect after you die?

_____

_____

_____

_____

The Victory of Jesus

22

I handed on to you as of first importance what I also received: that Christ died for our sins in accordance with the scriptures; that he was buried; that he was raised on the third day in accordance with the scriptures; that he appeared to Cephas, then to the Twelve.

1 CORINTHIANS 15:3–5

What do you believe about eternal life? Circle **T** if you believe the statement is true, and **F** if you believe it is false.

For everyone who believes in Jesus
    and listens to his words, eternal
    life has already begun.   T   F

You must have faith to believe in
    the Resurrection.   T   F

Christ's Resurrection is a promise
    of our future glory.   T   F

No one saw the Resurrection take
    place.   T   F

After we die we come back to Earth
    as other persons (reincarnated).   T   F

The Resurrection was the greatest
    event in human history.   T   F

He Is Risen

Jesus lives! The apostles were stunned to hear those words. Jesus of Nazareth, who died by crucifixion and was buried in a borrowed tomb, now was alive! He was still with them, appearing to his friends. Jesus was in Galilee! He was in Judea! He was eating fish! He was in the upper room! He was hiking to Emmaus!

No one saw the Resurrection happen. The Gospel accounts of it vary. But they agree on two facts: there was an open, empty tomb and the Christian believers had the experience of seeing Jesus risen! In the Gospel Easter stories, the early Christians convey something that is beyond human experience.

As you read the following Scripture passages, imagine you are a reporter in Jerusalem at the time of the Resurrection. Write one thing you learn from these witnesses:

Guards and women (Matthew 28:1–10)

_____

Mary Magdalene, Peter, John (John 20:1–18)

_____

Disciples on road to Emmaus (Luke 24:13–35)

_____

Thomas (John 20:24–29)

_____

Disciples fishing (John 21:1–14)

_____

Now pretend you are a follower of Jesus at the time of the Resurrection. What meaning would one of these stories have for you?

_____

_____

_____

Jesus Glorified

After Jesus died, his human soul united to his divine person went to the realm of the dead and opened the gates of heaven for the holy ones there. Then he appeared on Earth with his risen, glorious body. Jesus' appearances astounded the disciples and changed them forever. He had lived among them and had died. Now they saw him glorified. Death had no more power over him. As St. Paul wrote:

"Death is swallowed up in victory.
Where, O death, is your victory?
Where, O death, is your sting?"
1 Corinthians 15:54–55

Jesus was doing the same things he did before: teaching, forgiving, consoling, eating, and talking with his disciples. But they saw him full of power, mystery, and glory. He was not like Lazarus who had returned from the dead but would die again. He was the risen Lord who had passed beyond death. His words and his teachings were the authentic Word of God and would never pass away. Jesus had brought a totally new way of living—a way to share in eternal life, God's life. Looking at the risen Jesus, the disciples began to realize that they, too, would live as he did! Not until Pentecost, though, would they really understand who Jesus was and be empowered for their mission.

Read Luke 24:36–43. Suppose you were in the upper room and saw the risen Jesus. Later, a friend asked you about it. What would you say?

_____

_____

_____

Who Saw the Risen Jesus?

The Resurrection was for believers. Those who believed in Jesus saw him as the risen Lord. To recognize the risen Jesus required faith, because the Resurrection is a mystery of faith. The Gospels emphasize the doubt of different disciples when they heard about Jesus' resurrection. In each instance, Jesus took the initiative and revealed himself to them, and by his grace the disciples believed.

What if Jesus hadn't risen? Read 1 Corinthians 15:12–19. What do you conclude?

_____

_____

What kind of bodies will we have when we are raised? In 1 Corinthians 15:36–49, St. Paul says that our risen body will be as different from our present body as a seed buried in the ground is from the wheat that grows from it.

We Experience the Risen Jesus

By our baptism we share in the death, resurrection, and life of Jesus and witness to him. Through his death and resurrection, Jesus gives us the power to die to selfishness.

We are an Easter people. There is a contagious enthusiasm about the way we live and a freedom about the way we speak and act. Jesus' death and resurrection give meaning to our lives. We have the hope of eternal life. Our goal is to live as companions to the risen Jesus. By following his way we shall one day rise with him in glory.

Today we encounter the risen Lord especially in the *Eucharist,* in the *Scriptures,* and in the *faith community* of the Church.

A Witness Plan

Set up a plan to become a witness to the risen Jesus. Check your resolutions every day this week.

Eucharist

The spirit of the Eucharist I celebrate should influence my attitudes and actions toward others during the week. I will show a Christlike attitude by

Monday ❏	Tuesday ❏	Wednesday ❏	Thursday ❏	Friday ❏

Scriptures

The Resurrection showed that everything Jesus taught was pleasing to the Father. Every day I will deepen my understanding of his word by

Monday ❏	Tuesday ❏	Wednesday ❏	Thursday ❏	Friday ❏

Faith Community

The grace of the Resurrection helps me understand how I am to act like Jesus. To reach out to others, I will perform an act of generosity by

Monday ❏	Tuesday ❏	Wednesday ❏	Thursday ❏	Friday ❏

Signs That He's with Us

All seven *sacraments* are an opportunity to meet and grow closer to Jesus. Through them he acts in us and cares for us. They were instituted by him and increase grace in us directly. Other sacred signs called **sacramentals** have been given to us by the Church to remind us of God. The Church's prayers and the way we use sacramentals empower them to make us holy. Sacramentals may be blessed objects like medals and palms, or actions like the Sign of the Cross. They prepare us for the sacraments. The risen Lord is with us no less than he was with the first disciples.

Jesus' invisible but very real presence remained with them.

Read Acts 1:6–11. Name two unusual things that happened at Christ's leave-taking.

_____

_____

_____

_____

The Ascension: Jesus Is Lord

Good-byes can be sad. People who love each other find it hard to be separated. When have you experienced such a good-bye?

_____

The **Ascension** is Christ's return to his Father. In the person of Jesus, humanity is already with God! The early Christians believed that Jesus would come again soon in glory. But as time went on, they realized that the Second Coming might be in the far distant future. While they waited,

In the Apostles' Creed we pray, "He ascended into heaven and is seated at the right hand of the Father." The Ascension was more than just a good-bye. It completed the glorification of Jesus. Being seated at the right hand of the Father showed he was Lord of the universe. Before, Christ had limited his activity to Palestine. But now his influence extends to the ends of the universe. When we say Jesus is Lord, we say we believe he reigns over heaven and earth, the living and the dead. We see all things as subject to him—including ourselves. We believe his teachings are God's words.

Missioned to Make a Difference!

Jesus, filled with the Holy Spirit, promised this Spirit to his disciples. His Spirit would make them "other Christs." What did Jesus predict about them? See Acts 1:8.

_____

_____

We, too, witness to Christ Jesus and make the world aware of his justice and love. Our call to witness is a call to action! We are "givers" in a world of "takers." We are responsible for our acts and selfless in serving. We are not afraid to take risks for love of Jesus and to do the right things. We wait for Jesus to return and to remake our bodies "according to the pattern of his glorified body" (adapted from Philippians 3:21 JB).

> May the Son of God, who is already formed in you, grow in you so that for you he will become immeasurable, and that in you he will become laughter, exultation, the fullness of joy which no one will take from you.
>
> Isaac of Stella (?–1169)

Remember

Why is the Resurrection of Jesus significant?
The Resurrection of Jesus is significant because it shows that Jesus is the Son of God and that we will rise someday.

What is meant by the Ascension?
The Ascension means that Jesus returned to his Father in heaven and is Lord of the Universe.

How do we encounter the risen Lord today?
We encounter the risen Lord today in the sacraments, especially in the Eucharist, in the Scriptures, and in the faith community.

Words to Know

Ascension   sacrament
sacramental

Respond

How exciting it must have been for the disciples on the road to Emmaus to learn from Jesus himself the meaning of his passion, death, and resurrection. Their hearts were "burning within them" at his words. But he gave them more than words. He broke bread and opened their hearts. Write in your journal what you would have said to Jesus if you had been on the Emmaus journey (Luke 24:13–35). Then write a prayer telling how and where you will be a witness.

Reach Out

1. Read 1 Corinthians 15:3–58. This letter of St. Paul contains the earliest written statement about the Resurrection. It was probably written sometime between A.D. 54–56. Some Christian Corinthians had weakened in the faith, and Paul wanted them to know that the Resurrection was our greatest hope. With your family and friends, discuss how the Corinthians may have reacted to Paul's letter. Imagine that you are a member of their community and write a response to Paul expressing your belief.

2. Pray to become a peaceful person who brings the joy of the risen Jesus to others.

3. Jesus is life! Find Scripture verses from the Gospel of St. John and make holy cards for the elderly in a nursing home. Write a cheerful message on the back of each card.
   Here are possible references:

John 1:3–4	John 5:24	John 6:48
John 3:13–14	John 5:26	John 6:51
John 3:15–16	John 6:27	John 6:58
John 3:36	John 6:35	John 6:63
John 4:14	John 6:40	John 8:12
John 5:21	John 6:47	John 10:17–18

4. Bring to class one newspaper article that shows the needs of the world. Give the account to your teacher for posting, and then remember these needs in prayer.

5. Make a booklet of drawings and explanations of sacramentals. You could divide it into three sections: in the home, in church, and in your own life; or sacred objects, sacred actions, and sacred words.

Review

Who Am I?   Answer these riddles.

1. I am the first one Jesus appeared to according to the Gospels.

_____

2. I explained Scripture to two disciples on the road to Emmaus.

_____

3. I was invited to touch Jesus' wounds when I didn't believe the apostles had seen him.

_____

4. I was the first disciple to recognize that the stranger who helped us fish was Jesus.

_____

5. I was the first apostle to go into the tomb.

_____

6. I am the Lord of the universe.

_____

What Am I?   Answer these riddles.

1. I am what Jesus ate to prove he was alive.

_____

2. When Jesus broke me, the disciples recognized him.

_____

3. I am what you need to believe in the Resurrection.

_____

4. I was Jesus' first words to his apostles.

_____

5. I am Jesus' return to the Father in glory.

_____

6. I was conquered by Jesus.

_____

7. I am the great miracle that made all Jesus' words believable.

_____

8. I am a blessed object or action that has power to make you holy by the prayers of the Church.

_____

Meeting Jesus   Name four ways that we can encounter the risen Lord today.

1. _____

2. _____

3. _____

4. _____

The Church Alive with Jesus' Spirit

And behold, I am with you always,
until the end of the age.

MATTHEW 28:20

Many people have had "turning points": experiences that changed them and turned their lives around. Helen Keller was one of these people. An illness left her blind and deaf as an infant. By the time she was seven, she had become uncontrollable. Helen's family hired Anne Sullivan to teach her sign language, to reach somehow into the darkness of her life. It seemed like an impossible task, until one day Anne held one of Helen's hands under a pump and spelled "w-a-t-e-r" into her other hand. As Helen explained later:

> Somehow the mystery of language was revealed to me. I knew then that "w-a-t-e-r" meant the wonderful cool something that was flowing over my hand. That living word awakened my soul, gave it light, hope, joy, set it free! . . . Everything had a name, and each name gave birth to a new thought. As we returned to the house every object which I touched seemed to quiver with life. That was because I saw everything with the strange, new sight that had come to me.
> from *The Story of My Life* by Helen Keller

This was Helen's turning point. Although she would continue to struggle as she learned to cope in the world, her whole life had changed. She had been transformed.

Write about a turning point in your life or in the life of someone you know about.

Pentecost: Touched by the Spirit

A turning point occurred for all humanity the day Jesus' Spirit came to his Church. It was the harvest feast of Pentecost in Jerusalem, a time for pilgrims to gather in the holy city and praise Yahweh for fields of grain. Mary and the disciples were in the upper room. They were waiting. They had been commissioned by Christ to go and baptize, to bring the Good News of salvation and love to all people. But they needed help, power, and guidance. They needed Christ! So they put all their trust in him and waited, praying. Suddenly there was a tremendous sound—as if a powerful wind were filling the house. Something like tongues of fire appeared and rested on each person. The disciples were filled with the Holy Spirit. The Spirit of God touched and transformed them.

Spirit Alive

What the disciples experienced on Pentecost was beyond description. However, the two elements associated with the coming of the Spirit can help us understand how the Spirit changed their lives. In Scripture, wind and fire are signs of God's presence.

Name a characteristic of wind.

_____

How is the Holy Spirit's activity like wind?

_____

Name a characteristic of fire.

_____

How is the Holy Spirit's activity like fire?

_____

Out of Hiding

How did the coming of the Spirit affect the followers in the upper room? Read the verses listed. Then write what happened through the power of the Holy Spirit.

Acts 2:4, 11

_____

_____

Acts 2:14

_____

Acts 2:41

_____

_____

Acts 2:43

_____

_____

Acts 2:44–45

_____

_____

The Holy Spirit was present at the baptism of Jesus when he was anointed for his mission. Now the same Spirit empowered the disciples to fulfill their mission. Here is the mission Christ gave the disciples and to us.

> Go, therefore, and make disciples of all nations, baptizing them in the name of the Father, and of the Son, and of the holy Spirit, teaching them to observe all that I have commanded you.
>
> Matthew 28:19

The most important change the disciples experienced was inside, deep in their hearts. With the abiding presence of the Spirit, they became enthusiastic, courageous witnesses to Christ.

Fearless Followers

The Holy Spirit's power is not limited to the early Christians or to great saints and leaders. Through Baptism, you and all the faithful are gifted with the Spirit. Our encounter with the Spirit usually does not involve drastic changes, roaring winds, and tongues of fire. Instead, we grow a little each day through struggles and moments of love and understanding. In time, we become true followers of the Way.

One of the most effective ways to spread the Good News is to live caring lives. People are attracted to Christ when they see Christians living his message. But that kind of living takes courage: courage to say no to the evil spirit, courage to say yes to the Spirit of Christ. When have you shown Christian courage?

Community of Love: The Church

At Pentecost the Church was born as a society, with the Spirit as its strength and guiding force. A new era in salvation history was begun, as all that had been foretold by the prophets was accomplished.

After the Spirit had come upon the disciples, they did not just walk off to the farthest limits of the earth, preaching the Good News. Their first response was to form a community of believers. This community was a gift of God and, in many ways, also a miracle! For persecution and hardships surrounded the disciples.

The Christians had a common vision—a deep devotion to Christ, his way of life, and his kingdom. As they sought to love Jesus more, they showed a real concern for the poor and needy, and a thirst to spread the Good News. They also loved one another in Christ. They were bonded to one another more closely than a club or a team. They were the family of believers, the Mystical Body of Christ. In Jesus, the head of the Church, they were a new people reconciled to God. They shared his ministry. They celebrated his saving mysteries.

The unity among Christians is to resemble the unity among the Persons of the Trinity. Acts 2:42 names four things that bonded the community together:

✣ Devotion to the apostles' instruction
✣ Communal life
✣ The breaking of bread
✣ Prayers

Saint Paul Preaching at Athens by Raphael

Church Bonds

Read about these bonds and the growth of the early Christian community in Acts 2:42–47, Acts 4:32–35, and Acts 5:12–16. With your reading in mind, check possible endings to the following statement:

The description of the early Church in Acts
❑ seems impossible.
❑ is something I would like to experience.
❑ makes me want to try to be a better member of the community of believers.
❑ could never happen again.

Check the ways the people in the early Christian community were like people in your parish.
❑ The Eucharist was the center of the community's life.
❑ Not everyone agreed on what the Church and its practices should be.
❑ The people prayed together often.
❑ They showed concern for the needy and went out of their way to help them.
❑ They gathered in one another's homes for meals and sharing.
❑ They willingly gave money and possessions to others in the community.
❑ They spoke openly about their love for Christ and the Church.
❑ They attracted more and more people to their community.
❑ Some members seriously failed to live up to the ideals of Christian life.

You and the Family of Believers

You are a part of the community, the Church that was born on Pentecost. Like the apostles, you have a mission from Christ. You are to be a courageous witness to the Good News for the whole world *and* a loving, enthusiastic member of the community of believers, the Church.

Your role as a witness and disciple may not extend to all the world, but you are important and vital wherever you are. The Holy Spirit is at work in you this very moment. But remember, it may take a lifetime to be totally open to the transforming power of the Spirit.

Looking for Fruit

How can you tell you are open to the Spirit? What will your life be like? Galatians 5:22–23 contains a list of the qualities, or **fruits,** found in the life of a true disciple: love, joy, peace, patience, kindness, generosity, faithfulness, gentleness, and self-control.

Choose three fruits of the Spirit. Write how they show the presence of the Spirit in *your* life.

_____

_____

_____

_____

Remember

What is the significance of Pentecost?
At Pentecost the Holy Spirit was poured out upon Mary, the apostles, and other believers, empowering them to proclaim the Good News as courageous witnesses and to form a community of love, the Church. At Pentecost the Church as a social body was born and a new era of salvation history began.

How is the Church a community?
As a community, we are bonded by love for Christ and for one another, and by service to the world with the guidance and strength of the Holy Spirit. Like the early Christian community, we share in the teaching of the apostles (creed), community life, the breaking of the bread, and prayers (word and sacrament).

Words to Memorize
The fruits of the Holy Spirit

Respond

The Holy Spirit empowers you to be a courageous witness. There are times when you are called to stand up for what is right. Think of a time when you did what you knew to be right, even when it was difficult. Record the incident in your journal. Jot down how you felt before, during, and after making your decision. Then compose your own prayer to the Holy Spirit to use at times in the future when you will need strength and support.

Reach Out

1. Read a biography of St. Paul, St. Ignatius of Loyola, St. Bernadette Soubirous, or Matt Talbot. Find out about the turning points in their lives and report your findings to the class.
2. Your first experience of community was in your family. Write an essay about the "community life" of your family. Ask each member of the family to contribute something to your essay. Share with them Colossians 3:18–21. How well does your family reflect this teaching on family life?
3. The Spirit, the gift and power of God, directs the growth of the Christian community and enables its members to carry out the ministry of Christ through various gifts. Read 1 Corinthians 12–14, which lists many of these gifts and tells how they can be used for the Church. Then think of your own community—the parish. How evident are these gifts in the parish? Be ready to explain.
4. You can do much right now as a member of the family of believers. Read these Scripture references. Write a summary of each and two or three ways you can put Christ's message into action TODAY!
   Romans 12:9–13   Colossians 3:16–17
   1 Corinthians 10:31   1 Peter 4:10–11
5. Find out about the charismatic movement in the Church or in your parish. What is the turning point for the people in this movement? What gifts do they have? How is their experience similar to Pentecost? Ask someone who is involved in it what difference it has made in his or her life.

Review

Pentecost Acrostic   Use these clues to work the puzzle.

1. They were in the upper room with Mary when the Holy Spirit came
2. A visible sign of the Spirit's power to enlighten
3. A sign of the Spirit's invisible action
4. What the apostles spoke in after the Spirit came
5. The city where Pentecost took place
6. The community the followers became on Pentecost
7. What the Spirit gave the apostles
8. Qualities that are signs of the Spirit's presence in us
9. How many thousands of people were baptized on Pentecost

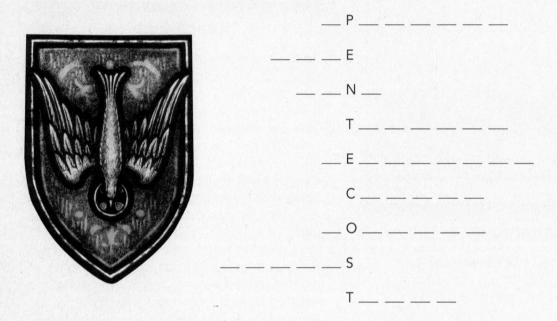

```
__ P __ __ __ __ __ __
      __ __ __ E
      __ __ N __
      T __ __ __ __ __ __
      __ E __ __ __ __ __ __ __
      C __ __ __ __ __ __
      __ O __ __ __ __ __
__ __ __ __ __ S
      T __ __ __ __
```

The Church: Ever Ancient, Ever New   Match each action you might do in the second column with a characteristic of the early Church.

a. Devotion to the apostles' instruction   _____   **1.** Celebrate Eucharist

b. Communal life   _____   **2.** Donate to Catholic Charities

c. The breaking of bread   _____   **3.** Attend religion classes

d. Prayers   _____   **4.** Participate in parish renewals and devotions

Your Mission   How can you follow Christ's command to baptize all nations and teach the Good News?

_____

_____

Jesus Emmanuel

Walking with Jesus in a Vocation: Matrimony and Holy Orders

24

There are different kinds of spiritual gifts but the same Spirit;
there are different forms of service but the same Lord;
there are different workings but the same God who produces
all of them in everyone.

1 CORINTHIANS 12:4–6

The activities of your everyday life are a part of God's plan for you at this time. List some of these activities here.

What responsibilities do you have at home?

_____

What responsibilities do you have in school?

_____

What do you do in your free time?

_____

What are you doing to grow spiritually?

_____

Are the activities you listed helping you to become your best self? If not, what is missing? Your life is like a puzzle, but God has a plan for putting all the pieces together. God calls you through the ordinary events of your life to become like his Son Jesus. God calls you to a special vocation in life and is preparing you for it now.

Your Life Call
You and all Christians have received one universal call from God at baptism. You can find it in 1 Thessalonians 4:3. Write the verse below.

_____

_____

Your call to holiness is a call to develop your talents so you can serve God and others better. It is a call to witness to God's love within your family and parish, among your friends and class-mates. In the future, God may call you to remain a member of the laity as a single or married person. God may call you to be a member of a secular institute, a sister or brother, a deacon, a religious or diocesan priest, or a bishop. God may even call you to several vocations.

In all of these lifestyles Jesus accompanies us on our journey. He is Emmanuel—God with us. He supports us with his grace. Every life call is meant to lead us to be holy and to share in Jesus' mission. The best way of life for you is the one to which God calls you.

Call to Single Life
God calls some people to the single life. Unmarried people can be involved in a wide range of activities and can spend their lives in service to others. They then become signs of God's love. They may make private vows. Some single people choose to live a vowed life as members of **secular institutes.** They live conse-crated lives of prayer and service, while keeping their jobs in the world.

Think of a single person you admire. How does he or she serve others?

_____

What qualities make him or her like Christ?

_____

Why can a single person serve in a way that others cannot serve?

_____

Call to Married Life

God calls most people to a lifelong commitment as husband or wife in marriage. By their generous love for each other and for the children God sends them, husbands and wives support and encourage each other to grow in holiness and to lead their children to holiness.

How can a couple help each other to be *holy*?

_____

_____

_____

A Covenant of Love

When 6:30 rolls around, Mrs. Rufo expects Kim to come over and babysit for her. Kim promised that she would come, and Mrs. Rufo trusts that Kim will be faithful to her promise.

To make a promise to someone is a sign of love. You might trust someone enough to make an agreement of friendship. If you love a person deeply, you might make a covenant. A **covenant** is a binding and solemn agreement.

On their wedding day, Catholic couples make a covenant of love with each other before God. Jesus raised the natural reality of marriage to the level of a sacrament, the Sacrament of Matrimony. The Church celebrates marriage as something holy. The priest represents Jesus as he witnesses the bridal couple's vows in the midst of the believing community. The man and woman act as ministers of the sacrament to each other. They bestow and receive the sacrament in the essential part of the ceremony: **the exchange of vows.** These promises bind them in a lifelong partnership. In the following version of the marriage vows, underline what Robert and Ann promise to do.

I, Robert (Ann), take you, Ann (Robert), to be my wife (husband). I promise to be true to you in good times and in bad, in sickness and in health. I will love you and honor you all the days of my life.

Covenant Fidelity

The love of Robert and Ann is a sign of Jesus' love for and union with the Church. Through the Sacrament of Matrimony Jesus enables married couples to remain faithful to their wedding promises. Their faithfulness, or fidelity, is symbolized by the rings they give each other. Christian marriage is founded on the sacredness of human life and the family. Children are the supreme gift God offers married people—a sign of their love.

> Before marrying, a person has to ask:
>
> ✤ Am I ready to share my life with another person for life?
> ✤ Am I aware what living with another person day after day really means?
> ✤ Do I really want to have children—with all that raising children involves?

Mission to Love

Throughout their married life, a husband and wife experience the effects of the sacrament. Jesus unites them and their children in a community of life and love. The family participates in the life and mission of Jesus by being king, priest, and prophet. It builds up the Church and upholds the rights of all.

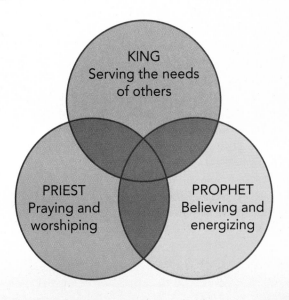

Call to Priesthood and Diaconate

God calls some men through the Church to an ordained ministry of service for the life and growth of the community. Through the Sacrament of Holy Orders, they become deacons, priests, or bishops forever.

A **deacon** assists the bishops and priests in teaching, preaching, celebrating the liturgy, and caring for those in need. Every priest is first a deacon. Some men are called to be permanent deacons. If they are married, they must be at least thirty-five years old.

A **priest** works with the bishop to bring Jesus to the world through word, sacrament, and service. His life is deeply rooted in the Christian community. He is committed to being a leader, a mediator, and a servant in God's family.

A **bishop** is ordained by another bishop with the laying on of hands. As successor to the apostles, he has the fullness of the priesthood. With his brother bishops, he is responsible for the People of God. In addition to exercising his priestly powers, he shepherds the people in a diocese, teaching, sanctifying, and governing them.

A Leader in Proclaiming God's Word

A main role of the priest is *to preach and teach the Gospel.* He helps us understand the teachings of Jesus and the Church. To do this well a priest reflects on the Word of God and studies what the Church teaches. He tries to proclaim the Word by his life as well as by his words.

A Mediator through Sacraments

Jesus was the perfect priest because he was the perfect mediator between God and all people. By Baptism all Christians share in his priesthood (the universal or common priesthood). We can participate in the Eucharist and in other sacraments. But bishops, priests, and deacons have a special share in Christ's priesthood (the ordained priesthood). *The greatest responsibility of a priest is to preside at the Eucharist where we offer Jesus and ourselves to the Father.* The priest also calls us to be reconciled to God and to others, forgives sins, and administers other sacraments.

A Servant of the Church

Jesus ministered to sinners, the sick, the troubled, the poor. He offered his life on the cross out of love. Ordained men have different gifts for different works, but they all minister to us as Jesus did. Some priests are diocesan priests who serve in a diocese under the local bishop. Together these priests and the bishop are responsible for the pastoral care of a diocese. Other priests, like the Jesuits, the Dominicans, and the Franciscans, belong to religious orders. They may serve in a diocese or in the special activities of their order.

An Interview with Father Robb

Sarah and Steve were assigned to report on Holy Orders for religion class. They decided to interview Father Robb.

Sarah: Father, what made you think of becoming a priest?

Father Robb: I knew my parish priest well and helped him out on weekends with yard work when I was in high school. He encouraged me to consider becoming a priest.

Steve: What do you do all day?

Father Robb: You mean when I'm not being interviewed? Let me give you a rundown of yesterday. After 8:00 Mass I was called to the hospital to anoint Grandma Samosa. Before I left the hospital I visited several other parishioners who were patients. When I got to my office, the secretary handed me this list.

MEMO: Father Robb

The publisher of the parish booklet "Year of Faith" is waiting in the living room to show you the manuscript.

The Marriage Encounter Group would like for you to give a talk and then celebrate Mass for them on Monday.

Sister Susan wants you to talk to Brian who's been in a fight again.

Mr. Berg dropped off four chairs for the poor.

Sister Juanita and the liturgy director need to meet with you to plan the Sacrament of Reconciliation for the seventh graders.

Steve (*reads the list, then hands it to Sarah*): Gee, Father, that's a pretty full day!

Father Robb: Right. But that evening when I was praying the Liturgy of the Hours, which every priest prays daily, I recalled the people I had met, consoled, advised, consulted, instructed, and prayed with that day. The thought came to me: how meaningful my vocation is!

Sarah: How do you learn to be a priest?

Father Robb: Men interested in the priesthood go to a **seminary** where they study theology and what it means to be a priest. Other priests help them decide if it is their vocation.

Steve: What happens at ordination?

Father Robb: Here, I have some pictures of my ordination. You see Bishop Wills in the sanctuary. Only a bishop ordains.

Sarah: Father, why are all the men lying on the floor in this picture?

Father Robb: This is **prostration,** Sarah. While the Litany of the Saints is sung, we prostrate as an act of humility and a sign of total acceptance of our call.

Steve: In this shot Bishop Wills has his hands on your head, Father. Is this ordination?

Father Robb: Yes, that is called the **laying on of hands.** By this act, the bishop passes on the power of the priesthood. Then all the priests present lay their hands on the men, too, as a sign of unity and brotherhood. The bishop then prays the consecration prayer.

Sarah: I see you are putting on your vestments in this photo.

Father Robb: Yes. After I vested, the bishop anointed my hands, a sign of consecration to Christ in service.

Steve: The bishop uses **chrism,** doesn't he, Father? That fits because the priest is Christ in a special way, and Sister told us that *Christ* means "anointed one."

Father Robb: After the anointing I received the gifts of bread and wine. I remember thinking how my hands would offer Christ's Body and Blood every day.

Sarah: And every day you're busy offering yourself for others. How can we help you?

Father Robb: Priests need your support and prayers. We want to make Christ's love real to all, but we know our limitations. Both of you are important members of the Church, too. When you use your talents to serve the community, you are supporting me also.

Steve: Thanks for the interview, Father. We have a lot to tell our class.

Call to Religious Life

God calls some people to dedicate their lives to his service as members of religious communities. Religious come from a variety of backgrounds and can be found serving in many different ways and in all parts of the world. But there are certain things that all religious have in common. All are called to be signs of Christ's love and his kingdom in a special way. Their life of **prayer,** which unites them to Christ, enables them to follow him more closely. Their **community life** provides them with the love and support of other religious. Their **vows** free them to love and serve God and others and to belong more completely to him. They share in a particular way in the mission of the Church.

Religious usually make three vows:

✤ **chastity**—being unmarried and chaste for the sake of the kingdom

✤ **poverty**—living a simple lifestyle and giving up control of material possessions

✤ **obedience**—listening to God particularly as he speaks through superiors.

Service in the Church

Name two religious communities in your diocese and tell how they serve Christ in others and bring people to him through the works of mercy. See the list of the works of mercy on page 198.

_____

_____

Get Ready

You probably won't receive a telegram from God telling you your vocation. The process of discovery is slow but can be exciting. To hear God's call, develop the skill of listening.

LISTEN to God.

Pray in quiet. Gradually you will hear God's gentle but persistent call.

LISTEN to yourself.

Find out your likes and dislikes, strengths and weaknesses, hopes and fears.

LISTEN to others.

Talk over your plans for the future with a counselor, coach, parent, priest, or teacher.

LISTEN to the needs of the world.

Choose a need that you want to help fill. Do something now to help fill it.

Prayer to Discover My Life Call

Lord Jesus,
help me to become a good listener.
Show me your plan for my life.
Bind me so close to you in friendship
    that I will be filled with your love.
Then I will bring your love to those
    who are struggling, confused, or
    lonely.
Show me the way I can best use my
    life to serve people in your name.
                Amen.

At this point in my life, God's call that appeals to

me is _____

because _____.

Remember

What is the universal call all Christians have received from God?
All Christians have received the universal call to holiness.

What is meant by a vocation?
A vocation is a call from God to a special way of life in which a person can share Christ's mission and reach holiness.

What is the love between a married couple a sign of?
The love between a married couple is a sign of Christ's love for his Church and his union with it.

What is the mission of bishops, priests, and deacons?
The mission of bishops, priests, and deacons is to give Jesus Christ to the world through word, sacrament, and service.

> I hope you come to find that which gives life a deep meaning . . .

Words to Know

laity	obedience
secular institute	deacon
fidelity	bishop
chastity	priest
poverty	ordination

Respond

The basis for every vocation is the call to be holy, the call to love. In your journal, write the important events of yesterday. Do any of these things show that you are aware of your call to be holy and to love others? Were there specific times when you blocked this call by refusing to pass on God's love to your parents? To your brothers and sisters? To your friends? To others? Read John 13:34 and evaluate how you responded to this message today.

Reach Out

1. Pray daily that you will hear the special life call that God has for you. Pray for your friends, too.
2. Write a newspaper article about the service given by lay Christians, religious, or priests in your parish. Give specific examples to show how they bring Christ to others.
3. List ways that people can be involved in your parish and diocese. Ask your parents to add to the list.
4. Read the life of a founder or foundress of a religious order. Find out the experiences that led him or her to start a religious community. Share your research with the class.
5. With a partner, create a colorful, appealing poster inviting young people to consider entering religious life or becoming a priest or deacon.
6. Interview a priest, perhaps a retired priest, and ask him to share how he experienced God's call to the priesthood and what it has meant to him.
7. Facing conflicts creatively is a way of caring for family members. Make up a short skit on some family conflict. Include a way to solve the problem so that family members grow in unity and love.

Review

Word Scramble   Unscramble the letters of the missing word and write it on the line.

1. God calls all Christians to be _____.

oylh

2. Single people who live in the world under vow belong to _____ _____.

rucleas   utttiissen

3. The _____ is the minister of the Sacrament of Matrimony for the bride.

omgor

4. The marriage vows bind a couple to each other in lifelong _____.

lidityef

5. By the vow of _____ religious promise to remain unmarried and chaste

thiscyat
for the sake of the kingdom.

6. A _____ has the fullness of priesthood.

spoibh

7. An ordained man who assists the bishop and priests is a _____.

noedac

8. A priest's greatest privilege is to preside at the _____.

hsiuEctar

9. The power of priesthood is passed on from a bishop by the laying on of _____.

nasdh

10. At their ordination, priests are anointed with _____.

shimrc

First Letters   Fill in the missing words.

Three things all religious have in common:

1. p_____   **2.** c_____   **3.** v_____

Two things Christian marriage is founded on: the sacredness of

4. h_____   **5.** f_____

Three things a bishop does:

6. t_____   **7.** g_____   **8.** s_____

Three roles of a priest:

9. l_____   **10.** m_____   **11.** s_____

The Mission of All
What must Christians be for the world in whatever vocation they follow? _____

Jesus the Life

When Christ your life appears,
then you too will appear with him in glory.

COLOSSIANS 3:4

Coin Flick

grace 1	raising of Lazarus 5	Liturgy of the Word 1	Last Supper 1	parousia 5	priest 2
virtues 3	Eucharist 2	Paschal Mystery 4	particular judgment 5	sacramental 3	Liturgy of the Eucharist 4
Trans-figuration 4	purgatory 3	Pentecost 3	suffering 2	Ascension 2	Jesus' Passion 2
multi-plication of loaves 2	sacrament 4	vocation 2	Resurrection 2	early Church 5	Sacrament of Matrimony 5
Sacramen-tary 2	Last Judgment 1	bishop 3	fruits of the Spirit 4	deacon 1	transubstan-tiation 3

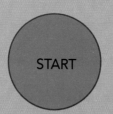

START

Put a coin on START. Flick it with your index finger onto the chart or tell about the words in all the squares the coin touches and win the points in the squares. If the coin lands off the chart, deduct five points. See who can reach 100 points first.

Find the Misfit

Put an *X* on the word in each group that doesn't match the rest. Write how the others are alike.

All are . . .

1. prudence   hope   justice   fortitude   _____

2. Eucharist   Jesus' death   Last Supper   Transfiguration   _____

3. Baptism   death   Resurrection   Ascension   _____

4. memorial   meal   vocation   sacrifice   _____

5. heaven   parousia   Last Judgment   Passover   _____

6. Mary Magdalene   apostle   disciples on way to Emmaus   Judas   _____

7. suffering   speaking in tongues   baptisms   birth of Church community   _____

8. breaking of bread   careers   prayer   possessions in common   _____

9. poverty   chastity   fidelity   obedience   _____

10. teach   sanctify   govern   write   _____

Life Savers

Tell how each of these situations has hurt the community and what can be done to rebuild it.

1. Peggy missed play practice because she was too tired to go.
2. Rick was crabby, so he started an argument during dinner.
3. Tom keeps borrowing money from different members of the class, but never gets around to paying it back.
4. Ellen was fooling around in the classroom with others and accidentally broke the pencil sharpener. The teacher doesn't know who did it.
5. Jessica and her friends wrote a note to one of the girls in the room telling her she was "weird" and they hated her.
6. When Miguel doesn't have enough time to study, his parents write a note to the teacher so he will be excused from tests. Then Miguel asks other students what was on the test so he knows what to study.

Find the Misfit

Looking Back

In the unit *Jesus Christ the Life* you studied the life, death, and resurrection of our Lord. You know that before he ascended into heaven he commanded you to witness to his teachings and to follow the example of his life. He sent the Holy Spirit to strengthen and guide you to love one another and form a community.

Not only have you learned about Jesus' life, but you understand your own life better. You know that Jesus offers you eternal life. Your spiritual life grows through daily prayer, frequent prayerful celebration of the sacraments (especially the Eucharist), reflection on the Scriptures, and the love and support of the faith community, the Church. As a disciple you reach out to serve your family, school, parish, and even the world. You prepare to use your gifts in the vocation to which God calls you. Then, following Jesus' way and living his truth will bring you his life!

As you complete this book, ask yourself three questions:

1. How has *Jesus Christ the Life* helped me become more loving and supportive in my family community, school community, and parish community?
2. How is my life like the life of Jesus in prayer, in helping the poor, and in forgiving others?
3. What practical steps can I take to deepen my friendship with Jesus?

Personal Inventory

Take a close look at your spiritual life. Put a check by the statements that indicate where you have grown.

My Life and God
Do I . . .

❏ pay more attention at Sunday Mass?
❏ celebrate the Sacrament of Reconciliation more frequently?
❏ think of Jesus at times during the day?
❏ really want to be a saint?
❏ have greater self-respect because I believe God loves me?

My Life and Other People
Do I . . .

❏ keep calmer when my parents and I disagree?
❏ talk kindly to people I dislike?
❏ trust my friends more?
❏ have the courage to decide as Jesus would want me to and stick to my decision?
❏ forgive others when they hurt me?

My Life and Situations
Do I . . .

❏ endure normal physical discomfort like hot or cold weather without complaining?
❏ try harder in my school work?
❏ remain content with what I have?
❏ volunteer to help where there is a need?
❏ take care of my health by eating the proper foods, exercising, and getting enough sleep?
❏ admit I make mistakes?
❏ take good care of the earth?

> ### Words to Ponder
> The bread you do not use
>   is the bread of the hungry;
> the garment hanging in your
>   wardrobe is the garment of him
>   who is naked;
> the shoes that you do not wear
>   are the shoes of one who is
>   barefoot;
> the money that you keep locked
>   away is the money of the poor;
> the acts of charity that you do not
>   perform are so many injustices
>   that you commit.
>
> St. Basil

Celebrating Our Journey in Life

Leader: The Father calls to us with love. The glory of the Son shines on us. The love of the Spirit fills us with life. Let us celebrate our journey of life by signing ourselves with the Sign of the Cross, the cross that brought us life.

All: In the name of the Father and of the Son and of the Holy Spirit. Amen.

Leader: Come, faithful pilgrims, and celebrate life.

Song, Procession, and Presentation of Symbols

Leader: Jesus has told us, "I am the Way, and the Truth, and the Life. I have come that you may have life and life to the full." Jesus taught people how to make the pilgrimage to eternal life.

First Reading (John 3:1–5, 16)

Reader 1: A Pharisee named Nicodemus, a leading Jew, came to Jesus at night and said,

Nicodemus: Rabbi, we know that you are a teacher who has come from God; for no one can do these signs that you are doing unless God is with him.

Jesus: Amen, Amen, I say to you no one can see the kingdom of God without being born from above.

Nicodemus: How can a person once grown old be born again?

Jesus: Amen, I say to you no one can enter the kingdom of God without being born of water and Spirit. . . . God so loved the world that he gave his only Son, so that everyone who believes in him might not perish but might have eternal life.

All: You will show me the path of life and guide me to joy forever.

Second Reading (John 4:47–53)

Reader 2: Now there was a royal official whose son was ill at Capernaum. Hearing that Jesus had arrived in Galilee from Judea, he went and asked him to come and cure his son who was near death.

Nobleman: Sir, come down before my child dies.

Jesus: You may go; your son will live.

Reader 2: The man believed what Jesus had said and left. While he was on his way back, his servants met him and told him that his boy would live.

Nobleman: When did my son begin to recover?

Servants: The fever left him yesterday about one in the afternoon.

Nobleman: That was the same time Jesus told me, "Your son will live."

All: You will show me the path of life and guide me to joy forever.

Third Reading (John 4:4–7, 9–11, 13–14)

Reader 3: Jesus came to the Samaritan town of Sychar and Jesus, tired by the journey, sat down by Jacob's well about noon. A Samaritan woman came for water.

Jesus: Give me a drink.

Woman: How can you, a Jew, ask me, a Samaritan woman, for a drink?

Jesus: If you knew the gift of God and who is saying to you, "Give me a drink," you would have asked him and he would have given you living water.

Woman: Sir, you have no bucket, and the well is deep. How could you get this living water?

Jesus: Whoever drinks this water will get thirsty again; but anyone who drinks the water I shall give will never thirst. The water I shall give will become in him a spring welling up to eternal life.

All: You will show me the path of life and guide me to joy forever.

Prayer

Leader: Jesus is with us on our journey. In each sacrament he acts to bring us to fullness of life.

Side 1: In you we have been baptized. We have put on Christ.

All: We are your people, Lord. Make us holy.

Side 2: We have been given the gift of the Spirit. We are to witness to you by lives of faith and love.

All: May we live the Gospel with courage, eager to proclaim the Good News to all.

Side 1: We have been nourished by the one bread and one cup and have been made one in you.

All: We are strengthened in love and promise to serve you, Lord, in one another.

Side 2: You have given us forgiveness and peace.

All: We are ready to change our lives by acts of charity, good example, and prayer.

Side 1: You have healed us. You conquered death and opened for us the way to eternal life.

All: Help us to imitate you, who went about doing good, healing and serving the sick.

Side 2: You have shown us the value of love and faithfulness by blessing marriage.

All: We will try to support our families by generous love and service.

Side 1: You have given us bishops, priests, and deacons to witness to the Gospel and celebrate the sacraments.

All: We pray that they draw close to you. Give many others the grace to devote themselves to your service.

Sign of Peace

Leader: As a sign of Christ's presence among us, let us give the sign of peace.
(*Sign of peace*)

Come, faithful pilgrims, let us continue to travel the path of the Gospel that Jesus has shown. Let us go now to love and serve the Lord.

Song

SUPPLEMENT

Christians Grow: Deepening Family Faith

The Scott family belongs to a family Bible study group. They began it in their neighborhood several years ago, when Father Joe pointed out that the primary place for Christian education is the home. The Scotts took these words to heart and discussed how they could grow in faith together. Realizing that they wanted to know more about the Bible, they decided to start a study group with their friends. They found a program that met their needs. It has a special component for children. Sometimes Father Joe comes to the meetings and talks about the particular book of the Bible they are reading and discussing.

There are other ways the Scotts learn more about Christ. They take advantage of a number of opportunities their parish church offers. They attend lectures and missions. During Lent this year they went to a course on the Church given by a visiting priest.

Sometimes Mr. or Mrs. Scott participates in a weekend retreat or in a day of recollection at a local spirituality center. The Scotts also get involved with parish programs and organizations. This puts their faith into action and makes it stronger.

From the time the Scott children were small, they have heard the stories of Jesus and the saints. Their parents have read books to them. The family also gets videos about the faith and views them together while enjoying a snack. The last one they saw was about the Holy Land. The Scotts subscribe to the diocesan newspaper and occasionally tune in to a Catholic station on the TV or radio.

You might wish to enrich your family's knowledge of the faith and practice of it by any of the means noted on this page. The more you know about our faith, the more you will want to know.

Advent: Jesus Comes

All kinds of comings brighten our lives: Santa's coming, Uncle Bob's coming, a plane's coming, a vacation's coming. Think of a time you waited for a special person to come. How did you feel?

_____

Every year for four weeks the Church celebrates the coming of God to Earth. This time is called **Advent,** which means "coming." During Advent we

✢ remember Jesus' coming in _history,_
✢ prepare for his coming in _mystery,_ and
✢ hope for his coming in _majesty._

Symbols of Comings

You are probably familiar with these Christian symbols for Christ:

Certain symbols remind us of the comings of Christ. Look up the Scripture references in the first and third columns and write the names of the symbols on the lines.

History	Mystery	Majesty
John 9:5		Rev. 22:13
_____	Bread and wine, wheat, grapes	_____
John 10:7		Rev. 1:5–6
_____	Shell, water	_____
Matthew 21:5–9		Rev. 1:17
_____	Cross	_____
John 19:18–19		Rev. 1:20
_____	Lectionary, Bible	_____
		Rev. 5:6
How will you prepare for his comings?		_____
_____		

Our Lenten Journey

Jesus' journey led to Jerusalem and death before he tasted the victory of the Resurrection. Each year we recall his journey of sorrow during the season of **Lent.** During Lent we are on a journey, too, moving closer toward our final destination.

Our Lenten journey has much in common with a family excursion. Complete the chart below, using the Scripture references to help you.

A Family Excursion	**Our Lenten Journey**
Discussion with family	**Discussion (Matthew 6:5–6)**
destination or goal	_____
length of trip	_____
route or plan	_____
side trips and stopovers	_____
Preparation	**Preparation (Matthew 6:1–4)**
light packing	_____
car check-up	_____
Journey	**Journey (Matthew 6:16–18)**
observing speed limits	_____
obeying traffic signs and signals	_____
following a map	_____
	_____

Pillars of the Spiritual Life

Write one example of something you could do during Lent in each of these categories:

prayer _____

almsgiving _____

fasting _____

Leader: God, come to my assistance.

All: Lord, make haste to help me.

Leader: Glory to the Father, and to the Son, and to the Holy Spirit:

All: As it was in the beginning, is now, and will be forever. Amen. Alleluia.

Song

Leader: Jesus said: Do not be afraid. Go and tell my brothers to set out for Galilee; there they will see me. Alleluia.

(Alleluias may be sung.)

Side 1: Alleluia. Salvation, glory, and power to our God: his judgments are honest and true.

Side 2: Alleluia. Sing praise to our God, all you his servants, all who worship him reverently, great and small.

Side 1: Alleluia. The Lord our all-powerful God is King; let us rejoice, sing praise, and give him glory.

Side 2: Alleluia. The wedding feast of the Lamb has begun, and his bride is prepared to welcome him.

Side 1: Glory to the Father, and to the Son, and to the Holy Spirit:

Side 2: As it was in the beginning, is now, and will be forever. Amen.

Reader: A reading from Acts of the Apostles 10:40–43. *(Passage is read.)*

All: This is the day the Lord has made; let us rejoice and be glad, alleluia.

Leader: With joy in our hearts, let us call upon Christ the Lord, who died and rose again, and lives always to intercede for us:

All: Victorious King, hear our prayer.

Leader: Light and salvation of all peoples, send into our hearts the fire of your Spirit, as we proclaim your resurrection.

All: Victorious King, hear our prayer.

Leader: Let Israel recognize in you her longed-for Messiah, and the whole earth be filled with the knowledge of your glory.

All: Victorious King, hear our prayer.

Leader: You have triumphed over death, your enemy; destroy in us the power of death, that we may live only for you, victorious and immortal Lord.

All: Victorious King, hear our prayer.

Leader: We pattern our prayer on the prayer of Christ our Lord and say:

All: Our Father . . .

Leader: God our Father,
by raising Christ your Son
you conquered the power of death
and opened for us the way to eternal life.
Let our celebration today raise us up and renew our lives
by the Spirit that is within us.
Grant this through our Lord Jesus Christ, your Son,
who lives and reigns with you and the Holy Spirit,
one God, for ever and ever.
    (from the *Liturgy of the Hours*)

All: Amen.

Leader: Go in peace. Alleluia, alleluia.

All: Thanks be to God. Alleluia, alleluia.

Song

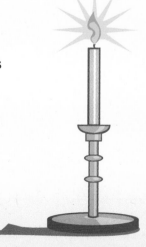

SACRAMENTS OF INITIATION

	BAPTISM	CONFIRMATION	EUCHARIST
Minister	Priest Deacon (in emergency, anyone)	Bishop Abbot (by delegation) Priest (by delegation)	For consecration: Bishop or priest For distributing: Bishop, priest, deacon, acolyte (in need, extraordinary minister)

Recipient	In general:
	  Any unbaptized person
	In particular:
	  Infants or persons not yet at the age of reason
	  Adults and those of the age of reason who desire baptism and are properly disposed
		Roman rite: Baptized persons not yet confirmed who are of the age of reason and wish to be confirmed	Baptized persons in the state of grace who are of the age of reason, believe in the Real Presence, and are properly disposed

Essentials of the Rite	Pouring of water or immersion into water with the words: "(Name), I baptize you in the name of the Father, and of the Son, and of the Holy Spirit."	Laying on of the hand and anointing with chrism on the forehead with the words: "(Name), be sealed with the gift of the Holy Spirit."	Changing bread and wine into the Body and Blood of Christ by the words: "Take this, all of you, and eat it: this is my body which will be given up for you . . . Take this, all of you, and drink from it: this is the cup of my blood of the new and everlasting covenant. It will be shed for you and for all so that sins may be forgiven. Do this in memory of me."
Effects	• cleanses the soul of sin: original and personal • makes one a child of God with the right to heaven • incorporates one into the faith community (Church) • bestows the gifts of the Holy Spirit • gives a share in God's life (sanctifying grace), in faith, hope, and love • indelibly marks the person • admits one into Christ's roles of priest, prophet, and king	• seals and strengthens one's baptismal call • indelibly marks the person • enables one to be more like Christ the Priest, Prophet, King (magnifies) • empowers one to witness to Christ courageously • strengthens one to serve others and to share the faith with them • makes one a more committed member of the Church	• nourishes the life of grace • deepens our union with Christ and through him with the Father and the Holy Spirit and with all the members of Christ • obtains forgiveness of venial sin and enables one to reach out in forgiveness to others • increases love for other people, impelling one to serve them and to share the Gospel with them
Some Responsibilities	• respond to the vocation to holiness, to live a life of love and loyalty to Jesus • reject Satan and sin • follow the teachings of Christ and his Church • participate in the liturgical and the sacramental life of the Church • serve others by sharing the faith and witnessing to it	• grow in faith and witness courageously to the Gospel • develop the ability to lead others to Christ • be willing to suffer for Christ and his Church • participate wholeheartedly in spreading God's kingdom	• celebrate the Eucharist for every Sunday and holy day of obligation • receive Holy Communion at each Mass • show devotion to Jesus in the Eucharist • grow in love for Christ and one another • sacrifice self in service to God and to others

SACRAMENTS OF HEALING		SACRAMENTS OF VOCATION	
RECONCILIATION/ PENANCE	**ANOINTING OF THE SICK**	**MARRIAGE**	**HOLY ORDERS**
Bishop Priest	Bishop Priest	Bride and groom (A priest or deacon is a witness in the name of the Church.)	Bishop
Baptized persons who have committed sin and are sincerely sorry for having offended God	Baptized persons whose health is seriously impaired by sickness or old age	Any man and woman who are baptized, are free to marry, and willingly enter into a life-long marriage agreement	Mature males who have completed Christian initiation and meet the age requirement, who knowingly and willingly wish to be ordained, and who have been accepted as candidates by the authority
Contrition, confession, act of penance, plus the words of absolution: "God the Father of mercies, through the death and resurrection of his Son has reconciled the world to himself and sent the Holy Spirit among us for the forgiveness of sins; through the ministry of the Church may God give you pardon and peace, and I absolve you from your sins in the name of the Father, and of the Son,† and of the Holy Spirit."	Anointing of the forehead and hands with the oil of the sick and the prayer: "Through this holy anointing may the Lord in his love and mercy help you with the grace of the Holy Spirit." "Amen." "May the Lord who frees you from sin save you and raise you up." "Amen."	The marriage covenant of the bride and groom consenting to give themselves permanently to each other in the presence of the priest (deacon) and the Church community	Laying on of hands and the words of the consecrating prayer
• forgives sin • reconciles one with God and the community • increases grace and the virtue of charity • increases self-knowledge and strengthens the will	• provides the grace of the Holy Spirit • encourages trust in God • gives strength to resist temptation and anxiety over death • gives patience and strength to bear suffering and fight against it • sometimes restores physical health • forgives sin and fulfills penance	• increases friendship with God (the grace life) • entitles the married couple to special graces that enable them to fulfill their duties • unites husband and wife with each other in Christ indissolubly • makes the couple a sign of God's love for his people	• increases friendship with God (the grace life) • confers the special powers of the order received: the diaconate, the priesthood, or the episcopate • indelibly marks the person • gives special graces, enabling the recipient to lead, teach, and sanctify the people
• celebrate the Sacrament of Penance regularly • be a reconciler in the faith community • strive for greater holiness by conversion of life	• accept suffering in patience and joy in union with Christ • look toward eternity with hope in God's mercy • suffer for the Church on Earth and for the souls in purgatory	• grow in love, care, and willingness to suffer for each other • share a common life • grow in faith and practice the works of mercy • provide for the physical, social, cultural, moral, and religious upbringing of their children • give an example of unselfish love	• Deacon: baptize, give Communion, bless marriages, conduct funeral services, minister to the needy • Priest: be a spiritual leader, celebrate the Eucharist, forgive sins, celebrate other sacraments, preach • Bishop: provide pastoral teaching, fulfill priestly duties, ordain priests, lead diocese

The Ten Commandments

1. I, the Lord, am your God. You shall not have other gods besides me.
2. You shall not take the name of the Lord, your God, in vain.
3. Remember to keep holy the Sabbath day.
4. Honor your father and your mother.
5. You shall not kill.
6. You shall not commit adultery.
7. You shall not steal.
8. You shall not bear false witness against your neighbor.
9. You shall not covet your neighbor's wife.
10. You shall not covet anything that belongs to your neighbor.

Precepts of the Church
(Duties of a Catholic Christian)

1. To keep holy the day of the Lord's resurrection (Sunday). To worship God by participating in Mass for every Sunday and holy day of obligation. To avoid those activities (like needless work) that would hinder worship, joy, or relaxation.
2. To lead a sacramental life. To receive Holy Communion frequently and the Sacrament of Reconciliation regularly.
3. To study Catholic teachings in preparation for the Sacrament of Confirmation, to be confirmed, and then to continue to study and advance the cause of Christ.
4. To observe the marriage laws of the Church. To give religious training, by word and example, to one's children. To use parish schools and catechetical programs.
5. To strengthen and support the Church—one's own parish community and parish priests, the worldwide Church, and the pope.
6. To do penance, including abstaining from meat and fasting from food on the days appointed.
7. To join in the missionary spirit and apostolate of the Church.

Days of Fast (for adults)

Ash Wednesday   Good Friday

Days of Abstinence (for all those over age 14)

Ash Wednesday   All Fridays in Lent

Holy Days of Obligation in the United States

Solemnity of Mary, Mother of God: January 1
We honor Mary, Mother of God.

Ascension: Fortieth day after Easter
Jesus ascended into heaven.

Assumption: August 15
Mary was taken into heaven, body and soul.

All Saints' Day: November 1
We honor all the saints in heaven.

Immaculate Conception: December 8
Mary was free from sin from the first moment of her life.

Christmas: December 25
We celebrate the birth of Jesus.

The Seven Sacraments

Baptism, Confirmation, Eucharist, Reconciliation (Penance), Anointing of the Sick, Matrimony, Holy Orders

Corporal Works of Mercy

Feed the hungry
Give drink to the thirsty
Clothe the naked
Visit the sick
Shelter the homeless
Visit the imprisoned
Bury the dead

Spiritual Works of Mercy

Warn the sinner
Instruct the ignorant
Counsel the doubtful
Comfort the sorrowing
Bear wrongs patiently
Forgive all injuries
Pray for the living and the dead

The Theological Virtues

faith, hope, love (charity)

The Cardinal Virtues

prudence, temperance, justice, fortitude

The Beatitudes (Matthew 5:3–10)

Blessed are the poor in spirit,
    for theirs is the kingdom of heaven.
Blessed are they who mourn,
    for they will be comforted.
Blessed are the meek,
    for they will inherit the land.
Blessed are they who hunger and thirst for
      righteousness,
    for they will be satisfied.
Blessed are the merciful,
    for they will be shown mercy.
Blessed are the clean of heart,
    for they will see God.
Blessed are the peacemakers,
    for they will be called children of God.
Blessed are they who are persecuted for
      the sake of righteousness,
    for theirs is the kingdom of heaven.

The Way of the Cross

I. Jesus is condemned to death on the cross.
II. Jesus accepts his cross.
III. Jesus falls the first time.
IV. Jesus meets his sorrowful mother.
V. Simon of Cyrene helps Jesus carry his cross.
VI. Veronica wipes the face of Jesus.
VII. Jesus falls the second time.
VIII. Jesus meets and speaks to the women of Jerusalem.
IX. Jesus falls the third time.
X. Jesus is stripped of his garments.
XI. Jesus is nailed to the cross.
XII. Jesus dies on the cross.
XIII. Jesus is taken down from the cross and laid in his mother's arms.
XIV. Jesus is placed in the tomb.
XV. Jesus rises from the dead.

Gifts of the Holy Spirit

wisdom, understanding, right judgment (counsel), courage, knowledge, reverence (piety), wonder and awe (fear of the Lord)

Fruits of the Holy Spirit

charity	benignity	faith
joy	goodness	modesty
peace	longanimity	continency
patience	mildness	chastity

The Mysteries of the Rosary

Joyful Mysteries
The Annunciation
The Visitation
The Nativity
The Presentation in the Temple
The Finding of Jesus in the Temple

Sorrowful Mysteries
The Agony in the Garden
The Scourging at the Pillar
The Crowning with Thorns
The Carrying of the Cross
The Crucifixion and Death of Jesus

Glorious Mysteries
The Resurrection
The Ascension
The Descent of the Holy Spirit
The Assumption of Mary
The Crowning of Mary as Queen of Heaven
    and Earth

The Divine Praises

Blessed be God.
Blessed be his holy name.
Blessed be Jesus Christ, true God and true man.
Blessed be the name of Jesus.
Blessed be his most Sacred Heart.
Blessed be his most Precious Blood.
Blessed be Jesus in the most Holy Sacrament
    of the Altar.
Blessed be the Holy Spirit, the Paraclete.
Blessed be the great Mother of God, Mary
    most holy.
Blessed be her holy and Immaculate Conception.
Blessed be her glorious Assumption.
Blessed be the name of Mary, Virgin and Mother.
Blessed be St. Joseph, her most chaste spouse.
Blessed be God in his angels and in his saints.

GLOSSARY

Pronunciation Key

a	h*a*llow	**ie**	l*ie*, sk*y*	**uh**	r*u*t, A*s*cen*sio*n, hom*i*ly	**kw**	*qu*it, *qu*arrel
ah	f*a*ther	**o**	l*o*t			**s**	*s*tart, pre*ss*, *c*ent
aw	str*aw*, bef*o*re	**oh**	*ow*n, l*oa*n, l*o*ne	**oo**	s*oo*n, allel*ui*a	**sh**	A*s*cen*s*ion, sta*ti*on
ay	m*ay*, tr*a*de	**ow**	c*ow*, h*ou*se	**yoo**	m*u*sic, b*eau*ty	**th**	*th*is, for*th*
e	p*e*t, f*ai*r, f*e*rret	**oy**	b*oy*, b*oi*l	**g**	*g*et	**z**	*z*oo, i*s*
ee	s*ee*n, sc*e*ne	**u**	f*u*ll, g*oo*d	**j**	*j*uice, e*dg*e	**zh**	mea*s*ure, vi*s*ion
i	h*i*t			**k**	*k*itten, *c*at		

A

Abortion (uh BOR shun): The deliberate killing of the fetus, the developing baby, before birth. Direct abortion is seriously wrong.

Absolution (ab suh LOO shun): Forgiveness or pardon for sin. In the Sacrament of Reconciliation, the priest acts with God's power to give absolution.

Acts of the Apostles: The book of the New Testament that describes how the Good News was proclaimed to the nations, how the Church grew under the guidance of the Holy Spirit, and how Peter, Paul, and the other disciples formed Christian communities after Jesus' Ascension. Acts is probably part two of Luke's Gospel.

Adultery (uh DUL tur ee): The act of being sexually unfaithful to one's husband or wife.

Ageism (AYJ ism): Prejudice against older people.

Annunciation (uh NUN see AY shun): Mary receives her call to be the Mother of God's Son, and the conception of Jesus within Mary takes place.

Anointing of the Sick: A sacrament in which a Christian whose health is seriously impaired by sickness or old age is anointed with holy oil. Immediate danger of death is not necessary. One of the sacraments of healing that always gives spiritual strength and at times restores physical health.

Apocalypse (uh POK uh lips): Another name for the Book of Revelation; the last book of the New Testament; a book that uses many symbols to tell how God is overcoming evil. It was written to encourage those who suffer to trust in God's promises.

Apostle (uh POS l): A word meaning "one sent." It is used most often to refer to the Twelve who were close to Jesus and specially chosen to preach the Good News of the risen Lord. The twelve apostles symbolize the New Israel, the Church.

Aramaic (air uh MAY ik): The language Jesus spoke.

Ascension (uh SEN shun): Jesus' returning to his Father in heaven forty days after his Resurrection. It is the final glorification of Jesus seated at the right hand of the Father.

Assumption (uh SUMP shun): The Catholic doctrine that Mary was assumed into heaven body and soul at the end of her life.

B

Baptism (BAP tiz um): The first sacrament through which one becomes a member of the Body of Christ, the Church, is cleansed of all sin by rebirth in Christ, and receives grace, God's life; the first sacrament of initiation.

Beatitudes (bee AT ih toods): In Matthew's Gospel a set of guidelines for Christlike living that will make us happy and lead us to eternal life. In each Beatitude a value is paired with a promise.

Bishop (BISH up): An ordained priest appointed by the pope who has received the fullness of Christ's priesthood through the prayers and the imposition of a consecrating bishop's hands; a successor of the apostles whose sphere of authority is called a diocese.

Blasphemy (BLAS fuh mee): Mocking or hateful speech concerning God. Blasphemy may include insulting or making fun of sacred persons or things.

Book of Revelation: The last book of the Bible; also called Apocalypse.

C

Cardinal virtues: The four main or "hinge" virtues that direct right living: prudence, justice, temperance, and fortitude.

Catechumen (kat uh KYOO mun): One who is in the second stage of the Rite of Christian Initiation of Adults, the catechumenate; one who is studying the teachings of the Gospel and of the Catholic Church in preparation for the sacraments of initiation.

Charity: A virtue or power by which a person loves God above all and loves other people for God's sake.

Chastity (CHAS tuh tee): A virtue or habit that helps us control the desire for sexual pleasure according to God's law; the virtue of those who keep the sixth and ninth commandments.

Christ: The title for Jesus, from the Greek word meaning "anointed" or "the anointed of God." The Hebrew word for Christ is *Messiah.*

Communion (kuh MYOON yun): The sharing of a deep and intimate unity; the reception of the Holy Eucharist; the Blessed Sacrament.

Community: A group of people who share the same beliefs, live together under the same authority, and work to benefit both their own members and others. The members of a Christian community are bonded by their love for Christ and for one another, and by their service to the world under the guidance of the Holy Spirit.

Compassion: Pity or sympathy for those who suffer in any way, with the desire to relieve their pain or to suffer in their place.

Confession (con FES shun): Telling sins to a priest in the Sacrament of Reconciliation for the purpose of receiving absolution and forgiveness from God.

Confirmation: A sacrament in which a baptized Christian receives a special outpouring of the Holy Spirit through the prayers, the imposition of hands, and the anointing with chrism by a bishop or his delegate; one of the sacraments of initiation.

Contrition (kun TRI shun): True sorrow for sin with the intention not to sin again. Contrition means to be sorry and ready to change and model one's life on Jesus.

Covenant (KUV uh nunt): A solemn, binding agreement between two or more persons.

Covet (KUV it): To desire enviously what belongs to another; to want to take.

Creed: A profession of faith.

D

Deacon (DEE kun): One ordained for the Church's ministry of service. A candidate for the priesthood is a temporary deacon; other deacons are permanent deacons.

Death: The passage or journey from one form of life to eternal life; the separation of the soul from the body. Death, the consequence of original sin, is not final for us. Through Jesus' Resurrection we too rise again, soul and body, to enjoy eternal life.

Despair (dih SPAIR): To lose hope in God, to give up hoping that it is possible to be saved. Despair is a distrust of God's mercy and goodness.

Disciple (dih SY pel): A word meaning one who has learned or been taught. The disciples were dedicated followers of Jesus.

Discourse (DIS kors): A long speech.

Doctrine (DOK trin): A truth taught by the Church.

Dogma: A truth or doctrine that has been revealed in Scripture or Tradition and defined by the Church as an article of faith for Catholics to believe.

E

Easter Triduum (TRID oo um): The liturgical time during which we celebrate the Paschal Mystery; the three days that begin with the Mass of the Lord's Supper on Holy Thursday and end on Easter Sunday evening.

Elect: One who has completed the catechumenate and is ready to enter the Lenten period of intense preparation for the sacraments of initiation.

Envy: Sadness at another's success, talent, possessions, good fortune, etc. Envy is a sin against charity.

Epiphany (ee PIF uh nee): A revelation or manifestation of God.

Epistle (ee PIS el): Letters in the New Testament, most of them by St. Paul, originally sent to communities or individuals. They tell how Christians can apply the message of Jesus to daily life. There are twenty-one epistles in the New Testament.

Essenes (eh SEENZ): Men who usually lived in desert communities in order to live a pure life, doing penance and waiting for the coming of God.

Eternal life: The life of perfect happiness promised by Christ to those who believe in him and live according to his teachings; a sharing in the life of God that lasts forever.

Eucharist (YOO kuh rist): The sacrament in which the Paschal Mystery of Jesus is called to mind and made present under the appearances of bread and wine. We offer Jesus with ourselves to the Father and are united through eucharistic communion with Jesus, with the Father and Holy Spirit, and with one another. It is one of the sacraments of initiation.

Euthanasia (yoo thuh NAY zhuh): The act or practice of putting people to death because they or others decide it will avoid pain or relieve others of the burden of caring for them. The word itself means "easy death."

Evangelist (ih VAN jul ist): Title given to Matthew, Mark, Luke, and John, the four Gospel writers; the word comes from the Greek word for "good news."

Evangelize (ih VAN juh lyz): To proclaim the Good News of Jesus to persons, especially for the first time.

F

Faith: As a virtue, the power of the mind to accept as true all that God has revealed; as an act, the conscious assent of the mind to what God has revealed. Faith is a free gift of God by which we believe and trust him.

Fidelity (fih DEL ih tee): Faithfulness to vows or obligations; loyalty based on strong affection.

Fortitude (FOR tuh tood): Moral courage; the cardinal virtue by which a person does what is good and right in spite of difficulties.

G

Galilee (GAL uh lee): The northern part of Palestine; the region where Jesus spent most of his public life.

Gentile (JEN tyle): Name given by the Jewish people to those who are not Jewish.

Gospel: The Good News that Jesus has saved us from the power of sin; the four New Testament books that tell us of the life, death, resurrection, and ascension of Jesus.

Grace: A free gift of God that enables us to share in his life and friendship on Earth and enjoy him forever in heaven; an inspiration and empowerment to do good.

Greed: Too great a desire for wealth, possessions, power, etc.

H

Heaven: The state of eternal happiness in which those who have loved unselfishly, as Jesus did, will see God face to face and be united with him; they will know, love, and enjoy God and others.

Hell: The state of eternal punishment and isolation for those who have freely and deliberately cut themselves off from God.

Hope: The power to desire the gift of eternal life and to know that God will provide the necessary help along the way to his kingdom; confidence in God.

Holy Orders: The sacrament in which men are ordained to receive the powers of Christ's priesthood by the imposition of the bishop's hands, by the anointing with chrism, and by the bishop's prayers. It also includes the diaconate and the episcopate. It is one of the sacraments of vocation.

I

Immaculate Conception (ih MAK yoo let cun SEP shun): The Catholic doctrine that at the time of her conception Mary was preserved from all sin, including original sin.

Incarnation (in kar NAY shun): The mystery of God becoming human.

Infancy narratives (IN fan see NAIR uh tivz): Stories about Jesus' birth and early life in the Gospels of Matthew and Luke.

Inquirer (in KWY ur ur): One who is in the first stage of the Rite of Christian Initiation of Adults, the precatechumenate; one who is interested in learning and studying about the Catholic faith.

Inspiration (in spuh RAY shun): The action of God moving the human authors of the Bible to communicate what he wanted made known.

J

Jesus: A name meaning "God saves" or "God is salvation"; the man from Palestine who is the Son of God and who redeemed the world.

Journal: A private notebook for written reflection to deepen a personal relationship with God.

Judea (ju DEE ah): Southern region of Palestine, the country where Jesus lived; a hot, dry territory including the Dead Sea, a wilderness, and the capital city Jerusalem with the Temple as the center of Jewish religion.

Justice: Fairness; the determination to give everyone what he or she deserves. Justice is one of the cardinal virtues that urges us to respect and protect the rights of all.

K

King: One who has highest power and authority in a kingdom.

L

Laity (LAY ih tee): All the faithful people of God who are not ordained and do not belong to the religious state; strictly speaking, all nonordained including nonordained religious.

Last Judgment: The revelation of the eternal destiny of every human person and humankind at the parousia. This judgment will be based on love of God and neighbor and on openness to the Good News.

Letters: Books in the New Testament that are mostly letters from St. Paul to early Christian communities and individuals that apply the message of Jesus to daily life; also called epistles.

Liturgy of the Eucharist (LIT ur jee of the YOO kuh rist): The second part of the Eucharist, in which we offer Jesus and ourselves to the Father, the bread and wine become Jesus, and we receive him in Communion.

Liturgy of the Word: The first part of the Eucharist, in which we hear and respond to the Word of God.

M

Magisterium (maj ih STAIR ee um): The teaching authority of the Church.

Marriage/Matrimony (MAT rih mo nee): The permanent, sacramental union of a man and woman who freely consent to a lasting covenant that promises total fidelity; sacrament that raises the natural union to become a permanent sign of the union between Christ and the Church; one of the sacraments of vocation.

Mercy killing: Another word for euthanasia.

Messiah (meh SY uh): The Hebrew word for "anointed one." The Greek word is *Christos.* The Messiah is the one promised by God to deliver all people from sin. The Messiah would bring peace, salvation, and happiness. Jesus is the Messiah promised in the Old Testament.

Miracle: An act of divine power, a wonder outside the laws of nature through which God gives a sign to his people.

Mission: The work of spreading the kingdom of God throughout the world.

Missionary: One who preaches the Gospel and leads others to friendship with Christ.

Modesty: A virtue that helps us choose appropriate dress and behavior so as not to call attention to one's sex or oneself.

Moral virtues: Good habits of right living or behavior.

Mortal sin: Serious offenses against God that destroy our friendship with him and cause us to lose grace and eternal life.

Mystagogy (MIS tuh GO jee): Postbaptismal catechesis; the last stage of the Rite of Christian Initiation of Adults. Christians in this stage grow in their relationship to Christ and to the Church community by sharing in the life and faith of Church members.

Mystical Body of Christ: The members of the Church united with the risen Christ as their head.

N

Nativity (nuh TIV ih tee): The birth of Jesus.

Natural law: The unchanging, immutable law written in the hearts of human beings. It flows from our participation in God's wisdom and goodness because we are made in God's image. Natural law expresses our dignity and forms the basis of our rights and duties. It is the foundation for moral rules and civil law.

New Testament: Twenty-seven books that form the second part of the Bible. The books are arranged according to the kind of writing (Gospels, Acts, Letters, Book of Revelation). The New Testament was originally written in the first century in Greek and Aramaic by authors writing under God's inspiration.

O

Obedience: Vow of religious to listen to God, particularly as God speaks through superiors.

Ordination (or din AY shun): The rite by which men become bishops, priests, and deacons.

Original sin: The first sin or the sin of Adam, who, as the head of the human race, offended God and thereby lost the right to heaven for himself and his posterity. Original sin is also the absence of sanctifying grace that we inherit from Adam when we enter the world.

P

Palestine (PAL uh styn): The Middle East land where Jesus lived.

Parable: A story that teaches about God and the kingdom of God through everyday experiences.

Parousia (par oo SEE uh, or, peh ROO zee uh): The second coming of Christ in glory, marking the completion of salvation history, when God's plan of salvation will be revealed. At the parousia, God's kingdom will come to perfection, the world as we know it will end, and the eternal destiny of every person will be revealed.

Particular judgment: The moment after death when a person realizes how much he or she has, or has not, become like Christ. Then, based on that degree of likeness, the person will learn how he or she does, or does not, fit into God's kingdom of love.

Paschal Mystery (PAS kuhl): The passion, death, resurrection, and ascension of Jesus; the whole redemptive work of Christ, especially the events from the Last Supper to Easter.

Passion: Suffering; the events surrounding the suffering and death of Jesus Christ.

Passion narrative: The record of the events surrounding the suffering and death of Jesus as found in the four Gospels.

Passover: The Jewish feast commemorating, with a religious meal, God's saving action of leading the Israelites from slavery in Egypt to the Promised Land.

Penance (PEN ans): A prayer, act of self-denial, or work of charity that makes up for damage or pain caused by sins and that helps overcome sin.

Pentecost (PEN tuh kost): The day the Holy Spirit descended upon the disciples and the Church was born as a society; originally a Jewish harvest feast.

Perseverance (pur suh VEER uns): The virtue of holding firmly to a belief or way of acting even when it is difficult to do so.

Pharisees (FAIR uh sees): An active religious Jewish group in the centuries before and after Christ appeared on Earth. Some schools of Pharisees emphasized strict obedience to the Law and legal aspects of religion. In the Gospels they are mostly represented as harsh and hostile to Jesus.

Poverty: Vow of religious to live a simple lifestyle and to give up control of material possessions.

Presentation: Jesus' being offered by Mary and Joseph to God in the Temple in keeping with Jewish law.

Presumption (pre ZUMP shun): To expect God automatically to give a person all he or she hopes for or desires, even though he or she does not cooperate with the graces and helps God has provided.

Priest: One ordained by the imposition of a bishop's hands and the consecrating prayers to serve in the Church's ministry, primarily by presiding at the eucharistic sacrifice and forgiving sins, preaching the Word of God, working with the bishop, and being a spiritual leader of the community.

Prophet: One who hears God's word and proclaims it; one who communicates a divine revelation.

Prudence (PROOD uns): Correct knowledge about what ought to be done and what should be avoided. Prudence is one of the cardinal virtues by which a person thinks before acting, makes wise choices, and follows through on decisions.

Purgatory (PUR guh TOR ee): The purification after death that transforms persons for the kingdom who are not yet perfect in love.

Q

"Q": An unknown source from which the writers of Matthew and Luke probably drew their material.

R

Racism (RAY cizm): Regarding a particular race as inferior.

Reconciliation (REK un sil ee AY shun): The restoring of a friendship through the asking for and receiving of forgiveness.

Reconciliation/Penance: The sacrament in which a repentant person has the guilt of sins committed after baptism removed by the Church through absolution spoken by the priest in Christ's name. In the sacrament, a Christian's love relationship with God is restored by sorrow and confession after having been damaged or destroyed by sin. It is one of the sacraments of healing.

Restitution (res tuh TOO shun): The act of repairing damage caused or returning to its rightful owner whatever had been unjustly taken from that person.

Resurrection (rez uh REK shun): The rising from the dead of Christ on the third day after his death and burial. The Resurrection is the victorious completion of our redemption.

Risen Jesus: The same Jesus of Nazareth, but a Jesus now glorified.

Rite: The words and actions used in a liturgical, religious ceremony. There are three rites for the Sacrament of Reconciliation.

Rite of Christian Initiation of Adults: The process that leads a non-Christian adult to full communion with the Catholic Church; abbreviated RCIA. It has four stages: evangelization and precatechumenate, catechumenate, purification and enlightenment, and postbaptismal catechesis or mystagogy.

S

Sacrament (SAK ruh ment): An outward sign of an inward grace instituted by Christ in which we encounter him at key points in our journey of life and grow in grace.

Sacramental (SAK ruh MEN tul): Objects, words, or actions that are sacred signs given by the Church that can make us holy by the prayers of the Church and by the way in which we use them.

Sacramentary (SAK ruh MEN tuh ree): The Church's official book that contains the prayers and directives for celebrating the eucharistic liturgy.

Sadducees (SAD yoo seez): A small group of wealthy and powerful political leaders, mostly priests, who worked closely with Rome and, unlike the Pharisees, did not believe in resurrection and in adding to the law.

Salvation history: The story of God's love for his people that tells how God entered into history and carried out a plan to save all people.

Samaria (sa MER ee uh): Central region of Palestine avoided by Jews. The Samaritans were considered heretics for intermarrying with foreigners and worshiping at their own temple on Mount Gerizim instead of in Jerusalem.

Sanctifying grace (SANK tih FY ing): Divine life; God dwelling within us to make us holy.

Sanhedrin (san HE drin): A group of seventy-one Jewish men in Judea who served as a supreme council with the chief high priest presiding.

Scandal (SKAN dul): Bad example that is likely to lead another person to sin. Scandal may be an act or an omission.

Scribes (SCRYBES): Well-educated Jewish people who studied, interpreted, and taught the law. Sometimes they were referred to as lawyers or rabbis. They were dedicated to defending and preserving the law.

Scripture (SKRIP chur): Sacred writings containing God's revelation. For Christians the Bible includes the Old Testament (Hebrew Scriptures) and the New Testament.

Secular institute (SEK yoo ler IN stih toot): A society of lay men and women and clergy who are consecrated by private vows of poverty, chastity, and obedience, but who retain their careers and social activities and do not live in community. They carry out apostolic works in their everyday lives.

Sermon on the Mount: A collection of some of the sayings and teachings of Jesus recorded in the Gospel of Matthew, chapters 5–7. The Sermon outlines the kind of life a follower of Christ lives if he or she seeks the kingdom of God.

Sexism: Treating members of a certain sex unfairly.

Shema (sheh MAH or SHEH mah): The main commandment for Jews, prayed twice daily: "Hear, O Israel! The LORD is our God, the LORD alone! Therefore, you shall love the LORD, your God, with all your heart, and with all your soul, and with all your strength." (Deuteronomy 6:4–5).

Social sin: An evil situation that harms people, especially the poor and minorities, and is opposed to the will of Christ. Christians must resist it and promote justice and respect.

Spiritual life: The life of grace, a life that is above our natural life and goes beyond the measure of space and time. The spiritual life is a life of friendship with God, a living of the Christ-life.

Sponsor (SPON ser): The person who assists the catechumen in the journey of faith.

Suicide: The deliberate taking of one's own life.

Synoptic (sin OP tik): Means same view; refers to the Gospels of Matthew, Mark, and Luke.

Synoptic Gospels: The name given to the first three Gospels (Matthew, Mark, Luke) because they basically present the "same view" of the life, death, and Resurrection of Jesus.

T

Temperance (TEM pur uns): The cardinal virtue by which one controls the desire for pleasure; moderation in eating, drinking, behavior, etc.

Temptation: Any person or thing that entices us to do what is evil or to omit doing what is good.

Theological virtues (thee uh LOJ i kuhl): Special powers from God, given us at Baptism and centered on him: faith, hope, and love. The theological virtues help us to know and love God as God knows and loves himself and to love others in him.

Torah (TOR ah): The Law; the first five books of the Bible; the Pentateuch.

Tradition (truh DISH un): Christian beliefs that have been passed down by words, customs, and example.

Transfiguration (TRANS fig yoo RAY shun): The glorified appearance of Jesus on one occasion before his death and Resurrection, as witnessed by the apostles Peter, James, and John according to the Gospels.

Transubstantiation (TRAN sub stan shee AY shun): The change of the substances of bread and wine into the Body and Blood of Jesus.

Trinity (TRIN uh tee): The central doctrine and mystery that in God there are three persons (God the Father, God the Son, and God the Holy Spirit) with one nature. The Three Persons of the Trinity are equal but distinct.

V

Venial sin (VEEN yel): Offenses that weaken but do not destroy our relationship with God.

Viaticum (vy AT ih kum): The reception of the Holy Eucharist by one who is in real or probable danger of death; Holy Communion received under this circumstance.

Virgin Birth: The Catholic doctrine that Mary conceived and gave birth to Jesus solely by the power of the Holy Spirit. Mary was a virgin before, during, and after the birth of Jesus.

Virtue (VER chu): A power or a habit for doing good.

Visitation (vis ih TAY shun): Mary's visit soon after the Annunciation to her relative Elizabeth; recognition by Elizabeth and John of the presence of Jesus within her.

Vocation (vo KAY shun): A call from God to holiness of life and to a specific state of life in order to achieve holiness. All Christians are called by God to holiness in baptism. God calls us to special states: marriage, single life, religious life, diaconate, or priesthood.

Vow: A free promise made to God to perform a good act that is not required to achieve salvation. A vow may be temporary or permanent.

W

Witness (WIT nis): One whose life, words, and actions give testimony to his or her beliefs. The Greek translation of this word is *martyr*.

Z

Zealots (ZEL uts): A group of Jewish freedom fighters who sometimes used violence to help Israel overthrow Roman rule.

INDEX

My Lenten Plan

SUNDAY	MONDAY	TUESDAY	WEDNESDAY	THURSDAY	FRIDAY	SATURDAY
Each Sunday in Lent, I will read and meditate on the Sunday Gospel.	Each weekday I'll write a resolution. At the end of the day, I'll color the cross completely if I did my resolution well, partly if I did fairly well, and not at all if I did not do it.	✝	✝	I'll try to be especially kind to someone who isn't a close friend. ✝	✝	✝
1. A. Matthew 4:1–11 B. Mark 1:12–15 C. Luke 4:1–13	✝	✝	✝	✝	I'll do an extra chore at home. ✝	✝
2. A. Matthew 17:1–9 B. Mark 9:2–9 C. Luke 9:28–36	✝	I'll avoid wasting food. ✝	✝	✝	✝	✝
3. A. John 4:5–42 B. John 2:13–25 C. Luke 13:1–9	I'll write a cheerful note to a sick person. ✝	✝	✝	✝	✝	✝
4. A. John 9:1–41 B. John 3:14–21 C. Luke 15:1–3, 11–32	✝	✝	I'll offer to help someone who needs a hand. ✝	✝	✝	✝
5. A. John 11:1–45 B. John 12:20–33 C. John 8:1–11	✝	✝	✝	✝	✝	I'll pray a decade of the rosary for sinners. ✝
6. A. Matthew 21:1–11 B. Mark 11:1–10 C. Luke 19:29–40	✝	✝	✝	I'll pray short prayers at times when I'm silent. ✝	✝	✝

A: Gospels for 1999, 2002, 2005; B: Gospels for 1997, 2000, 2003; C: Gospels for 1998, 2001, 2004

Praying the Rosary

Catholics have prayed and loved the rosary for centuries. On the beads we pray Hail Marys in sets of ten called **decades.** Each decade is framed by an Our Father and a Doxology (Glory to the Father). While praying these prayers, we reflect on the *mysteries* of the life of Jesus, a different mystery for each decade.

Did you know . . .

✤ a blessed rosary is a sacramental, a means of growing in grace?

✤ Pope John XXIII prayed the rosary every day?

✤ October is the month of the rosary, and October 7 is the memorial of Our Lady of the Rosary?

✤ it is said that in appearances at Lourdes and Fatima, Mary asked us to pray the rosary?

✤ the rosary is a good prayer for families to pray together?

Hints:
Make an intention for each decade.
Memorize the mysteries.
Make up your own mysteries from the life of Jesus.

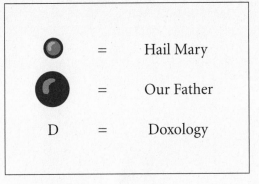

⬤	=	Hail Mary
⬤	=	Our Father
D	=	Doxology

Joyful Mysteries
Annunciation
Visitation
Nativity
Presentation
Finding of Jesus

Luminous Mysteries
Jesus' Baptism
Wedding Feast at Cana
Proclamation of the Kingdom
Transfiguration
Institution of the Eucharist

Sorrowful Mysteries
Agony in the Garden
Scourging
Crowning with Thorns
Carrying of the Cross
Crucifixion

Glorious Mysteries
Resurrection
Ascension
Descent of the Holy Spirit
Assumption
Crowning of Mary

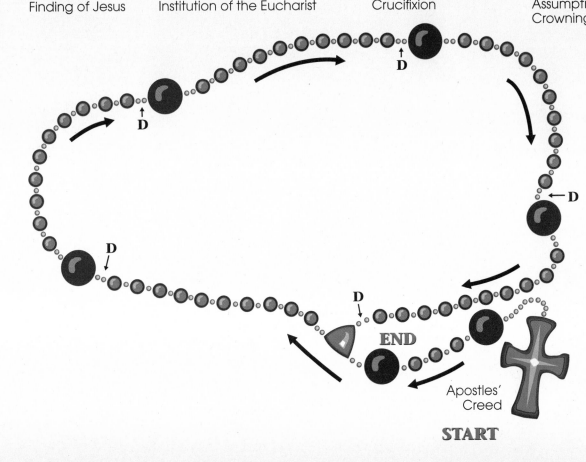

D

D

D

D

D

END

Apostles' Creed

START

Family Activities

Write activities the members of your family could do together to make Sunday special. Then check each family activity when it is completed.

Making Sunday special in the _____ Family,

this year of _____

☐ _____

☐ _____

☐ _____

☐ _____

☐ _____

☐ _____

☐ _____

Our Family Prayer

Compose a prayer for your family, or write one that your family prays together.

_____

Our Family Pledge

Have family members pledge to make Sunday special in a particular way.

I, _____, pledge to make our Sundays special by _____

I, _____, pledge to make our Sundays special by _____

I, _____, pledge to make our Sundays special by _____

I, _____, pledge to make our Sundays special by _____

I, _____, pledge to make our Sundays special by _____

Making Sunday Special

My Family
Draw a picture or place a photo of your family here.

My Family's Activities on a Sunday

_____

_____

_____

_____

Fold this page on the lines and stand it up in a prominent place at home as a reminder to make Sunday special.

- Have I taken anything that is not mine? Have I returned things I borrowed? Have I damaged anything that belongs to someone else? Did I pay for or repair the damage?
- Have I always spoken the truth? Have I been kind in talking about other people? Have I guarded the good reputation of others as I would want them to guard mine? Have I kept secrets and promises? Can others depend on my word?
- Do I choose good friends? Those who will help me be the person God calls me to be? Am I willing to be friendly to everyone? Or do I belong to a closed group of friends?
- Do I do what I can to help those who are poorer than I am?
- Have I omitted doing good things when I could and should have done them?
- Is something else I did bothering me?
- Is Jesus pleased with my behavior? Am I the person he expects me to be?

Examine Your Conscience

The Lord says: "You shall love the Lord your God with your whole heart."

- Do I believe that God truly loves me? Have I spent time talking to God each day? Am I willing to have others know I am a follower of Jesus?
- Do I show respect for God's name and for all that is holy? Do I curse or swear? Why?
- Have I participated in Mass for every Sunday and holy day? If I missed Mass, came late, or left early, was it for an important reason or because I did not want to be there? Have I really tried to pray and sing at Mass? Or did I do things to distract myself and others?
- Have I thanked God for his goodness to me? Have I told God I was sorry when I sinned? Do I truly try to live as a son or daughter of God and a friend of Jesus? Do I ask the Holy Spirit to help me?

The Lord says: "You shall love your neighbor as yourself."

- Have I been obedient and respectful to my parents and others who care for me? Have I loved and prayed for them?

Rite of Reconciliation

- Greet the priest.
- Make the Sign of the Cross.
- Listen as the priest prays.
- Read or listen to the Word of God (optional).
- Confess your sins. (Mention how long it has been since your last confession. For mortal sin, tell how often it has occurred.)
- Speak about anything that is troubling you.
- Listen to the priest's advice.
- Accept your penance.
- Pray an act of contrition. (You may use your own words.)
- Receive absolution, silently making the Sign of the Cross. Respond, "Amen."
- Proclamation of praise and dismissal:
  Priest: Give thanks to the Lord for he is good.
  Response: His mercy endures forever.
- Say, "Thank you, Father."

Spend some time in prayer and thanksgiving.

DO YOUR PENANCE!

Jesus Saves

Jesus, for your name's sake,
do that which your name proclaims.
Jesus, pardon the pride that pained you,
and look upon the unhappy one
that calls on your tender name;
name of comfort,
name of delight, and, to sinners,
name of blessed hope.
For what does your name mean, Jesus,
but "Savior"?
Therefore, for your name's sake,
be to me, Jesus, a merciful Savior.

St. Augustine

Name _____

- Have I tried to bring peace and joy to my family? By helping with the work? By being kind? By controlling my feelings? By being pleasant? Have I talked back to my parents?
- Have I been responsible for my duties as a student? Obeyed and respected my teachers and others in authority? Paid attention in class? Studied and done my assignments? Been Christian in my behavior on the playground, the bus, in the gym, and other public places?
- When I was a leader, did I try to do what I thought was best for everyone? If someone told me to do something wrong, was I strong enough to refuse?
- Have I taken care of the gift of life? My life and the lives of others? Have I hurt myself with the use of drugs or alcohol? Have I hurt anyone by fighting, by playing jokes? By calling them names? By any unkind words? Have I mocked or made fun of others? Put them down? If I became angry or jealous, did I handle my feelings in a positive way?
- Have I encouraged or led others to sin? Have I accepted the responsibility for my own actions? Have I forgiven anyone who hurt me?

- Have I asked forgiveness when I hurt someone? Have I used the gifts of mind, spirit, and body that God has given me to bring happiness to others and glory to God?
- Have I shown respect for my body and the bodies of others? Have I told stories, used crude language, read magazines, looked at pictures, or watched movies that lack respect for the human body? Do I enjoy and prolong daydreams about such pictures or stories? Have I touched the private parts of my body or another's body in the wrong way?
- Do I respect the act of sex as a part of God's beautiful plan of life which is to be protected by the love of married people? Am I open to learning God's plan for sex, or do I think it is all right to do whatever I feel like doing?
- Have I tried to take care of my things? Things that belong to others? Things in public places? Have I been careful not to waste God's gifts so that others can use them too? Am I satisfied with what I have, or would I like to take what belongs to others?

Prayer to the Holy Spirit

Breathe in me, O Holy Spirit,
That my thoughts may all be holy;
Act in me, O Holy Spirit,
That my work, too, may be holy;
Draw my heart, O Holy Spirit,
That I love but what is holy;
Strengthen me, O Holy Spirit,
To defend all that is holy;
Guard me, then, O Holy Spirit,
That I always may be holy.

St. Augustine

Read the Word of God

Be imitators of God, as beloved children, and live in love, as Christ loved us and handed himself over for us as a sacrificial offering to God for a fragrant aroma. (Ephesians 5:1–2)

Other Readings:
Matthew 26:69–75   Luke 15:11–32
Matthew 9:9–13   John 20:19–23

Pray an Act of Contrition

My God,
I am sorry for my sins with all my heart.
In choosing to do wrong,
and failing to do good,
I have sinned against you
whom I should love above all things.
I firmly intend, with your help,
to do penance,
to sin no more,
and to avoid whatever leads me to sin.
Our Savior Jesus Christ
suffered and died for us.
In his name, my God, have mercy.
(from the *Rite of Reconciliation*)

Plan for the Future

I must truly intend to change my life and live according to the teachings of Jesus.

What must I change to follow Jesus more faithfully? What resolution and promise will I make?

Moments with the Lord

The Book of Revelation

Jesus continues to invite you to a deeper relationship with him. The Book of Revelation tells how God will triumph. Read the following sections thoughtfully. Write your prayer response in the space provided.

Reference	Prayer Response
Revelation 3:20	
Revelation 4:11	
Revelation 14:13	
Revelation 22:17	

COME, LORD JESUS!
Rev. 22:20

Name _____

God loves you and asks you to believe and trust. God invites you to follow the way Jesus his Son has shown, the way to life.

It takes time to form deep friendships. If you want to come to know Jesus better, spend a few minutes with him each day reading, thinking, and praying about the Scriptures. Help yourself form the habit of using the Scriptures for prayer. Get a calendar and place a checkmark or some other sign over each day during which you have spent some time with the Lord. Begin on any day—today if possible.

Before you begin your reading of Scripture, place yourself in the presence of Jesus and pray:

Jesus, I believe you are the Savior of the world.
I praise and thank you for calling me to live in your love.
Send your Spirit to enlighten my mind.
Give me the strength I need to follow your way of love.
I love you, Lord, above all things!

October

Sunday	Monday	Tuesday	Wednesday	Thursday	Friday	Saturday
	1	2	3	4	5	6
7	8 ✗	9 ✗	10 ✗	11 ✗	12	13
14	15	16	17	18	19	20
21	22	23	24	25	26	27
28	29	30	31			

Acts of the Apostles

The Acts of the Apostles describes the first Christian communities. It has many stories about how people were brought to the Lord. Read the passages here. Write a headline for each story that proclaims the wonders of the Lord shared in it.

Reference	Headline
Acts 3:1–10	
Acts 4:32–35	
Acts 9:1–19	
Acts 14:8–18	

Other sections to read:
Acts 1:15–26   Acts 9:32–43   Acts 16:16–34
Acts 4:1–12   Acts 12:1–19   Acts 22:1–21

Psalms

Think about times when you experienced God's power and loving care. Read the psalm verses here. Then write your thanks on the lines.

It is good to give thanks to the LORD,
to sing praise to your name, Most High,
To proclaim your love in the morning,
your faithfulness in the night,
With the ten-stringed harp,
with melody upon the lyre.
For you make me jubilant, LORD, by your deeds;
at the works of your hands I shout for joy.
Psalm 92:2–5

I will praise the LORD with all my heart
in the assembled congregation of the upright.
Great are the works of the LORD,
to be treasured for all their delights.
Majestic and glorious is your work,
your wise design endures forever.
You won renown for your wondrous deeds;
gracious and merciful is the LORD.
Psalm 111:1–4

I bow low toward your holy temple;
I praise your name for your fidelity and love.
For you have exalted over all
your name and your promise.
When I cried out, you answered;
you strengthened my spirit.
Psalm 138:2–3

Our soul waits for the LORD,
who is our help and shield.
For in God our hearts rejoice;
in your holy name we trust.
May your kindness, LORD, be upon us;
we have put our hope in you.
Psalm 33:20–22

3

Words for Life

Write God's message to you at the following times:

Are you afraid or worried about something? Read Mark 4:35–41.	
Has a friend disappointed you? Read Luke 6:36–38.	
Do you wonder if God will hear your prayer? Read Luke 11:10–13.	
Do you think that God can never forgive you for something you've done? Read Luke 15:1–10.	
Do you feel that others have more to share than you do? Read Luke 21:1–4.	

10

Sayings of Jesus

Select a saying of Jesus. Read it slowly and prayerfully, conscious that Jesus is speaking to you. As you read, ask yourself:

✤ What is Jesus saying?
✤ What do his words mean to me?
✤ What is he asking me to do?

Then pray, thanking Jesus for his message. Tell him how you want to respond, what difficulties you see, and how you'd like him to help you.

Scripture Saying	Your Prayer Response
John 6:37	
Luke 6:37	
John 8:31	
Luke 11:9	
Matthew 5:16	

Gospels

Read the following sections when you are in the kind of situation described and write your prayer response.

When you've hurt someone, read Matthew 5:23–24.	
When someone has hurt you, read Matthew 18:21–35.	
When you feel troubled or confused, read John 14:27.	
When you're in trouble, read Matthew 11:28–30.	
When you think of death, read John 11:21–26.	

Print your favorite Scripture text here: _____

Parables of Jesus

The parables are stories Jesus told about us. Each day choose a different parable. Read it slowly and prayerfully. As you read, ask yourself:

✤ What does it tell me about following Jesus?
✤ What does it mean for my life right now?
✤ How do I want to respond to it?

Then pray, talking to Jesus about what his message means to you and how you need his help to follow his way. Record your thoughts in your journal.

Check the parables you read.

- ☐ The Rich Fool—Luke 12:16–21
- ☐ The Great Feast—Luke 14:16–24
- ☐ The Talents—Matthew 25:14–30
- ☐ The Pearl—Matthew 13:45–46
- ☐ The Lost Coin—Luke 15:8–10
- ☐ The Two Sons—Matthew 21:28–32
- ☐ The Sower—Mark 4:3–9
- ☐ The Gatekeeper—Mark 13:33–37

John 8:47	
Mark 6:50	
John 13:35	
Matthew 6:15	

Other sayings you can use:

Mark 1:15	Mark 1:17	Mark 2:17
Matthew 11:28	Matthew 18:20	Matthew 23:11
Luke 12:15	Luke 12:32	Luke 18:41
John 4:10	John 6:35	John 7:24

5

8

The Letters

The epistles apply the message of Jesus to daily life. Each day read one verse of Scripture listed here, and think how the message applies to a situation in your life. Then write the maxim and ask the Lord to help you do it! Memorize and pray your maxim.

Reference	Maxim
Colossians 3:13	
Galatians 6:2	
Romans 15:2	
Romans 12:21	
1 Peter 2:1	
1 Corinthians 13:6	

Romans 15:17	
2 Thessalonians 3:13	
James 4:8	
1 Peter 4:8	
1 Thessalonians 5:14	
1 Timothy 6:10	

Other maxims for you to read:
1 Corinthians 6:20   1 Peter 5:7
2 Timothy 3:12   1 John 4:16
James 4:17   1 Thessalonians 5:11